HOW TO CHOOSE & CARE FOR YOUR
CAT

White and Red Tabby British Shorthair kittens.

A Blue Dilute Calico Persian.

HOW TO CHOOSE & CARE FOR YOUR

CAT

BY

DOROTHY SILKSTONE RICHARDS

CONSULTANTS

CHARLENE BEANE
MICHAEL FINDLAY

Illustrated by
JOHN FRANCIS

HPBooks

©1982 Fisher Publishing, Inc.
Printed in U.S.A.

ISBN 0-89586-173-9
Library of Congress Catalog Card Number: 82-82676

First Published 1980 by
Salamander Books, Ltd.

Published in the United States by
HPBooks
P.O. Box 5367
Tucson, AZ 85703
602/888-2150

Publishers: Bill and Helen Fisher
Executive Editor: Rick Bailey
Editorial Director: Randy Summerlin
Editor: Judith Schuler
Art Director: Don Burton
Book Design: Kathleen Koopman

A Silver Tabby American Shorthair.

Salamander Books, Ltd. (1982)
A Salamander book first produced by
Salamander Books Limited of Salamander
House, 27 Old Gloucester St., London
WC1N3AF, England.
Not to be sold outside of the United States and its
territories, and Canada.

A Lilac-Point Siamese.

Author

Dorothy Silkstone Richards writes about cats from practical experience. Until recently Ms. Richards bred Burmese. Her cats have won many prizes at shows and their offspring are still seen on show benches around the world. From breeding cats, Ms. Richards ventured into the commercial world of cat care. She runs a company marketing cat accessories for pet owners and has written two books on cat breeding and co-authored one on the Burmese. She served on committees of various cat clubs and the Pet Trade Association. Her first-hand experience has given her a valuable insight into the problems and temperaments of cats.

Consultants
Charlene Beane has a wide knowledge of the American cat scene and is a regular contributor to *International Cat Fancy Magazine*.
Michael A. Findlay is a veterinarian in England. He has written or contributed to several books on pet care.

CONTENTS

PROFILES

Detailed profiles of more than 100 breeds and color varieties

A Chocolate Tortoiseshell Persian.

CONTENTS

PRACTICAL GUIDE
Essential information for cat owners.

Terminology: If some of the cat terms in this book are new or unclear to you, refer to the Glossary on page 156. Many terms are defined and clarified.

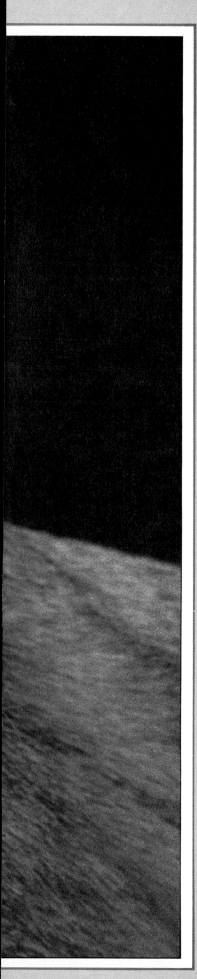

PROFILES

Detailed profiles of more than 100
breeds and color varieties.

Part One of this book provides a comprehensive guide to help you choose a cat. Full-color illustrations show cats of each breed. Detailed drawings show the body shape and head shape of each cat. Coat colors and patterns are shown in color photographs.

There are two body types in cats. The powerfully built cat with a round head is typified by the Persian, and Exotic and British Shorthairs. The more lightly built cat with a wedge-shape head is typified by the Siamese, Balinese and other foreign breeds. There are five coat types: longhair, shorthair, curly, wirehair and hairless. A hairless cat is not really hairless because it has fine hair on several parts of its body. Various coat colors and patterns are reviewed on pages 12 to 17.

In the breed profiles section starting on page 19, each breed, and sometimes each color, is discussed. *Advantages* and *Disadvantages* are listed, detailing good and bad characteristics you should consider before making a choice.

Grooming requirements for each breed are outlined. Do not choose a cat with long hair unless you have the time and interest to groom it. For people with less time, there are shorthair cats that need little grooming.

The *Origin And History* section provides background information about each breed. It explains which breeds are natural, and which have been developed by selective genetic breeding. Under *Breeding* and *Kittens,* you can learn how to breed cats to achieve desired results.

Show Requirements list standard points for each breed under the headings of coat, body, tail, head and eyes. These descriptions outline what is required of a top show specimen. Each breed profile concludes with a list of colors and coat patterns available within the breed.

Cats may not be available in each country. The seven American cat associations recognize more breeds than any other country, so most breeds are available in the United States. Choose a breed that suits your taste and temperament. You may enjoy up to 20 years of devotion and companionship from your pet.

A Chocolate-Tortie Shaded
Silver Oriental Shorthair.

COLOR & COAT PATTERNS

Self-color cats, which are solid color, and bicolors have been known for centuries. Some colors are more prolific in the wild because they are genetically dominant. Recessive colors do not show up as often.

Black—Black is one of the earliest-known coat colors. It is shown here by an American Shorthair. Blacks may be longhair as in the Persian, Angora, Norwegian Forest, Maine Coon and Cymric or shorthair as in the American, British and Exotic Shorthairs, Scottish Folds, Manx, American Wirehair, Cornish and Devon Rex, and Sphynx. Black also appears in the Bombay, Oriental Shorthair and the Japanese Bobtail.

Blue—A Blue Persian is shown here. Blue is a recessive color and prized on the show bench. Blue is selectively bred. Blue longhair cats may be Persian, Norwegian Forest, Angora, Maine Coon or Cymric. Shorthair cats may be British Blues, Chartreux, American Wirehair, Manx, Scottish, Sphynx or Exotic Shorthair. Russian Blues, Korats, Oriental Blues or Blue Burmese may also have this coloring.

Red—Shown here is a Red Cornish Rex. The gene for red is sex linked. In some breeds, red females are rare or non-existent. Instead, males are red and females tortoiseshell. Red longhair cats may be Persian, Peke-Face Persian, Angora, Cymric,

Maine Coon or Norwegian Forest. In shorthair cats, red appears in American and Exotic Shorthairs, Scottish Folds, Sphynx, Manx, American Wirehairs and Rex. Red occurs in Oriental Shorthairs, the Japanese Bobtail and Red Burmese. The deep red required on the show bench is different from the ginger color of non-pedigree cats. It is obtained by selective breeding. Apricot, a dilution, is now appearing on the show bench.

Cream—The Cream British Shorthair shown here represents the dilute form of red. Cream is a recessive color and obtained only by selective breeding. It is not seen frequently among free-roaming

cats. Longhair cream cats may be Persians, Peke-Face Persians, Cymric, Maine Coon or Norwegian Forest. Shorthair creams may be British, American and Exotic Shorthairs, Scottish Fold, Manx, Sphynx, American Wirehair, and Cornish and Devon Rex. Foreign-shape cats may be Oriental Creams, Japanese Bobtail or Cream Burmese. Beige is a new shade of cream.

White—The Oriental White looks like porcelain. The white coat pattern may carry a gene for deafness. In many breeds,

Black
American Shorthair

Blue
Persian

Red
Cornish Rex

Cream
British Shorthair

blue-eyed Whites may be deaf. Longhair white cats may be Persian, Angora, Maine Coon, Norwegian Forest or Cymric. White shorthairs are American Wirehair, Rex and Sphynx. White also appears in the Japanese Bobtail.

Chocolate—The true chocolate cat is represented here by the Havana. Chocolate is a dilute form of black. It is a recessive color and not usually seen in the wild. Longhair chocolate cats are Chocolate Persian, the Self-Chocolate Himalayan or Kashmir, and the Chocolate Angora. In shorthair cats only the foreign breeds, such as the Havana and Chocolate Burmese, recognize brown or chocolate coloring. The Chocolate Burmese is actually black, but appears brown because of a gene restricting coat color. Dilutions are Cinnamon and Caramel.

Lilac—Lilac is genetically a dilute form of chocolate, as shown here in a Lilac Angora. Another lilac longhair breed is the Self-Lilac Himalayan or Kashmir. Shorthair lilac breeds are the Oriental Lilac and Lilac Burmese.

Bicolor—The bicolor coat pattern may be black and white, blue and white, or red and white. It should be mainly white on the underparts and symmetrical elsewhere, with an inverted *V* covering the nose. It is an old coat pattern. Shown here is a Black-And-White Maine Coon. Longhair bicolors may be Maine Coon, Persian, Ragdoll, Norwegian Forest and Cymric. Shorthair cats include the American, British and Exotic Shorthairs, the Scottish Folds, Manx, American Wirehair and Sphynx, if symmetrical. Cornish Rex may be bicolor if symmetrical, but not Devon Rex. The Japanese Bobtail includes bicolors.

Piebald—A piebald is a white cat with color restricted to odd patches on the head and tail. Featured in ancient Chinese and Oriental paintings, it is sometimes known as *Harlequin*. This piebald spotting is common in non-pedigree cats. Cats with this pattern, with more white on the body, are known as *Van*. Patches are solid, tortoiseshell or blue-cream. In the Van pattern, Persian, Turkish and Turkish Angora may display it in the longhairs. In shorthairs, American, Exotics and the Japanese Bobtail may display it.

White
Oriental Shorthair

Chocolate
Havana

Lilac
Angora

Bicolor
Black-And-White Maine Coon

Piebald
Black-And-White Harlequin Shorthair

COLOR & COAT PATTERNS

Genes for a white undercoat are dominant. This has made it possible to develop tipped cats. **Light Tipping**—Shown here is a Cymric with a Chinchilla pattern. In this pattern, guard hairs are tipped with a darker color for about 1/32 of their length. It gives a sparkling effect over the underlying white or paler color. Black tipping is called Chinchilla. If tipping is blue, it is Blue Chinchilla; if brown, it is Gold Chinchilla; if red, it is Shell Cameo or Red Chinchilla. It is possible to get tortoiseshell, also called tortie, or blue-cream tipping and cats tipped lightly in a tabby pattern. Light tipping is found in Maine Coon and Persian longhairs, American, British and Exotic Shorthairs and the Scottish Fold, Manx, Wirehair and Orientals.

Medium Tipping—This is a Red-Shaded American Shorthair. Coats in which the tipping on the guard hairs is restricted to approximately 1/3 of the length are known as *shaded cats*. It gives an effect of a mantle over the underlying coat. If tipping is black, the coat is called Shaded Silver. Tipping can also be brown, tortoiseshell, red, chocolate or lilac. Medium tipping is found in Persians, Maine Coon and Cymric in longhairs. In shorthairs, it can be found in the Rex, American, British, Exotic, Wirehair, Scottish Fold, Manx and Orientals.

Heavy Tipping—Shown here is a Blue Smoke Persian. When the coat is heavily tipped 3/4 of its length or more, it is known as *Smoke*. Tipping may be black, tortoiseshell, blue or red. Longhairs with this coat pattern may be Persians, Maine Coon or Cymric. Shorthairs may be British, American, Exotic, Scottish Fold, Manx, American Wirehair or Rex. There are also Oriental Smokes.

Tortoiseshell—This is a Tortoiseshell British Shorthair. The tortoiseshell coat pattern is a female-only pattern. Males that produce this coat pattern in their offspring are solid color. In nature, the black and red or cream coats are intermingled rather than patched, but become more patched as white is added to the coat. In longhair cats, this coat pattern can be found in Persians, Norwegian Forest, Maine Coon, Angora and Cymric. In shorthairs, it is found in British, American, Exotic, Scottish, Manx, Wirehair, Sphynx and Rex. Foreign-shape cats include Oriental Torties and the Japanese Bobtail. The dilution of tortie is blue-cream.

Light Tipping
Chinchilla Cymric or
Longhair Manx

Medium Tipping
Shaded Red
American Shorthair

Tortoiseshell
Brown Tortoiseshell
British Shorthair

Heavy Tipping
Blue Smoke Persian

Chocolate Tortoiseshell—This is a Chocolate-Tortoiseshell Longhair Persian. The brightly colored patches are distinct and well-broken on the face and body. This is a new coat color that appeared during selective breeding programs. Black pigment was replaced by chocolate, but with red and cream added. This coloring can be found in the Burmese and Orientals. The dilute form of chocolate tortie is lilac-cream or lilac tortie. Both are female-only.

Blue-Cream—This Scottish Fold shows a blue-cream patched coat. It is a dilute form of tortoiseshell coloring and consists of patches of blue and cream. The natural form is mingled, but it is patched when combined with white. It is a female-only variety. Males are blue or cream. Genetically, blue is a dilute form of black, and cream is a dilute of red. Many cats share this coloring. Persian, Maine Coon, Cymric and Norwegian Forest can be this color. American, British, Exotic, Scottish, Manx, American Wirehair, Rex and Sphynx shorthair cats share this color. In the foreign cats, there are Blue Tortie Orientals and Blue Tortie Burmese.

Lilac-Cream—Here is a Lilac-Tortie Burmese. Lilac tortie is the dilute form of chocolate-tortoiseshell. The chocolate color has been replaced by lilac with cream. There are few cats with this coloring, but breeders are beginning to breed this coat color in other cats. Chocolate and lilac colors are still rare. The Persian has a lilac-tortie coat. The Oriental Lilac Tortie has the same color coat.

Calico—This American Wirehair has a coat that is tortie and white. It is an old coat pattern. Before selective breeding began, cats with white in the coat, as well as black and red, had large, well-defined patches of color. The pedigree calico cat must have mainly white on the underparts, as though a red and black spotted cat had been dipped in milk. Longhairs with this coloring are Persian, Maine Coon, Cymric or Norwegian Forest.

Shorthairs are British, Manx, American Wirehair, Rex or Sphynx. The Japanese Bobtail also has this coloring. Its coat usually has more white than other pedigree cats. This pattern is called *Mi-Ke*.

Dilute Calico—Dilute calico is a form of blue-cream and white. Black in the coat is replaced with blue. Red is replaced with cream. These two colors are combined with white.

If you like these colors and coat patterns, turn to the breeds in which they appear and read more about them. There may be a cat suitable for you in your choice of color.

Chocolate Tortoiseshell
Persian

Lilac Tortie
Burmese

Blue-Cream
Scottish Fold

Calico
American Wirehair

COLOR & COAT PATTERNS

The tabby coat pattern has been known for centuries. Thousands of years ago, tabby cats were depicted in Egyptian paintings, Pompeiian relics and Far Eastern mythology. Sometimes cats were striped, sometimes spotted. Many of today's wild cats have this coat pattern.

Classic Tabby—The classic tabby coat pattern is shown here on a Silver Tabby British Shorthair. The pattern can be silver, brown, blue, red or cream in almost any breed except one-color or one-pattern breeds. The ground color contrasts with the overlying pattern color. The

pattern is seen best in shorthairs. Persians, Peke-Face Persians, Maine Coon, Norwegian Forest and Cymric have this pattern. In shorthairs, British, American, Exotic, Scottish, Manx, Sphynx, Rex and Wirehair, as well as some Oriental tabbies, have this coat pattern.

Mackerel Tabby—This is a Cream Persian, with a mackerel-tabby coat pattern. This pattern has vertical stripes down its flanks. Stripes are less visible in a longhair, particularly paler varieties. Mackerel tabbies can be the same breeds as classic or blotched tabbies.

Spotted Tabby—Shown here is an Oriental Cameo Tabby cat. In the spotted tabby, stripes have been broken into spots, giving a coat pattern like a miniature leopard. Spotted tabbies are usually British shorthairs, Manx or Rex. Foreign spotted cats may be Oriental, the Ocicat or the Egyptian Mau.

Ticked Tabby—This is a Blue Abyssinian. Blue is a new color in this breed. The ticked coat occurs in the Somali and Angoras. The shorthair Singapura, where ticking is brown and the ground color beige, is one of the newest-pedigree cats. There are

also Oriental ticked tabbies. This type of ticked coat is known genetically as *Agouti.*

Patched Tabby—The patched tabby coat is seen opposite on a Brown Torbie Exotic Shorthair. A torbie is a tabby with tortoiseshell patches. Torbie has become a recognized coat pattern in some countries and some breeds. It is often seen in the wild. Torbies may be brown, blue or silver tabby with bold patches of red, cream, or red and cream. Patched tabbies occur in Persians, Norwegian Forest and Cymric in the longhairs.

Mackerel Tabby
Cream Persian

Ticked Tabby
Blue Abyssinian

Classic Tabby
Silver Tabby British Shorthair

Spotted Tabby
Cameo Tabby Oriental Shorthair

Shorthairs with this pattern are American and Exotic Shorthairs, Rex and Manx. Oriental torbies come in standard and silver tabby coat patterns in black, blue, chocolate and lilac.

Combination Coat—A combination coat is shown here on a Japanese Bobtail. It is a white coat, with bold patches of black and brown tabby. Many cats have a combination of one of the earlier-mentioned coats with white. These are called *combination coat patterns*. In longhairs, this may be seen on Maine Coon, Norwegian Forest and Cymric. In shorthairs, the Sphynx may have a combination coat. The American Wirehair and Japanese Bobtail may also have combination coats. The Manx may not have combinations with chocolate or lilac.

Himalayan Coat—Shown here is a Seal-point Siamese. In the Himalayan coat pattern, the color is concentrated in the points—the mask, ears, legs and tail. The points may be seal, chocolate, blue, lilac, tortie, blue-cream, tabby, torbie, red or cream, according to breed. Longhairs with the Himalayan coat pattern are the Colorpoint Longhair, Balinese and Ragdoll. Shorthairs are Siamese, Colorpoint Shorthairs and the Devon Si-Rex and Burmese kittens.

Himalayan Combination Coat—This is a Lilac-point Birman. It has four symmetrical white feet. This coat combines the Himalayan pattern with white, produced genetically by a gene for white spotting. Another longhair in this coat pattern is the Mitted Ragdoll. Chocolate and lilac bicolors are being produced in Self-Chocolate and Lilac longhairs. Usually, bicolor does not include combinations with chocolate and lilac. The Snowshoe is a Siamese-color cat with white feet and often a white muzzle. This is a new breed, still awaiting recognition.

Summary

Pages 12 to 17 illustrate the range of coats, patterns and coat types found in cats. Patterns are solid colors, bicolors, piebald, tabbies, particolors, combination coats, Himalayan and Himalayan combinations. Coat types are shorthair, longhair, curly coat, wirehair and hairless.

Choose the coat color, pattern and coat type you find most attractive. Then look in the breed profiles for the breeds listed under each coat pattern. Choose a cat for its temperament and availability as well as good looks. One will be right for you.

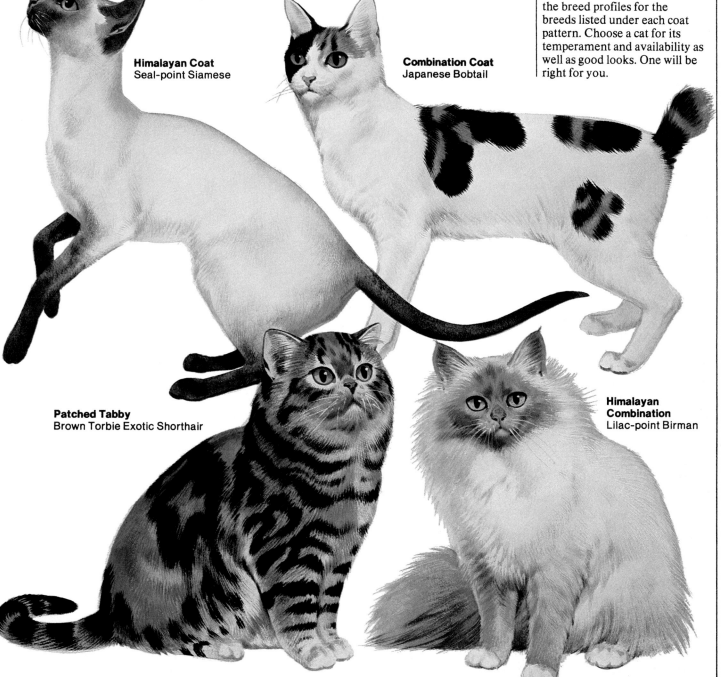

Himalayan Coat
Seal-point Siamese

Combination Coat
Japanese Bobtail

Patched Tabby
Brown Torbie Exotic Shorthair

Himalayan Combination
Lilac-point Birman

LONGHAIR CATS

Longhair cats are beautiful, but they need a lot of attention. When you have a longhair cat, you must groom it every day. Show-quality Persians with long coats may need two grooming sessions a day to keep them looking beautiful. Grooming helps prevent them from swallowing their fur or getting knots in the coat. Some longhair breeds, such as the Balinese or Maine Coon, are easier to groom than Persians. Make grooming a factor when choosing a kitten.

You will find many lovely cats in this section. Persians are available in over 30 color varieties. You may prefer the Birman. For an outdoor life, the Maine Coon is ideal. For adaptability and grace, consider the Angora. The tailless Cymric or the charming Somali may be more to your taste. Whichever breed you choose, be sure its temperament and personality suit you. Do not judge by looks alone.

A Shaded Cameo Persian.

PERSIAN
Longhair

Advantages
- **Affectionate**
- **Companionable**
- **Docile**
- **Quiet**
- **Suitable for an apartment**
- **Even-tempered**

Disadvantages
- **Needs daily grooming**
- **Sheds**

The Persian is an attractive, undemanding pet. It is docile, quiet, friendly and elegant. It is even-tempered and likes being with people.

This cat is quieter and less adventurous than other cats. It lives happily in an apartment if given the run of the house and plenty of fresh air.

The Persian *must* be groomed daily. The cat sheds all year, especially in the summer. If the cat swallows large quantities of hair, fur balls may form and cause an obstruction in the stomach. In extreme cases, fur balls must be removed surgically. Combing must be thorough because the undercoat, particularly under the legs and neck, knots into hard balls. Their removal can be painful.

Owning a Persian cat requires a lot of time and work on the owner's part to keep it in top condition. But if you have time to look after one, you will find it an excellent, loving, devoted companion.

Persians do not have as large a litter as some shorthair or foreign varieties. They may cost more to buy. However, if you want a pet rather than a show champion, it is possible to purchase a non-show quality kitten that will make a wonderful pet.

GROOMING
Daily grooming is essential. Remove knots and tangles, which may not be visible, with a wide-tooth comb. Then use a fine-tooth comb to remove dead hairs. Finally, brush the coat with a long-handle, pure-bristle brush. This creates less static electricity than brushes with synthetic fibers. Comb tufts between toes carefully. Mats here are uncomfortable for the cat. Check eyes regularly, because Persians can have blocked tear ducts. Any discharge from the eyes discolors fur around the nose.

If destined for showing, pale-color Persians will benefit from a bath a week before the show. A few days after bathing, powder the coat to remove grease marks. Rub the powder to the roots, then brush it out. For darker colors, apply bay rum to the coat.

Do not use powder because it could mar the color. Hair is whipped up with the brush so each hair stands away from the body and frames the face.

ORIGIN AND HISTORY
Longhair cats have been known in Europe since the 16th century, but their origin remains obscure. Records show there were two types of longhair cat. One came from Turkey—*the Angora*—and the other from Persia—*the Persian*. It is likely both types originated in Russia and were brought to Europe by traders. Although longhair cats are found today in Turkey and Iran (Persia), they are more common in parts of Russia. It is possible the harsh climate there may have caused the evolution of the long coat.

Cats in Persia had broader, rounder heads, smaller ears, shorter bodies and plusher coats than Angoras. They were probably the forerunner of the modern Persian. Selective breeding of these cats, particularly in the last 100 years, has produced the typical Persian type and numerous color varieties known today. The Persian is one of the oldest and most popular show breeds.

SHOW REQUIREMENTS
Sturdy cat with gently curving lines. Medium to large with a long, flowing coat. An ethereal look and pretty face.

Coat—Long, thick and shining, up to 6 inches (15cm) in length. Fine, soft and silky, standing away from the body, ideally with every hair separate. A full ruff forms a halo around the head and a long frill between the front legs.

Body—Cobby, solid and round. Low lying on the legs. Deep in the chest, massive across the shoulders and rump. Legs short, thick and strong with straight forelegs. Feet large, firm, round and tufted.

Tail—Short and full, especially at the base. No kinks.

Head—Broad, round and massive on a short, thick neck. Face round and pretty, with no hint of wedginess. Jaw broad. Chin strong, not undershot. Cheeks full. Nose almost snub. Short and broad with a break or stop where it meets the forehead. Stop is particularly pronounced in American Persians. Ears tiny, round at the tips, set wide apart and tilted forward. Set low on the head with long ear tufts.

Eyes—Large, round and set wide apart. Full, with a sweet expression. Slanted, oval or deepset eyes are faults. Eye color may fade with age or breeding.

COLORS
There are at least 30 color varieties of Persian today, although not all are recognized for competition in all countries. Colors are listed as varieties of Persian. In the United Kingdom, each color variety is regarded as a separate breed and classified by the name Longhair rather than Persian.

White Persian

White Persian is an old variety. It was regarded as a status symbol in London at the turn of the century. It has been known in Europe for about 300 years. The earliest cats had blue eyes, long, pointed faces and were frequently deaf. The White Persian began to attract attention in the late 1800s. They were first shown in the United States around 1900. They also became popular in Great Britain at that time.

Today there are three varieties: blue-eye White; orange-eye White; and odd-eye White, one eye of each color. This is due to outcrossing to other Persians, notably blues. It is difficult to breed Persian types with blue eyes. The blue-eye White on the show bench has a slightly longer face and ears, although it usually has better coats than orange-eye Whites.

Many blue-eye Whites are born deaf. Some odd-eye Whites are deaf on the blue-eye side. Deafness may be difficult to detect at first because the cat's other senses compensate for the deafness.

GROOMING
To keep the coat white, dust with talc or grooming powder. Brush and comb thoroughly. Any grease in the coat of a White Persian will show as yellow marks, particularly on the tail and especially in male cats. To remove these stains, wash the tail in warm water with borax. Rinse thoroughly. For a show cat, a bath a few days before a show may be necessary.

BREEDING
Blue-eye Whites are not as numerous as orange-eye Whites. They have smaller litters. Deafness may also account for their lack of popularity. Cats with normal hearing may produce deaf kittens. Do not use a deaf cat for breeding. A deaf queen requires more supervision because she cannot hear her kittens.

KITTENS
All White kittens are born with blue eyes. It may be some weeks before you can tell whether they will be blue-eye, orange-eye or odd-eye. The depth of eye color also takes months to develop. Orange eyes should be deep orange or copper. If a kitten does not have deep eye color by the time it is 6 or 7 months old, it is unlikely the color will intensify later. When born, kittens are pink. The baby coat soon disappears and they develop fluffy white coats. Some kittens are born with a smudge of black hairs on top of their heads.

This is an indication they have normal hearing, at least in one ear. The spot disappears as the adult coat starts to come in at about 9 months.

COLOR
The coat must be white, with no shadow markings or black hairs. Noseleather and paw pads pink. Eyes deep blue; orange or copper; or one orange or copper and one deep blue. Pale or green-tinged eyes are faults.

Black Persian

The Black Persian is an old variety and a natural breed. It is rare because a perfect black is difficult to obtain. Black Persians were known in Europe at the end of the 16th century, but it is not known where they came from. They first appeared on the British show bench in 1871. Early black cats were more like Angoras than Persians, with long noses and big ears. These features have now been bred out and current champions have the typical snub nose, round head and tiny ears.

GROOMING
Daily grooming with brush and comb is essential. Bathing before a show may not be necessary, except to make the coat more fluffy. Adding bay rum to the coat enhances the shine. Do not use powder because it is impossible to brush it all out and it dulls the color. Dampness or strong sunlight produce a rusty tinge on the coat. Keep a show cat away from these conditions whenever possible.

BREEDING
Mating two Black Persians produces black kittens. To improve type, it is necessary to outcross to other colors, usually Blue or White. In this case, only females from such crosses are used for further breeding. Black males from Black-to-Black matings are used to produce Tortoiseshells, Calicos, Whites, Smokes, Creams and Bicolors.

KITTENS
Kittens are born with blue eyes, which gradually change to copper. They are born black but often have rusty coats or some white hairs until the adult coat appears. The worst kitten coats at 6 months old often become the densest black adults at 12 to 18 months.

COLOR
The coat must be a solid, even black all over. Each hair must be black from tip to root. A jet black is required, with no tinge of rustiness, white hairs or tabby markings. Noseleather and paw pads black. Eyes orange or deep copper.

Persian

Black Persian

Blue-Eye White Persian

Blue Persian

Blue Persians are popular cats. They have long, flowing coats, delicate looks and sweet faces. It is said they came from Persia, Turkey, China, Burma, Afghanistan and Russia! They have been featured in paintings for several centuries, but were largely unknown in Europe before the end of the 16th century. They were known in Italy during the Renaissance and they were prized in India. Bred principally in France and England, they were later exported to the United States.

The blue color is genetically a dilution of black. It may have originally resulted from crossing a black cat with a white cat. Blue cats did not appear in a separate class until 1889. Before then, they were shown in mixed classes with Blue-And-White Bicolors and Blue Tabbies.

GROOMING
Daily grooming with a brush and comb is essential. Bathing before a show is not usually necessary. Grease marks can be removed by dusting the coat with grooming powder.

BREEDING
Blues are often used to produce Blue-Creams. Because they seem to excel in Persian type, Blues are used to improve the type and eye color of other Persians.

KITTENS
When born, Blue kittens may have tabby markings. These usually disappear as the adult coat develops. Heavily marked kittens often have the best overall blue coats. Kittens are born with blue eyes, which change to deep orange over the next few months.

COLOR
The coat should be an even, pale gray-blue all over. Color is the same depth from root to tip, with no sign of a paler undercoat, tabby markings or white hairs. Paler blue coats are preferred. Noseleather and paw pads slate-blue. Eyes copper or deep orange with no green tinge.

Red Persian

The name *red* is misleading, because the coat color is more orange than scarlet. Although red cats have appeared in shows since the beginning of the century, a good specimen is rare. It is almost impossible to produce without some tabby markings in the coat.

GROOMING
Daily grooming is essential. Powder before a show or apply a little bay rum to enhance the coat for a show appearance.

BREEDING
Despite the predominance of male red cats in the wild, red females do occur. They can be obtained by mating a Red male with a Tortoiseshell or a Blue-Cream female, if the male does not carry the blue color factor in his genetic makeup. Do not mate Reds to Red Tabbies. It reintroduces tabby markings. Outcross to other solid-color cats, such as Blacks. Reds are used to breed Tortoiseshells and Calicos.

KITTENS
Red kittens are usually born with tabby markings, which they may lose when the adult coat is grown. It is often difficult to tell whether the kittens will be Red or Red-Tabby. Breeding for Red Persians is a challenge.

COLOR
The coat is a deep red, without any markings or white hairs. Noseleather and paw pads brick-red. Eyes deep copper.

Cream Persian

Cream Persians are not as numerous as other Persian varieties. Generally, they have small litters. The Cream was first recorded in Great Britain in 1890. At first, they were regarded as Reds too pale to meet show standards. Many were sold as pets. Others were exported to the United States, where breeders became interested in Cream Persians. Serious breeding of Creams did not start until the 1920s.

Cream kittens may have appeared first in litters born to Tortoiseshells mated to Red-Tabby males. Tortoiseshells have red, black and cream in their coats. This mating can produce all-cream kittens.

GROOMING
Daily grooming is essential. A bath may be necessary a few days before a show. Grooming powder and brushing fluffs the coat into show condition.

BREEDING
Continuous matings between Cream Persians produce gradual loss of type. Outcrosses to other-color varieties are necessary. Cream is genetically a dilution of red and is easier to achieve than solid red. Creams are produced most reliably from matings between Blues and Creams. A Cream female mated to a Blue male produces Cream male and Blue-Cream female kittens. A Cream male mated to a Blue female produces Cream kittens of either sex, Blue males and Blue-Cream females.

KITTENS
Cream kittens are often born with faint tabby markings. These usually disappear when the adult coat starts to develop at about 9 months of age.

COLOR
Coat is cream, without any markings or darker area down the spine. American associations prefer a pale buff-cream. Too-red is a fault. There should be no paler undercoat. Hair is the same color from root to tip. The coat color may be darker in older cats or just before shedding. Noseleather and paw pads pink. Eyes copper.

Bicolor Persian

The Bicolor cat, which is two colors, has been known since early times but is a newcomer to the show bench. It was originally regarded as an alley cat without known parentage. It can be black and white, blue and white, red and white, or cream and white. Cream and white is rare. In pedigree breeding, it has been difficult to meet the standard, which requires the coat to have symmetrical patches of color on the head and body. Symmetry seems to be an elusive characteristic and few perfect Bicolors are seen.

GROOMING
Daily grooming is essential. For showing, a bath may be necessary. Powder is not used on the coat because it deadens the contrast between the color and the white.

BREEDING
Bicolors may result from mating two Bicolors, a Bicolor with a Calico, a Bicolor with a solid color or a solid color with a White. Bicolors are the best sires for producing Calico kittens. Litters usually contain a colorful assortment of three or four kittens in any of the above patterns.

KITTENS
Bicolor kittens are robust and hardy. If kept for breeding, they produce almost any color kitten, depending on their ancestry and mating partner. Kittens are large and mature early.

COLOR
To show the Bicolor Persian, it must have a patched coat with no more than two-thirds of the body colored or more than one-half white. The pattern should be symmetrical, with patches of color on the face, head, back, flanks and tail. Accepted colors are black and white, blue and white, red and white, and cream and white. Tabby markings and white hairs within color patches are faults. White is desirable on the underparts, chest, feet, legs, chin and lips. A facial blaze is preferred and a white collar is permitted. Noseleather and paw pads generally pink, otherwise in keeping with the coat color. Eyes deep copper to orange.

Red and Cream Persian kittens. The faint tabby markings fade at about 9 months.

Persian

Blue Persian

Black-And-White
Bicolor Persian

Cream Persian kitten

Red Persian

Persian Chinchilla and Shell Cameo

The Persian Chinchilla and Shell Cameo belong to a group that contains some of the most beautiful longhair cats. These cats have a tipped coat pattern. The characteristic feature is an undercoat of one color—white or cream—with guard hairs tipped to varying extents with a different, contrasting color. These cats are classified according to whether the color tipping is light, such as on Chinchillas and Shell Cameos; medium, as on Shaded Silvers and Shaded Cameos; or heavy, as on Smokes.

The Chinchilla and Shell Cameo undercoats are usually white. The ends of some guard hairs, for one-eighth of the hair length, are lightly tipped with a contrasting color, giving a shimmering, sparkling effect to the coat.

The name chinchilla is misleading. The South American chinchilla has fur that is dark at the roots and white at the tips, the opposite of the cat's coat. Early Persian Chinchillas were more heavily marked and probably more like today's Shaded Silvers. They are believed to have been developed from cats with silver genes, probably Silver Tabbies, whose markings were indistinct or almost absent. These were mated to Blue Persians or Smokes. Further selective breeding used only the palest kittens or non-tabby kittens mated to White Persians with blue eyes. Early Silver Tabbies had hazel or gold eyes. The first chinchillas also had hazel eyes. When these were mated to blue-eye White Persians, some of the kittens had green or blue-green eyes. These kittens were popular and altered the standard. After World War II, there was a shortage of all types of pedigree cats in Europe. American Chinchillas

This Shaded Golden Persian shows the typical seal-brown tipping over the cream undercoat.

were imported to improve the stamina of the variety.

A Chinchilla's delicate appearance belies its hardy nature. It is not fragile, but robust and healthy. Its sweet, baby face has made it popular worldwide.

In recent years, the name chinchilla has been extended to cats of similar appearance and coat pattern but of different colors. The most notable is the Golden Chinchilla. It is a brown-tipped variety now becoming popular.

The Shell Cameo is similar to the Chinchilla in coat pattern. It was developed in the late 1950s. Selective breeding of Silver Persians with red cats and cream cats produced this pattern. Mating with Chinchillas produced kittens with green eyes, which was not desired for Shell Cameos. Smokes with copper eyes were introduced and mated to Reds and Tortoiseshells. No tabbies of any color were used, except to produce the Cameo Tabby, to keep from reintroducing tabby markings. Mixed breeding has produced a wide variety of colored Shell Cameos, from red to tortoiseshell and blue-cream.

GROOMING

For showing, bathe Chinchillas and Shell Cameos a week before the show and apply baby powder. Powder them every day for four or five days to give body to the coat. Daily combing is necessary to prevent knots. The day before the show, all traces of powder must be removed. Each hair should stand out from the body. This is true show condition: every hair separate in the fluffy coat.

Sunlight tends to give the white fur a yellow tinge. If showing the cat, try to keep it out of direct sunlight.

BREEDING

Female Persians develop relatively slowly. Do not mate the cat until it is 12 to 18 months old. This gives her time to develop fully before bearing kittens. Once mated she usually becomes a good mother. To preserve the variety as it is, Chinchillas are now mated only to other Chinchillas. Mate a queen to a stud possessing all the qualities missing or less-than-perfect in the queen. If the queen has poor eye color, choose a stud that excels in the color of his eyes.

Breeding for Shell Cameos is more complex. Crosses of copper-eye Smokes to Red or Cream Persians, without blue in the background, or to Tortoiseshells, produces Shell Cameo males. When these Shell Cameo males are mated to Blue-Cream, Tortoiseshell, Shaded Tortoiseshell or Shaded Blue-Cream cats, they produce Shell Cameo females. Blue-Cream and Tortoiseshell females can be mated to Red or Cream males. Mating cats of different parents may be better than mating brothers and sisters. It also saves waiting two years until kittens mature.

KITTENS

The average Chinchilla and Shell Cameo litter contains 3 or 4 kittens. Chinchilla kittens are born with dark and tabby markings, particularly on the tail. These disappear by the time they are 4 to 6 weeks old. If a kitten still shows markings after 10 weeks, it is not showable. Cameo kittens are born white, with tipping gradually appearing.

COLORS

Chinchilla—Conforms to the standard for Persians. The undercoat should be white. The last 1/8 of each hair on the back, flanks, legs, head and tail tipped with black, giving a sparkling silver appearance to the coat. The chin, ear tufts, stomach and chest are white. The lips, nose and eyes are outlined in black or deep brown. Whiskers are white, but may be black near the face. Noseleather brick-red. A pale noseleather is considered a fault. Paw pads black. Eyes green.

Masked Silver—A white undercoat and topcoat tipped lightly with black on the back, flanks and tail, but with darker, heavier tipping on the face and paws. Noseleather brick-red. Paw pads black or deep brown. Eyes green.

Chinchilla Golden—Undercoat is a rich, warm cream. The coat on the back, flanks, head and tail is lightly tipped with seal-brown to give a sparkling gold appearance. Legs may be lightly tipped. Chin, ear tufts, stomach and chest are cream. The lips, nose and eyes are outlined with seal-brown. Noseleather deep rose. Paw pads seal-brown. Eyes green or blue-green.

Shell Cameo—Undercoat white with the coat on the back, flanks, legs and tail lightly tipped with red, giving a pink effect. Chin, ear tufts, stomach and chest white. Tabby markings are a fault. Noseleather and paw pads rose. Eyes copper, outlined in rose.

Shell Tortoiseshell—Females only. Undercoat white, lightly tipped with red, black and cream in defined patches and broken on the face. Chin, ear tufts, stomach and chest white. A blaze of red or cream tipping on the face is desirable. Noseleather and paw pads black, pink or a combination of the two. Eyes copper.

Blue-Cream Particolor Cameo—Females only. Undercoat white and the coat on the back, flanks, legs and tail lightly tipped with blue and cream softly intermingled to give the effect of a mother-of-pearl mantle. Noseleather and paw pads blue, pink or a combination. Eyes deep copper.

Cameo Tabby—Undercoat off-white, lightly tipped with red in either classic or mackerel tabby coat pattern. Noseleather and paw pads rose. Eyes copper.

Cameo Tabby Persian

Shell Cameo Persian

Persian

Chinchilla Persian

Shaded Persian

Similar to the Chinchilla and Shell Cameo, the Shaded Persian also has a pale undercoat. About a quarter of the hair length is tipped with a contrasting color, giving the effect of a colored mantle over the body.

Shaded kittens appear in the same litters as Chinchillas and Shell Cameos. In early pedigree cat breeding, when Chinchillas were darker than they are today, it was difficult to distinguish between the two types. Interest in shaded cats has been revived and a standard has been introduced for them. They are bred in several colors. The original variety was silver. They can be bred in any coat color or pattern.

GROOMING
Daily grooming is necessary. Show preparation requires the same treatment as for Chinchillas and Shell Cameos.

COLORS
Shaded Silver—Undercoat white. Topcoat tipped in black to give the effect of a black mantle over the undercoat, back, flanks, face legs and tail. Usually darker than the Chinchilla. Noseleather and paw pads brick-red. Eyes green or blue-green, rimmed with black.
Shaded Cameo—Undercoat white. Topcoat tipped in red, giving the effect of a red mantle overlying the undercoat, back, flanks, face, legs and tail. Usually darker than the Shell Cameo. Noseleather and paw pads rose. Eyes copper, rimmed with rose.
Shaded Golden—Undercoat cream. Topcoat tipped in seal-brown to give the effect of a gold overcoat. Usually darker than the Chinchilla Golden. Noseleather deep rose. Paw pads seal-brown. Eyes green or blue-green, rimmed in seal-brown.
Shaded Tortoiseshell—Undercoat white. Topcoat tipped in black, red and cream in defined patches of the tortoiseshell pattern. A blaze of red or cream on the face desirable. Noseleather and paw pads black, pink or a combination. Eyes copper.
Pewter—Undercoat white. Topcoat tipped in black, giving the effect of a black mantle overlying the undercoat. Darker than the Chinchilla but similar to the Shaded Silver. Lips, nose and eyes outlined in black. Noseleather brick-red. Paw pad black. Eyes orange or copper, with no green tinge.

Smoke Persian

Like the Chinchilla and Shaded Persian, the Smoke is characterized by its white undercoat and contrasting-tipped topcoat. The topcoat hairs are tipped with color for at least half their length. The Smoke Persian may look like a solid-color cat until it moves and the pale undercoat shows. Ruff and ear tufts are usually a paler color.

Smoke-color cats have been recorded in Great Britain since the 1860s. They appeared originally as the result of chance matings of Chinchilla, Black, Blue and White Persians. Their popularity declined until interest revived in the 1960s. Now several colors are being bred, but not all are recognized for competition in every country.

GROOMING
The Smoke Persian requires frequent and expert grooming. It may take many weeks of careful grooming before the cat is ready to be shown.

Bathe the cat a week before a show to remove grease. The undercoat must be brushed to show through the dark topcoat. This requires patience and skill. Too much brushing may pull out the undercoat. Strong sunlight bleaches the coat, so Smokes are best shown during winter months.

BREEDING
Outcrosses to improve type can be made to Tortoiseshell, Black or Blue Persians, resulting in Black, Blue or Tortoiseshell Smokes. This preserves the copper eyes. Silver Tabbies should not be used because they reintroduce the green eye and tabby markings, which are not desirable. Another good cross is to a Chinchilla, to improve the undercoat. But this may introduce the green eye color.

In order to produce All-Smoke kittens, parents must have a Smoke in their backgrounds. Black is dominant over Smoke; Black-to-Smoke mating produces all-Black kittens. Even Smoke-to-Smoke matings may produce some all-Black kittens. Mating Smokes with Smokes repeatedly results in loss of Persian type.

A Black Smoke Persian with its pale undercoat showing through.

KITTENS
Smokes are difficult to distinguish at birth from solid-color kittens. Smoke kittens may have white around the eyes and a paler stomach. It may take months to distinguish Smokes. The full coat color and pattern is sometimes not seen until the adult is about two years old. Kittens whose undercoats pale the fastest usually become the best adult Smokes. The undercoat begins to show through at about 3 weeks. By 6 to 8 weeks, kittens have a mottled appearance. At 6 months they are ready to be shown. Kittens with unsatisfactory coats can be sold as affectionate, even-tempered pets.

COLORS
Black Smoke—Undercoat white, heavily tipped on the back and flanks with black, giving the effect of a solid-color cat until the animal moves. Coat shades to silver on the lower flanks. Face and feet are black, with no markings. Color white at the roots. The ruff and ear tufts are silver. Noseleather and paw pads black. Eyes copper or orange.

Blue Smoke—Undercoat white, heavily tipped with blue on the back and flanks, giving the appearance of a solid blue cat until the animal moves. Face and feet are blue, without markings. Color white at the roots. The ruff and ear tufts are silver. Noseleather and paw pads blue. Eyes orange or copper.
Cameo Smoke—Undercoat white, heavily tipped with red on the back and flanks, giving the appearance of a solid red cat until the animal moves. Face and feet are red, without markings. Color white at the roots. The ruff and ear tufts are white. Noseleather and paw pads rose. Eyes orange or copper.

Tortoiseshell Smoke—Undercoat white, heavily tipped with black, red and cream in clearly defined patches on the back and flanks, giving the appearance of a tortoiseshell until the animal moves. Face and feet solid red, black and cream, with preference given to a facial blaze of red or cream. Colors white at the roots. Ruff and ear tufts white. Noseleather and paw pads charcoal, rose, pink or a combination. Eyes copper.

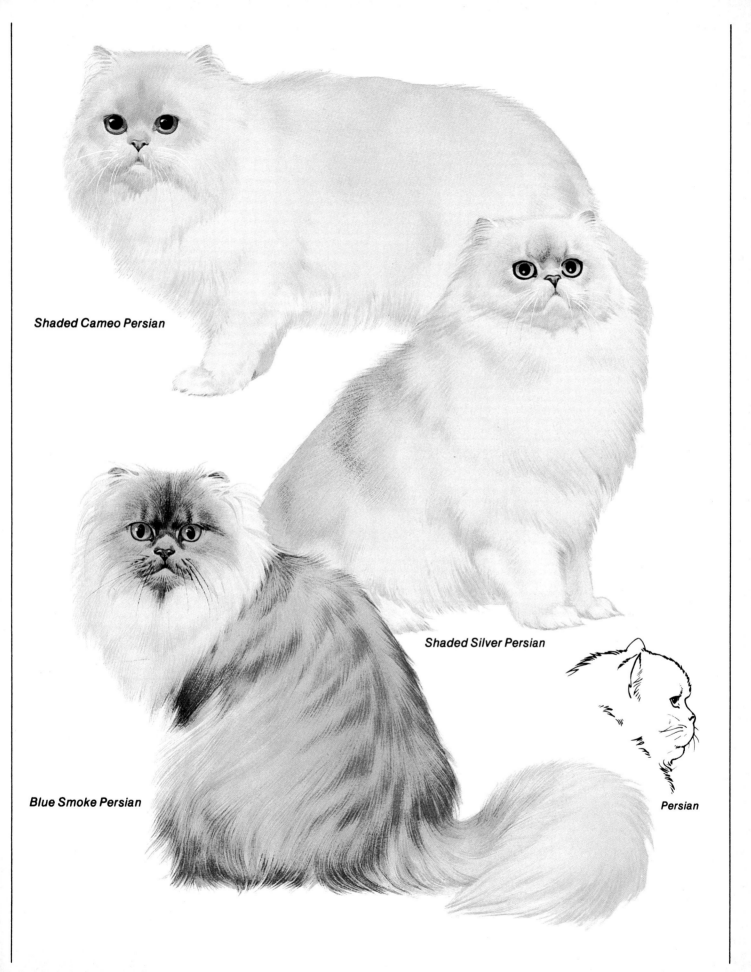

Shaded Cameo Persian

Shaded Silver Persian

Blue Smoke Persian

Persian

Tortoiseshell Persian

The longhair Tortoiseshell was not recorded before the end of the 19th century. The Tortoiseshell first appeared at shows in the early 1900s. It soon became popular on both sides of the Atlantic. Because it is difficult to breed, it is still rare. The demand for Tortoiseshell kittens usually exceeds the supply. They may be more expensive than other Persians.

GROOMING
Daily grooming with brush and comb throughout the year is necessary to keep the coat in condition. Do not use grooming powder because it deadens the color.

BREEDING
This is a female-only variety. The rare male is usually sterile. Like-to-like mating is not possible; breeding is difficult and unpredictable. Mating Tortoiseshells to solid-color males or to bicolors cannot be relied on to produce Tortoiseshell kittens. It is more by luck that one appears in a litter. Tabby sires introduce unwanted bars and markings.

KITTENS
When Tortoiseshells are mated to males of different colors, a colorful assortment of kittens results.

COLORS
The coat is evenly patched with red, cream and black. All colors are clear and brilliant, not mingled. Black should not predominate. Large patches of any one color are considered a fault. A red or cream blaze from the forehead to the nose is desirable. Colors are broken up on the head and ears. The fur is long on the ruff and tail. White hairs and tabby markings are faults. Noseleather and paw pads pink or black. Eyes copper or deep orange.

Blue-Cream Persian

The Blue-Cream is a female-only variety, genetically a dilute form of the Tortoiseshell. It is an attractive and popular cat. It has been slow to gain championship status and did not achieve official recognition until 1930. It has appeared in litters resulting from Blue and Cream matings. It was first shown as a Blue Tortoiseshell in the early 1900s.

It is now recognized as valuable breeding stock for Blues, Creams and Blue-Creams. The crossing of these varieties has given stamina to both Blues and Creams. The Blue-Creams are a healthy, robust variety.

American and British standards are different. American standards call for broken patches of blue and cream. British standards call for evenly intermingled blue and cream throughout the coat.

GROOMING
Daily grooming with brush and comb is essential. A bath may be necessary before a show. Use grooming powder to fluff the coat into show condition.

BREEDING
If a Blue-Cream is mated to a Cream sire, the resulting kittens are anything except Blue females. If a Blue-Cream female is mated to a Blue sire, the resulting kittens are anything except Cream females. A Blue female mated to a Cream male produces Blue-Cream female and Blue male kittens. A Blue male mated to a Cream female produces Blue-Cream females and Cream males.

KITTENS
Kittens are colorful. There may be Blues, Creams and Blue-Creams in a litter. Those with the palest coats develop into the best adults for competition. Often a fine Blue-Cream looks pale blue in the first few weeks.

COLOR
Coat blue, patched with solid cream clearly defined and broken on body, legs, tail and face. Noseleather and paw pads blue, pink or a combination. Eyes deep copper or orange.

Calico Persian
Tortoiseshell-And-White

The Calico Persian is another female-only variety. It has a patched coat of black, red and cream with white. It is always in demand.

Although shorthair calico cats have been known in Europe for centuries, the origin of the longhair variety is obscure. Like the Tortoiseshell, it probably appeared by chance in litters of solid-color Persians with mixed-color backgrounds.

The color is sex-linked genetically and produces only females. The rare male is sterile. Cats with this coat pattern were known in the past as *Chintz* because of the bright, bold color patches.

This pedigree variety has only been recognized since the 1950s. Since then, the dilute variety, the Blue Calico, also attained recognition. These cats often appear in the same litter as Calicos and have patched coats of blue and cream with white.

White concentrated on the underparts is preferred. One American association describes the cat as a Tortoiseshell that has been dropped into a pail of milk, the milk splashing on the face and neck.

GROOMING
This coat does not mat as much as most Persian varieties, but a daily brushing and combing is advisable. If being prepared for a show, powder can be rubbed into the lighter parts of the coat and then thoroughly brushed out.

BREEDING
Calicos produce kittens in an assortment of colors. More Calico kittens are born when sired by red-and-white or black-and-white bicolor cats. Those producing the best patched coats are males with too much white in their own coats, according to the bicolor standard. Tabbies should not be used because they may introduce undesirable bars and markings.

KITTENS
Kittens often have patches of dull blue, dark cream or drab white in their coats when young. These usually turn into jet black, bright red and pure white patches in an adult. Blue-Calico kittens often appear in the same litter and are usually paler in color. It is difficult to assess the quality of the coat coloring when kittens are young.

COLORS
Calico—Coat patched with black, red and cream, interspersed with white. Patches are equally distributed, bright and clear, without white hairs or tabby markings. They should be spread evenly over the body with white on the legs, feet, chest and face. Too much white is a fault. White is concentrated on the underparts. A cream or white blaze from the top of the head to the nose is desirable, especially when it sharply divides the black side of the face from the red side. Noseleather and paw pads pink, black or a combination. Eyes copper.

Blue-Calico—Coat patched with blue and cream. Patches evenly distributed over the body, clear and unbrindled, with white on the legs, feet, chest and face, and concentrated on the underparts. A cream or white blaze on the face is desirable. Noseleather and paw pads pink. Eyes copper or orange.

A Blue-Calico Persian.

Persian

Calico Persian

Tortoiseshell
Persian

Blue-Cream Persian

Chocolate Tortoiseshell and Lilac-Cream Persians

These new varieties developed from the Himalayan (Colorpoint) breeding program, with outcrossing to Tortoiseshell Persians and Cream Persians. They are regarded as Himalayan hybrids and cannot be shown. They are bred in two colors.

Chocolate Tortoiseshell—Coat patched with chocolate, red and cream. Colors are bright, rich and broken on the face. Noseleather and paw pads brown. Eyes copper.

Lilac-Cream—Throughout the coat, shades of lilac and cream are softly intermingled. No white hairs. Noseleather and paw pads pink. Eyes copper.

Tabby Persians

Tabby Persians are excellent pets for people who have the time to devote to grooming. They are healthy, docile and more independent than other Persian varieties.

The name *tabby* comes from the similarity of the cat's coat pattern to plain-woven watered silk or taffeta, known as *tabbisilk*. This type of weaving produces a striped or ridged effect on the cloth.

The tabby pattern is common among domestic cats, although longhair tabbies were not recorded in Europe until the end of the 16th century. Judging from the markings of many wild cats, the original domestic tabby was probably a striped cat, resembling the Mackerel Tabby of today. The classic or blotched pattern, more common now in pedigree cats, is a mutation of the striped form that first appeared in Europe among domestic and wild cats. It was common by the middle of the 17th century.

Although original tabby colors were probably brown, red or ginger, selective breeding over the last 100 years has produced several others. The Brown Tabby is not a common variety in pedigree circles, possibly because it is difficult to breed a cat to the required color standard. Affectionately known as *Brownies,* they are noted for their health, strength and longevity.

Red Tabbies and Silver Tabbies are popular. Silver Tabbies were bred before organized cat shows were held.

Recently, the Blue Tabby has been recognized for competition. Blue is a genetic dilution of black. Kittens of this color appear ocassionally in Brown Tabby litters, especially if there is blue in the ancestry.

Clearly defined tabby markings required by show standards are difficult to achieve in tabbies, especially the Cream Tabby. Genetically a dilute form of the Red, it shows little contrast between ground color and markings. As a result, a good specimen is rare. This variety is recognized for competition in the United States only.

GROOMING
To show a Tabby Persian to perfection, the coat must be brushed to enhance markings. This means brushing and combing only from head to tail. Do not brush forward to fluff up the coat as done with some varieties. The use of powder on the coat is not recommended because it deadens the contrast between the color and markings. Use bay rum to remove grease before a show.

BREEDING
Mating two Tabbies of the required color together gives several generations of good type. Eventually, outcrossing to a solid color is necessary, using the solid color of the overlay coat pattern or a Tortoiseshell. In the Brown Tabby, this means an outcross to a solid Black Persian, in the Red Tabby to a Tortoiseshell or Red, in the Silver Tabby to a Black, in the Blue Tabby to a Blue Persian and in the Cream Tabby to a Cream. A Silver Tabby may introduce the gold eye color, which is undesirable, so a Chinchilla can be used.

KITTENS
Tabby kittens are colorful, with markings showing as soon as they are born. Often the darker striped they are at birth, the clearer the adult coat pattern will be. Kittens unsuitable for showing make excellent pets. These include those with white hairs in the darker markings, white patches, a white tip on the tail, a white chin, too-solid a color down the back or incorrect eye color. In Silver Tabbies, a brown or yellow tinge to the fur makes it unsuitable for showing.

COLORS
Classic Tabby Pattern—All markings are clearly defined from the ground color. The characteristic head marking is a letter *M*, resembling frown marks on the forehead. Unbroken lines run from the outer corners of the eyes toward the back of the head. There are other pencil markings on the face, especially swirls on the cheeks. Lines extend back from the top of the head to the shoulder markings, which are shaped in a butterfly pattern. Three unbroken lines run parallel to each other down the spine from the shoulder markings to the base of the tail. A large blotch on each flank is circled

by one or more unbroken rings. These markings should be symmetrical on either side of the body. There should be several unbroken necklaces on the neck and upper chest. A double row of buttons runs from chest to stomach. Both legs and tail are evenly ringed.

Mackerel Tabby—Rare in Persians, but recognized. Head is marked with the characteristic *M* and there is an unbroken line running from the outer corner of the eyes toward the back of the head. There are other pencil markings on the cheeks. A narrow unbroken line runs from the back of the head to the base of the tail. The rest of the body is marked with narrow unbroken lines running vertically down from the spine line. These lines should be narrow, numerous and clearly defined from the ground color. There should be several unbroken necklaces on the neck and upper chest. A double row of buttons runs from chest to stomach. Legs are evenly barred with narrow bracelets and the tail evenly ringed.

Brown Tabby—Ground color tawny-sable to copper-brown. Markings jet black. No white hairs. Noseleather brick-red. Paw pads black or dark brown, the dark color extending up the back of the hind legs from paw to heel. Eyes copper or hazel.

Red Tabby—Ground color red. Markings dark red. Lips and chin red. No white hairs or patches. Noseleather brick-red. Paw pads pink. Eyes copper or gold.

Silver Tabby—Ground color silver. Markings jet black and clearly defined. Noseleather brick-red. Paw pads black. Eyes green or hazel.

Blue Tabby—Ground color, lips and chin pale blue-ivory. Markings deep slate-blue. Noseleather deep rose-pink. Paw pads rose-pink. Eyes copper.

A Blue Classic-Tabby Persian.

Cream Tabby—Ground color, lips and chin pale cream. Markings rich cream, not too red but dark enough to contrast with the ground color. Noseleather and paw pads pink. Eyes copper.

Cameo Tabby—Ground color, lips and chin off-white. Markings red. Noseleather and paw pads rose. Eyes copper to gold.

Patched Tabby—Markings classic or mackerel tabby with red, cream, or red and cream patches. Facial blaze preferred.

Brown—Ground color copper-brown. Markings jet black with red, cream, or red and cream. Noseleather brick-red. Paw pads black or brown. Eyes copper.

Silver—Ground color pale silver. Markings jet black with red, cream, or red and cream. Noseleather and paw pads rose-pink. Eyes copper or hazel.

Blue—Ground color pale blue-ivory. Markings deep slate-blue with red, cream, or red and cream. Eyes copper.

Van Persians

These cats are almost entirely white, with patches of color on head, legs and tail. Noseleather and paw pads in keeping with coat color or pink. Eyes copper-gold.

Van Bicolor—Patches of black, blue, red or cream.

Van Calico—Patches of black and red.

Van Blue-Cream—Patches of blue and cream.

Brown Classic-Tabby Persian

Silver Classic-Tabby Persian

Persian

Red Mackerel-Tabby Persian

PEKE-FACE PERSIAN

Advantages
- *Affectionate*
- *Intelligent*
- *Quiet*
- *Suitable for an apartment*

Disadvantages
- *Needs daily grooming*
- *May have breathing problems*
- *May have feeding problems*

Occasionally, in Red Tabby Persian litters, a kitten with a face resembling a Pekingese dog appears. It has a shorter nose and an indentation between the eyes. It is called a Peke-Face Persian. It is as sweet and companionable as other Persians. Because of its snub nose and large jowls, it may suffer from breathing and feeding problems if upper and lower teeth do not meet in an even bite. The Peke-Face Persian is almost unknown outside the United States.

GROOMING
Like all Persians, the Peke-Face requires daily grooming with brush and comb to remove knots and tangles from its long coat. Attention must also be paid to the eyes. Tear ducts may become blocked. Sponge away any mucus collecting in the corners of the eyes with warm water. Examine ears and teeth regularly.

ORIGIN AND HISTORY
Peke-Face Persians have been bred for many years. They are popular and have been shown since the 1930s. The breed has attracted criticism, especially from veterinarians, because its extreme facial characteristics may cause breathing and feeding difficulties.

BREEDING
Two Peke-Face cats mated together do not necessarily produce Peke-Face kittens. The best ones come from Red Tabby and Peke-Face matings.

It is not immediately obvious whether there are any Peke-Face kittens in a litter of Red Tabbies. The Peke characteristics do not appear for some weeks. Breeders must take special care to make sure the physical features that cause problems are reduced. These features have limited the breed's popularity.

KITTENS
There is a high mortality rate among Peke-Face kittens because of the difficulties in feeding and breathing. Kittens often try to feed by using their paws to bring food to their mouths. If they do not have an even bite, they may not be able to get enough to eat. They develop slowly and seem to remain kittenish longer than other Persians.

Kittens with facial Peke-Face characteristics, but without the problems associated with overtyping, develop normally.

SHOW REQUIREMENTS
The Peke-Face Persian is a solid, cobby cat of Persian type, with a distinctive face that resembles a Pekingese dog.
Coat—Long, flowing, silky and soft with a large ruff around the neck.
Body—Short, cobby and massive. Legs short. Paws large, with tufts.
Tail—Short, plumed and full at the base.
Head—Large, round and heavy with a short snub nose. Indented between the eyes, giving an obvious nose break. Muzzle is wrinkled with a fold of skin running from the corner of the eye to the mouth. The forehead bulges out above the nose and eyes. The neck is short and thick. Ears are small, although slightly larger than in other Persians.
Eyes—Prominent, almost bulging, round and full.

COLORS
Only two colors are recognized for competition, although Peke-Face cats also appear in Dilute Red.
Red—Body color an even deep red throughout with no markings or white hairs. Noseleather and paw pads brick-red. Eyes copper.
Red Tabby—Ground color red. Markings in either classic or mackerel tabby pattern, deep rich red. Noseleather and paw pads brick-red. Eyes copper.

RAGDOLL

Advantages
- *Gentle*
- *Affectionate*
- *Quiet*
- *Playful*
- *Intelligent*
- *Suitable for an apartment*

Disadvantages
- *Vulnerable to injury*
- *Does not feel pain*

The Ragdoll is a large, cuddly cat that is fun to have around. Its thick fur does not mat. It is quiet, loyal, affectionate and dependent on its owner. Because it is believed it does not feel pain, the Ragdoll is vulnerable to injury. An injury may go unnoticed. If you are thinking about owning a Ragdoll, be aware that this cat requires mothering.

The Ragdoll has another unique feature. When picked up and carried, it relaxes completely, becoming limp like a ragdoll. Although this has given the breed its name, scientific tests show this cat is physiologically the same as other cats.

GROOMING
The Ragdoll has a long coat and needs daily grooming to remove dead hairs. It sheds heavily in the summer; thorough grooming is important. Tangles should be combed out using a wide-tooth comb. Brush the coat gently and thoroughly with a long-bristle brush.

ORIGIN AND HISTORY
The Ragdoll originated in California and is of mixed ancestry. The foundation stock seems to have involved a white Angora, a Birman and a non-pedigree Burmese. This mixed blood resulted in large and vigorous descendants. Within accepted colors and patterns, Ragdolls breed true. Today, Ragdolls are mated only to Ragdolls, although in the early days of the breed there were many crosses back to the foundation sires. The breed was first recognized for competition in 1965, but it has not gained acceptance by all American cat associations. At present, Ragdolls are unknown outside the United States.

BREEDING
To preserve the distinguishing features of the breed, Ragdolls are mated only to Ragdolls. It is possible to produce Ragdoll kittens in one of the desired coat patterns and colors in every litter.

KITTENS
Kittens are born all-white. The point colors and coat shading develop gradually. Ragdoll kittens are slow to mature. It may take three years for the full adult coat to develop.

SHOW REQUIREMENTS
The Ragdoll is a large, heavily built cat with a long flowing coat and a characteristic limpness when held.
Coat—Long, full and silky. Non-matting. Luxuriant ruff and extra-long fur on the chest and stomach. Shorter on the face. The coat is likely to be longer in cold than warm climates. It sheds heavily during summer months.
Body—Large and heavy with strong bones. Males 15 to 20 pounds (6.8 to 9kg). Females 9 to 12 pounds (4 to 5.4kg) and shorter in the body than males. Hindquarters are heavy. The cat has a furry, loose stomach pad. As broad across the shoulders as across the rump, with a deep chest. Legs medium in length and heavy, with hind legs slightly longer than forelegs. Paws large, round and firm with tufts of hair between toes.
Tail—Long and furry. Medium thick at the base with a slight taper toward the tip. A short or kinked tail is a fault.
Head—Medium size with a modified wedge. Wider in the male than in the female. The skull between the ears is flat. Cheeks are full, tapering to a round chin. There is a gentle nose break that gives a distinctive profile. Neck is strong, short and thick. Ears medium size, broad at the base, round at the tips, tilting forward with ear tufts. Large, small or pointed ears are faults.
Eyes—Large, oval, set wide apart. Round or almond-shape eyes or squints are faults.

COLORS
Ragdolls are bred in three coat patterns: colorpoint, mitted and bicolor. Point colors within these patterns are seal, chocolate, blue and lilac. All are recognized for competition in some associations.
Colorpoint—Body color an even shade to the roots. Points—ears, mask, legs and tail—darker to provide a distinct contrast with the body color. Chest, bib and chin a lighter shade of body color. Ticking and white spotting not accepted.
Mitted—Body color an even shade to the roots. Points darker, providing a distinct contrast with the body color. Chest, bib and chin white. A white stripe runs from the bib between the forelegs to the base of the tail. White mittens on both front paws evenly matched and scalloped. White boots on hind legs also match. Color spots in white areas or ticking on colored areas are faults.
Bicolor—Body color an even shade to the roots. The ears, mask, with the exception of an inverted white V down the nose, and tail are darker and clearly defined. Chest, stomach and legs white. The symmetrical inverted V on the face starts between the ears, covers the nose, whisker pads, neck and bib. It should not extend beyond the outer edge of the eyes. No color spots on the white areas. Body areas may have small spots of white.
Seal-Point—Body color a pale fawn shading to pale cream on the underparts. Points dense seal-brown. Noseleather dark brown. Paw pads dark brown or black. Eyes deep blue.
Chocolate-Point—Body color an even ivory all over. Points warm milk-chocolate. Noseleather rose. Paw pads salmon. Eyes deep blue.
Blue-Point—Body color an even platinum blue-gray, shading to lighter blue on the underparts. Points deep blue-gray. Noseleather and paw pads dark blue-gray. Eyes deep blue.
Lilac-Point—Body color an even milk-white all over. Points gray-pink. Inside ears pale pink. Noseleather lilac. Paw pads coral pink. Eyes deep blue.

Ragdoll

Chocolate-Point
Bicolor Ragdoll

Lilac-Point Bicolor
Ragdoll kitten

Peke-Face
Persian

Red Tabby Peke-Face
Persian

HIMALAYAN
Colorpoint

Advantages
- *Affectionate*
- *Devoted*
- *Intelligent*
- *Learns quickly*
- *Good with children*

Disadvantages
- *Needs daily grooming*
- *Does not like to be caged*

A Himalayan is a Persian with Siamese coloring, called the Himalayan pattern. It is more demanding and independent than many Persians, although more docile and less demonstrative than a Siamese. The Himalayan, or Himmy, likes to choose its own activities and is happiest if given the run of the house.

Do not have a Himalayan as a pet unless you are prepared to devote a lot of time to grooming. The Himalayan is beautiful and makes an affectionate, devoted pet.

Show cats are expensive but kittens that do not meet show standards are lower priced.

GROOMING
Daily grooming is essential. If neglected, the undercoat mats into tight knots. In extreme cases, knots might have to be cut out under anesthetic. Despite regular attention, mats sometimes form, particularly if the cat spends a lot of time outside. A mat cutter designed for dogs can be used to cut through a mat to remove it rather than cutting it out and leaving a bare spot. Have your vet or a professional do this for you.

Use a wide-tooth comb to remove knots, followed by a medium-tooth comb to remove dead hairs. Brush the coat with a long-handle, pure-bristle brush. Repeated daily, this keeps the coat healthy. A little powder dusted into the coat before brushing helps untangle fur, but brush it out thoroughly afterwards. Inspection of eyes for blocked tear ducts and ears for mites completes the daily routine.

ORIGIN AND HISTORY
The Himalayan is a manufactured breed, specifically produced by breeders. It is not a Siamese with long hair, but a Persian with Siamese coloring. The name Himalayan comes from the coat pattern of the Himalayan rabbit, where darker color is confined to the face, legs and tail, as in the Siamese.

The breeding of the Himmy involved complex scientific techniques and took years to perfect into the correct Persian type. Breeders crossed Siamese with Persians for many years but had gotten only solid shorthair kittens. In the 1940s, a series of scientific experiments was made, crossing Siamese with longhair Black Persians and Blue Persians. The resulting shorthair self-color kittens proved useful for breeding. They carried the genes required to produce the Himalayan. They were mated together and back to their parents until Himalayan kittens were produced. Further selective breeding back to longhair Blacks and Blues to develop Persian type was carried out. The resulting cats, when mated back to Himalayans, produced excellent new generation Himalayans.

After 10 years of selective breeding, the long noses and large ears of the Siamese were bred out, but the colorpoint coat pattern, blue eyes and Persian type were fixed. It was recognized independently as the Himalayan in 1957.

BREEDING
Himalayan-to-Himalayan breeding produces 100% Himalayan kittens. To preserve type, outcrosses are still made to solid-color Persians and the offspring mated back to the original Himalayans. With outcrossing to other-color Persians, all point colors are possible. Mixed breeding has made the Himalayan a hardy breed. Litters containing 6 kittens are not uncommon.

KITTENS
The kittens are born with white fur and pink paw pads, noses and ears. The point color gradually develops over the first few weeks. Kittens have a lot of energy and curiosity.

SHOW REQUIREMENTS
The Himalayan is a Persian-type cat, although slightly larger, with the Himalayan coat pattern. The main color is confined to the mask, legs and tail.

Coat—Long, thick, soft and silky, standing away from the body. The ruff is full and extends to a frill between the front legs.
Body—Cobby and low on the legs. Deep in the chest. Massive across the shoulders and rump, short and round in between. Long, svelte Siamese lines are a fault. Legs are short, thick, straight and strong. Paws are large, round and firm with long toe tufts.
Tail—Short, full and carried low. A long or kinked tail is a fault.
Head—Broad and round, with width between the ears. The neck is short and thick. Face is round. Nose is short and broad with a definite break in profile. Ears are small, round at the tips, tilting forward and not too open at the base. They are set far apart, low on the head and furnished with long tufts.
Eyes—Large, round and full. Set wide apart.

COLORS
All point colors are possible, although not all are recognized at present. More recently developed varieties include the female-only Chocolate Tortie-point and Lilac Cream-point. The Smoke-points and the Tabby-points are now recognized in Europe.
Coat Pattern—Body an even, pale color with the main contrasting color confined to the points—mask, ears, legs and tail. The mask covers the whole face, but not the top of the head, and is connected to the ears by tracings.
Seal-Point—Body an even pale fawn to warm cream, shading to a lighter cream on chest and stomach. Points deep seal-brown. Noseleather and paw pads seal-brown. Eyes deep blue.
Chocolate-Point—Body ivory all over. Points milk-chocolate color. Noseleather and paw pads cinnamon-pink. Eyes deep blue.
Blue-Point—Body blue-white, shading to a warmer white on the chest and stomach. Points slate-blue. Noseleather and paw pads slate-blue. Eyes deep blue.
Lilac-Point—Body white. Points gray with a pink tone. Noseleather and paw pads lavender-pink. Eyes deep blue.
Red-Point—Body cream-white. Points light orange to red. Noseleather and paw pads flesh-pink or coral-pink. Eyes deep blue.
Cream-Point—Body cream-white. Points buff-cream. Noseleather and paw pads flesh-color or coral-pink. Eyes deep blue.
Tortie-Point—Body color and basic point color as appropriate to Seal-point and Chocolate-point. Points patched with red, cream, or red and cream. A blaze of red or cream on the face is desirable.

Noseleather and paw pads pink or in keeping with the basic point color. Eyes deep blue.
Blue-Cream-Point—Body blue-white or cream-white, shading to white on the chest and stomach. Points blue, with patches of cream. Noseleather and paw pads slate-blue, pink, or slate-blue and pink. Eyes deep blue.
Lilac-Cream-Point—Body white. Points pink-gray, patched with pale cream. A facial blaze is desirable. Noseleather and paw pads lavender-pink or pink. Eyes deep blue.
Tabby-Point—Body color as appropriate to the point color, which can be seal, chocolate, blue, lilac or red. Points carry characteristic *M* marking on forehead, bars on face and fainter rings on legs and tail, in the appropriate solid color. Defined from a paler background. Noseleather and paw pads in keeping with point color. Eyes deep blue.

HIMALAYAN HYBRIDS

Outcrossing to Persians to improve the Colorpoint resulted in other-color longhair kittens in litters. These cats are regarded as Himalayan hybrids. They are useful for breeding Himalayans because they carry the appropriate genes. But they cannot be shown. They look like Persians, but are usually less expensive and make excellent pets for people wanting a Persian-type cat not intended for show.

Self-Color Himalayan
Kashmir

Chocolate and lilac cats that appeared when breeding the Colorpoint are classed as Solid-Color Himalayans. They first appeared in Himalayan or hybrid litters when an outcross to a Persian had been made to improve type. It has taken several years to achieve an even body color with the long flowing coat required by the standard. Lilac is a dilute form of Chocolate. The show standard is the same as for the Himalayan.

COLORS
Chocolate—Medium to dark chocolate-brown, with the same depth of color from the root to the tip of each hair. No sign of a paler undercoat. Noseleather and paw pads brown. Eyes deep orange or copper.
Lilac—Pink-gray all over with no sign of a paler undercoat. Noseleather pink. Paw pads pale pink. Eyes pale orange.

Lilac Kashmir

Tortie-Point
Colorpoint

Colorpoint
and Kashmir

Seal-Point Himalayan

BALINESE
Longhair Siamese

Advantages
- *Quieter than the Siamese*
- *Lively*
- *Affectionate*
- *Good with children*

Disadvantages
- *Dislikes being left alone*
- *Needs daily grooming*

A Balinese makes an excellent pet. It enjoys fun with the family and loves people. It resembles the Siamese in its graceful beauty, but is quieter in voice and temperament. It is easy to care for.

Although still a rare breed, the Balinese is becoming more popular because of its delightful personality. It makes a good pet for a person who likes the Siamese look, but prefers a less overwhelming personality!

GROOMING
The Balinese is easy to groom. The coat is long, silky and non-matting. It needs daily grooming to remove dead hairs. Brushing for a few minutes with a soft-bristle brush is all that is required.

ORIGIN AND HISTORY
The Balinese is a natural mutation, derived from Siamese parents with a mutant gene for long hair. A few longhair kittens first appeared in Siamese litters and were selectively bred together. The breed was first recognized in 1963. By 1970, the Balinese was being shown in Europe.

The name is unconnected with its origin. It was named because of its graceful agility. Its movements resemble those of Balinese dancers.

BREEDING
Longhair Siamese kittens appear from time to time in Siamese litters. When mated together they breed true, producing all-Balinese kittens. Outcrossing to Siamese is necessary to improve type. Balinese litters normally contain 5 or 6 kittens.

KITTENS
Kittens are born white. Point markings gradually appear over the first few weeks.

SHOW REQUIREMENTS
The Balinese is medium size, svelte and dainty. Lithe and muscular, it has long, tapering Siamese lines and a silky coat.

Coat—Erminelike and soft. Silky and flowing, 2 inches (5cm) or more in length. It may be shorter in summer. No downy undercoat or ruff around the neck.

Body—Medium size, long and svelte. Fine boned but muscular. Males may be larger than females. Legs long and slim, hind legs longer than forelegs. Feet dainty, small and oval.

Tail—Long, thin and tapering to a point. Plumed.

Head—Long, tapering wedge, making a straight-edge triangle from jaw to ears. No whisker break. Nose is long and straight with no nose break. Neck long and slender. Ears wide at the base, large and pointed. Not less than the width of an eye between eyes.

Eyes—Medium size and almond shape. Slanted toward the nose. No squints allowed.

COLORS
Only seal, chocolate, blue and lilac are recognized for competition. Cats with other Siamese colors are known as Javanese, but carry the same standard for type as the Balinese.

Coat Pattern—Body an even, pale color. The main contrasting color confined to the mask, ears, legs and tail. The mask covers the whole face, but not the top of the head. It is connected to the ears by tracings. Older cats may have darker body color.

Seal-Point—Body color pale fawn to warm cream, shading to a lighter cream on the chest and stomach. Points seal-brown. Noseleather and paw pads seal-brown. Eyes deep blue.

Chocolate-Point—Body color ivory. Points warm milk-chocolate color. Noseleather and paw pads cinnamon-pink. Eyes deep blue.

Blue-Point—Body color blue-white, shading to a warmer white on the chest and stomach. Points slate-blue. Noseleather and paw pads slate-blue. Eyes deep blue.

Lilac-Point—Body color white. Points gray with a pink tone. Noseleather and paw pads lavender-pink. Eyes deep blue.

Red-Point—Body color cream-white. Points delicate orange to red. Noseleather and paw pads flesh-pink or coral-pink. Eyes deep blue.

Cream-Point—Body color cream-white. Points buff-cream. Noseleather and paw pads flesh-color or coral-pink. Eyes deep blue.

Tortie-Point—Body color and basic point color as appropriate to Seal-point and Chocolate-point. Points patched with red, cream, or red and cream. A blaze of red or cream is desirable. Noseleather and paw pads of the basic point color or pink. Eyes deep blue.

Blue-Cream-Point—Body color blue-white or cream-white, shading to white on the chest and stomach. Points blue with patches of cream. Noseleather and paw pads slate-blue or pink. Eyes deep blue.

Lilac-Cream-Point—Body color white. Points pink-gray, patched with pale cream. A facial blaze is desirable. Noseleather and paw pads lavender-pink or pink. Eyes deep blue.

Tabby-Point—Body color as appropriate to the point color, which can be seal, chocolate, blue, lilac or red. Points carry an *M* mark on forehead, bars on face and fainter rings on legs and tail in appropriate solid color. Defined from a paler background. Noseleather and paw pads in keeping with point color. Eyes deep blue.

BIRMAN
Sacred Cat Of Burma

Advantages
- *Intelligent*
- *Adaptable*
- *Easy to train*
- *Good with children*
- *Quiet*

Disadvantages
- *Needs daily grooming*
- *Does not like to be caged*

The Birman is as individual in its personality as in its looks. It has a quiet, gentle charm. Intelligent and friendly, a Birman enjoys being part of the family. It mixes with other animals, is adaptable, playful and likes freedom to roam around the house.

GROOMING
The Birman's coat does not mat, but must be brushed and combed daily to remove dead hair. For a show cat, grooming powder dusted into the paler areas of the coat removes grease marks.

ORIGIN AND HISTORY
The Birman, or Sacred Cat of Burma, originated in the temples of Burma. It probably developed by natural crosses between Siamese and bicolor longhair cats. In France, it was established in the 1920s, and first recognized there in 1925. At about the same time, another line was established in Germany. In 1959, the first Birmans arrived in the United States.

BREEDING
Birmans breed true to type. Litters usually contain 4 kittens.

KITTENS
Birman kittens are large and healthy. They maintain their playful behavior into adulthood.

SHOW REQUIREMENTS
The Birman is a large, longhair cat with the Himalayan coat pattern, but with four white paws.

Coat—Long and silky with a tendency to wave on the stomach. Non-matting. Thick, heavy ruff around the neck.

Body—Medium long, but stocky and low on the legs. Legs heavy, medium in length. Paws round, firm and large with toes close together.

Tail—Medium in length and bushy. No kinks allowed.

Head—Strong, broad and round. Cheeks full. Roman nose with low nostrils. Ears wide apart, as wide at the base as tall, round at the tips.

Eyes—Almost round.

COLORS
Only four colors occur naturally within the breed: seal-point, chocolate-point, blue-point and lilac-point. All have white feet or gloves.

Coat Pattern—Body a pale color with the main contrasting color confined to the mask, ears, legs and tail. A mask covers the whole face, including the whisker pads. It is connected to the ears by tracings. Front paws have white gloves ending in an even line across the paw over the knuckles. A white glove covers hind paws and extends up the back of the legs to a point just below the hocks. These markings are known as *laces* or *gauntlets*.

Seal-Point—Body color a pale beige to cream, warm in tone with a characteristic golden glow over the back. Especially obvious in adult males. Underparts and chest slightly paler. Points, except gloves, dark seal-brown. Gloves white. Noseleather seal-brown. Paw pads pink. Eyes violet-blue.

Chocolate-Point—Body color ivory. Points, except gloves, warm milk-chocolate. Gloves white. Noseleather cinnamon-pink. Paw pads pink. Eyes violet-blue.

Blue-Point—Body color blue-white. Cold in tone, becoming less cold on the stomach and chest. Points, except gloves, deep blue. Gloves white. Noseleather slate-gray. Paw pads pink. Eyes violet-blue.

Lilac-Point—Body color white. Points, except gloves, frosty gray-pink. Gloves white. Noseleather lavender-pink. Paw pads pink. Eyes violet-blue.

Balinese

Blue-Point Balinese

Seal-Point Birman

Birman

NORWEGIAN FOREST CAT
Norsk Skogkatt

Advantages
- *Athletic*
- *Waterproof coat*
- *Good hunter*
- *Playful*

Disadvantages
- *Needs daily grooming*
- *Prefers outdoor life*
- *Sheds in spring and summer*
- *Not common in the United States*

The Norwegian Forest Cat loves the outdoors. It is active, with a robust, hardy disposition and loves to climb trees. Its unique waterproof coat dries in about 15 minutes after heavy rain. It loves to show off in front of an audience and is affectionate, intelligent and extremely playful.

The Norwegian Forest Cat is used to a rough life and is a good rodent catcher. This cat is happiest living outdoors where it is free to roam. Confined in an apartment, it might soon become bored.

GROOMING
The Norwegian Forest Cat has a double coat. Its undercoat is tight and woolly. The topcoat is water resistant and silky. The coat does not mat, but needs careful daily grooming if the cat is shown. To prevent fur balls, groom daily with a brush and comb, especially during the early summer months when the undercoat is being shed. After this, less attention is necessary until the full coat is grown again in the autumn.

ORIGIN AND HISTORY
Despite its name, which suggests a wild origin, the Norwegian Forest Cat has been domesticated in Norway for several centuries. Cats of this type are frequently kept on farms.

The breed is believed to have evolved as a result of the harsh Scandinavian climate. It is likely the cat's ancestors were shorthair cats from Southern Europe and longhair cats from Asia Minor, brought to Scandinavia by traders and travelers. Kept as mousers, not as pets, they led an outdoor life. The harsh climate may have meant that only cats with heavier coats survived the winters.

In recent years, pedigree breeding lines of Norwegian Forest Cats have been established. Now there are about 500 registered. The breed was recognized by Federation Internationale Feline d'Europe in 1977. It is accepted for competition at all European shows. The breed is little known outside Europe. Most cats are bred in Norway. It is not recognized or bred in the United States.

BREEDING
Queens kitten easily and make attentive mothers.

KITTENS
Norwegian Forest kittens are healthy and playful. The first adult coat begins to grow at 3 to 5 months of age.

SHOW REQUIREMENTS
The Norwegian Forest Cat gives the impression of strength. It is muscular, with a long body and long legs. A characteristic feature is its shaggy, weather-resistant coat.
Coat—Long topcoat. Guard hairs are smooth and oily, making the coat water repellent. Tight woolly undercoat. In autumn, a ruff grows around the neck and chest, but is shed the following summer. Coat quality may vary with living conditions. Cats kept indoors most of the time have softer, shorter coats.
Body—Long, large and heavily built. Legs long. Hind legs longer than forelegs. Feet wide with heavy paws. Slender body is a fault.
Tail—Long and well-furnished.
Head—Triangular in shape, with a long, wide straight nose without a nose break. Neck long, cheeks full, chin heavy. Ears long, set high on the head, upright and pointed. Furnished inside with long ear tufts. Whiskers prominent and long. Faults include a short nose, small or wide-set ears.
Eyes—Large, open and set wide apart.

COLORS
Any coat color or pattern is permitted with or without white. White often appears on the chest and paws. Tabby cats generally have heavier coats than solid and bicolor varieties. Eye color same as coat color.

MAINE COON

Advantages
- *Hardy*
- *Active*
- *Quiet, unique voice*
- *Adaptable*
- *Good with children*
- *Even-tempered*
- *Easy to care for*
- *Good mouser*

Disadvantages
- *No drawbacks known*

The Maine Coon is a large cat, hardy and active. It is good with children, but shy. It is even-tempered, and easy to groom and care for. It loves playing and performing tricks and has a quiet, chirping voice. No two Maine Coons sound alike. Distinctive in appearance, the cat is almost shorthair in front and longhair along the back and stomach. The Maine Coon is apt to sleep in strange positions and in peculiar places. Although adaptable to indoor or outdoor life, this cat prefers plenty of space to roam.

Requiring little grooming, it makes an ideal pet for the person who likes the beauty of a longhair cat, but does not have the time to devote to daily grooming.

GROOMING
The Maine Coon's undercoat is thin, so the cat is easy to groom. A gentle brushing and combing every few days removes dead hairs.

ORIGIN AND HISTORY
Like many breeds of cat, the Maine Coon's origin is unknown. It probably developed from matings between domestic shorthair cats and longhair cats brought by traders from Asia to Maine.

It is possible in its early days that the Maine Coon may have roamed free and was given the name *coon cat* because of its similarity in appearance and habits to the native raccoon. Both have long fur and are similar in color, climb trees and have ringed tails.

Although no early records were kept, Maine Coons were known in the East Coast states by the end of the 19th century. They were kept as mousers long before they became show cats. But they were one of the earliest breeds seen at cat shows. Many Maine Coons were exhibited at the first New York cat show in 1860. A Maine Coon was Best in Show at a Madison Square Garden cat show in New York in 1895. After that time, interest in the breed almost died out until the formation of the Maine Coon Cat Club in 1953, which held regular one-breed shows for them.

The Maine Coon is no longer confined to the state from which it takes its name. It is known and bred in Europe.

BREEDING
Maine Coons usually have only one litter per year and make good mothers. Because of the breed's mixed background, the litters often contain a colorful assortment of kittens.

KITTENS
The large, robust kittens mature slowly. They may take up to four years to develop their full beauty.

SHOW REQUIREMENTS
The Maine Coon is tough, large and rugged, solidly built, with a smooth, shaggy coat.
Coat—Heavy and shaggy, yet silky in texture. Lustrous and flowing. Short on the face and shoulders but longer on the stomach and hind legs, where it forms long shaggy breeches.
Body—Long body with a broad chest and level back, giving a rectangular appearance. Males 10 to 12 pounds (4.5 to 5.4kg), females smaller, 8 to 10 pounds (3.6 to 4.5kg). Muscular, with strong legs set wide apart. Feet large and round. Paws tufted.
Tail—Blunt end, furnished with long fur. Plumelike. Wider at the base. No kinks allowed.
Head—Medium length and width, set on a powerful neck. Square muzzle. Firm chin, not undershot. High cheekbones. Nose medium length, with a slight upward tilt. Ears large and tufted, wide at the base and tapering to a point. Set high on the head.
Eyes—Slightly slanting, large and set wide apart.

COLORS
Maine Coons are bred in all coat colors and patterns, with combinations of colors and patterns, such as tabby with white. Eye color can be green, gold or copper. White cats may also be blue-eye or odd-eye. There is no relationship between eye color and coat color or patterns. Color standards for show cats are the same as those for Persians.

Maine Coon kittens take an active interest in life.

Norwegian Forest Cat

Brown Tabby-And-White Norwegian Forest Cat

Blue-And-White Bicolor Maine Coon

Maine Coon

TURKISH ANGORA
Angora

Advantages
- *Intelligent*
- *Loyal*
- *Friendly*
- *Quiet*
- *Adaptable*

Disadvantages
- *Needs daily grooming*
- *Sheds in spring and summer*

The Angora makes a charming, dainty companion. It is attractive, with its long lithe body and plumed tail. It is not a talkative cat but is loyal, affectionate and adaptable. An Angora is happy living in town or in the country, but prefers the run of the house. Alert, lively and intelligent, it loves to play games and to show off for an audience.

Angoras are bred in most colors and patterns, although white is probably the most popular. Some of the blue-eye and odd-eye Whites may be deaf. Have a vet check a kitten before you purchase one to be certain it is not deaf.

The Angora is still a rare breed and may be expensive to buy. It is possible to purchase a non-show kitten for a reasonable price.

GROOMING
Although the Angora is easier to groom than a Persian, it still needs daily grooming. Use a medium-tooth comb to remove dead hair. Grooming is important in spring and early summer when the coat is shed.

ORIGIN AND HISTORY
The Angora may be the oldest longhair breed in Europe. It originally came from Ankara, Turkey. It exists there today as a free-roaming domestic cat.

Angoras arrived in Great Britain via France at the end of the 16th century. They were known for a time as French cats. In the early days they were mated with Persians. The Persian type was dominant and the Angora type was lost, until recently. Early Persians had long, thick coats, lacking the silkiness of the Angora coat. Angoras may have been used to improve the Persian coat.

The breed has been revived with cats imported directly from the Ankara Zoo. These cats are white, but other colors have been bred. Many colors are now recognized for showing.

A blue-eye White Angora. Some blue-eye Whites are born deaf. Have a kitten checked before you buy it.

BREEDING
Angora litters usually contain 4 to 5 kittens, though a litter of 6 or 7 is not uncommon. Although many colors occur naturally within the breed, white is so dominant that it almost always appears in the coat. It is difficult to produce show-quality Angoras in other colors. Deafness is common among blue-eye and odd-eye white Angoras.

KITTENS
Angora kittens are charming, fluffy and playful. White kittens born with a smudge of black hairs on the top of their heads usually have good hearing in at least one ear. Kittens mature slowly and the coat is not fully developed until two years old.

SHOW REQUIREMENTS
The Angora is medium size, solidly built, but graceful and lithe with a long, flowing coat.
Coat—Medium-length silky hair. Slightly wavy, especially on the stomach. No thick woolly undercoat. Hair is long on the underparts and ruff, and shorter along the back and on the face.
Body—Medium size, long, graceful and lithe. Fine but strong boned. Long, sturdy legs. Hind legs slightly longer than forelegs. Feet small, oval to round, and dainty. Toes tufted.
Tail—Long and tapering. Wider at the base and plumed. When moving, tail is carried horizontally over the body, sometimes almost touching the head.
Head—Medium size and wide. Gently pointed wedge. Nose straight without a stop. Neck long and slim. Ears set high on head, large and pointed. Broad based and tufted.
Eyes—Large, round-to-oval in shape and slightly slanted.

COLORS
Chalky white is the favorite color, but these colors are also accepted: black, blue, chocolate and lilac in tabby patterns, red, tortoiseshell, cinnamon and bicolors. Chocolate and lilac are not accepted. Eyes are amber in all colors. Brown and Silver Tabbies may have green or hazel eyes. White may be blue-eye or odd-eye—one blue, one amber.

TURKISH
Turkish Van Cat

Advantages
- *Intelligent*
- *Hardy*
- *Lively*
- *Likes water and swims*

Disadvantages
- *Needs daily grooming*
- *Sheds in spring and summer*
- *Not shown in the United States*

This breed is not recognized for competition. Some Turkish are bred and kept as pets. This cat is beautiful, with its white coat and striking auburn face and tail. It enjoys swimming and playing with water. In colder climates, care must be taken to make sure the cat does not catch cold.

This is still a rare breed, so you may have to pay a lot of money for one. You may have to wait for a kitten, as demand will probably exceed the supply. It is worth the wait because it is lively, affectionate and makes a charming, intelligent companion. A neutered male makes an excellent pet and may be obtained more reasonably because not as many studs are kept for breeding as female kittens.

GROOMING
A light daily combing removes dead hairs, particularly when the cat is shedding in spring and summer. A little grooming powder may be dusted into the coat to remove grease marks, which mar the white appearance. Unlike many other cats, the Turkish enjoys a bath.

ORIGIN AND HISTORY
Turkish cats are believed to have originated from natural selection due to interbreeding within the Van region of Turkey, a geographically isolated area. They have been domesticated there for centuries. They were first brought to Great Britain from Turkey by an English breeder in the 1950s. The line was gradually established with more cats imported from Turkey.

BREEDING
Turkish cats breed true. Kittens always resemble their parents. The breed is being kept pure by not outcrossing to any other breed or color variety. The average litter contains 4 kittens.

KITTENS
Kittens are born white, not pink. Auburn markings are clearly visible. Their eyes open early, at 4 or 5 days. Eyes are blue and gradually change to pale amber.

SHOW REQUIREMENTS
The Turkish is medium size, sturdy and strong. It has a long, silky coat. Males are larger and more muscular than females.
Coat—Silky, long, straight fur, without a thick woolly undercoat.
Body—Long but sturdy, with medium-length legs. Feet small and round, with tufted toes.
Tail—Medium length and full.
Head—Short and wedge shape. Medium-length neck. Nose long, not snub. Ears large, upright, close together. Ears shell-pink inside and tufted.
Eyes—Round, pink rimmed.

COLOR
Chalk white with auburn markings on the face, around and below the ears. A white blaze continues up between the ears. Nose, cheeks and chin are white. Tail is ringed in two shades of auburn. Markings are obvious in kittens. Small auburn markings are allowed elsewhere on the body. Noseleather and paw pads pale pink. Eyes pale amber.

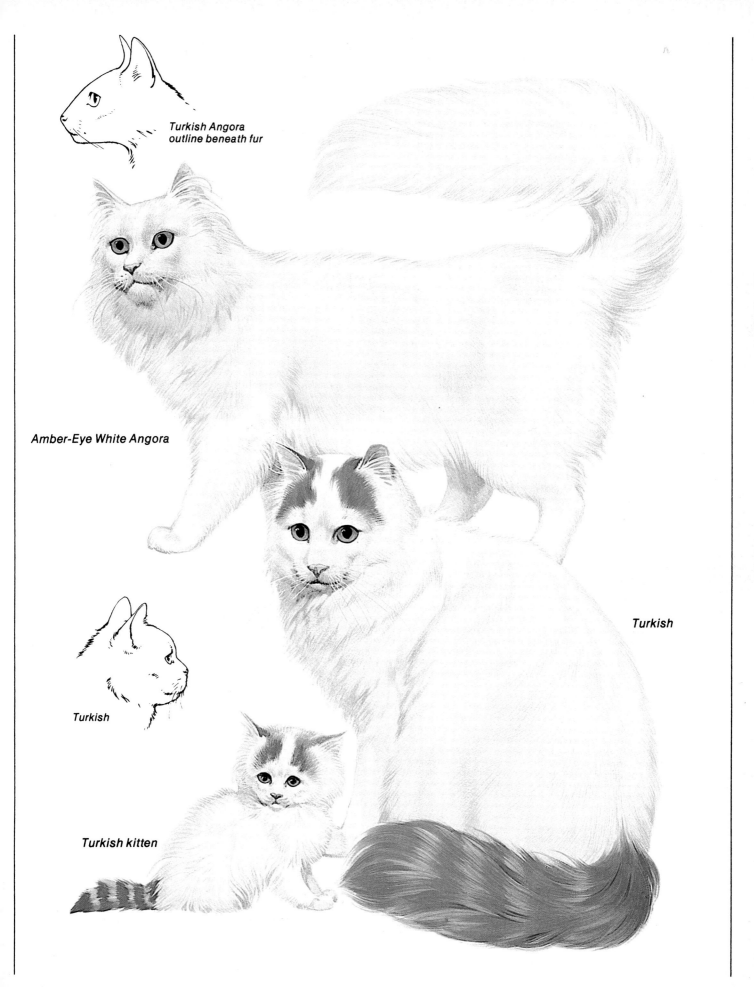

Turkish Angora outline beneath fur

Amber-Eye White Angora

Turkish

Turkish

Turkish kitten

CYMRIC
Longhair Manx

Advantages
- *Intelligent*
- *Quiet*
- *Loyal*
- *Affectionate*
- *Strong*
- *Gentle*
- *Good mouser*
- *Good with children*
- *Good with dogs*

Disadvantages
- *Needs daily grooming*

The Cymric, pronounced *kum-rick,* has a unique appearance. It has no tail, but it has long hair, which makes it different from the Manx. The Cymric is loyal, affectionate, gentle, intelligent, courageous and strong. It makes an excellent pet and is good with children and dogs. It is amusing and sensitive. A fast runner and good hunter, the Cymric needs space to roam.

GROOMING
Although it has long hair, fur does not mat easily. The cat is easy to groom. A daily combing is necessary to remove dead hairs. Examine eyes and ears regularly for dirt or ear mites.

ORIGIN AND HISTORY
The Cymric is a longhair Manx. The Manx is an established breed. Cymrics first appeared in Manx litters in Canada in the 1960s. The Manx was not knowingly outcrossed to a longhair cat, but a recessive gene for long hair must have been present for many generations. The Cymric is one of the newer breeds in the show ring and is confined to North America. It has not yet attained full championship status in all associations.

BREEDING
Mating two Cymrics produces 100% Cymric kittens. But tailless cats carry a lethal factor when mated together too often. For best results, tailed or stumpy-tailed cats should be mated to tailless cats. The show animal must be completely tailless, with a hollow where the root of the tail normally is. Many tailed or stumpy-tailed kittens born in the same litters make excellent pets and are intelligent and affectionate.

KITTENS
Cymric kittens are courageous, adventurous and playful.

SHOW REQUIREMENTS
The principal feature in a show Cymric is a complete absence of tail. The cat has a round, rabbit look, with a short back and long hind legs.
Coat—Medium-to-long and double. Undercoat is thick and cottony. Topcoat is silky and glossy.
Body—Solid and round, with a short back, round rump, deep flanks and muscular thighs. Forelegs are set apart, short and heavily boned. Hind legs are longer than forelegs. Back is arched from the shoulder to the rump. Feet are neat and round.
Tail—Absent, with a decided hollow at the end of the spine. A residual tail is a fault.
Head—Large and round, with prominent cheekbones. Short, thick neck and strong chin. Nose medium length with a gentle nose dip. Whisker pads are round, with a decided whisker break. Ears are large, wide at the base, tapering to slightly pointed tips. Set on top of the head, with ear tufts at the ends.
Eyes—Large, round and expressive. Set at an angle to the nose. Outer corners are slightly higher than inner corners.

COLORS
All coat colors, patterns and combinations of coat colors and patterns are accepted, except chocolate, lilac and the Himalayan pattern, or these colors with white. For color standards, see Persians.

SOMALI

Advantages
- *Easy to groom*
- *Almost voiceless*
- *Amusing*
- *Affectionate*
- *Gentle*
- *Even-tempered*
- *Good with children*

Disadvantages
- *Does not like to be caged*

The Somali is a longhair Abyssinian. It is similar to the Abyssinian in temperament and coloring, but is less noisy. The Somali is playful and lively, yet quiet to have around. It is almost voiceless. Gentle and well-mannered, the Somali is an excellent pet and usually even-tempered.

A Somali is happiest if given plenty of freedom and space to run. It may fret if caged.

GROOMING
Although fairly long, the Somali's coat does not mat. Daily grooming is not essential. A combing with a medium-tooth comb is advisable to remove dead hairs.

ORIGIN AND HISTORY
Longhair kittens appeared in Abyssinian litters in the 1960s. They were thought to be a natural mutation, but their ancestry can be traced back to Abyssinians mated to longhair cats. The gene for long hair was introduced by breeders. The export of American-bred Abyssinians to all parts of the world has spread the longhair factor abroad. Some Abyssinian breeders in Australia now concentrate on breeding Somalis instead of Abyssinians.

The first breed club was formed in 1972. By 1978, the breed was officially recognized by various American and Canadian governing bodies.

BREEDING
Mating two Somalis produces all-Somali kittens. They may also appear in Abyssinian litters when both parents carry the gene for long hair. Somalis can also be mated to Abyssinians to improve type.

KITTENS
Somali litters rarely contain more than 3 or 4 kittens. The ratio of males to females is high. Somali kittens are slightly larger than Abyssinian kittens and are slower to develop their full adult coats.

SHOW REQUIREMENTS
The Somali is medium size, firm and muscular, with a long coat and distinctive coloring.
Coat—Full, dense, silky and fine textured. Ruffs around the neck and breeches are desirable. Coat is longer on the stomach and shorter over the shoulders. The full beauty of the coat may take as long as 2 years to develop.
Body—Medium length, lithe, graceful and muscular. Rib cage round. Back slightly arched. Legs long and slim. Paws small and oval with tufted toes.

A Red Somali. This breed is an Abyssinian with long hair. It is gentle and easy to care for.

Tail—Full brush. Thick at the base and gently tapering.
Head—Round, short wedge. All lines curve gently. Wide between the ears. Ears are large, alert, pointed and wide at the base. Set apart, toward the back of the head. Furnished with long ear tufts. Chin round, firm and full. No whisker break. Slight nose break.
Eyes—Almond shape, large and expressive.

COLORS
The Somali is recognized in two colors—Ruddy and Red. With Abyssinians bred in different colors, more colors are likely to appear.
Ruddy—Orange-brown. Each hair ticked with black. The first band starts next to the skin. Double or triple banding is preferred. On the back, darker shading forms a line along the spine that continues along the tail, ending in a black tip. Ears tipped with black or dark brown. The face is marked with a short, dark vertical line above each eye. Another line continues from the upper eyelid toward the ear. Eyes are dark rimmed and surrounded by a pale area. The underside, insides of the legs and chest are an even ruddy color, without ticking or other markings. Toe tufts on all four feet are black or dark brown. Black between the toes extends up the back of the hind legs. White or off-white is allowed only on the upper throat, lips and nostrils. Noseleather brick-red. Paw pads black or brown. Eyes gold or green; deeper colors preferred.
Red—Body red ticked with chocolate-brown. Deeper shades of red preferred. Ears and tail tipped with chocolate-brown. The underside, insides of the legs and chest are red-brown without ticking or other markings. Toe tufts are chocolate-brown. Color extends slightly beyond the paws. Noseleather rose-pink. Paw pads pink. Eyes gold or green; deeper colors preferred.

Cymric

Blue-Calico Cymric

Ruddy Somali

Red Somali kitten

Somali

SHORTHAIR CATS

If you do not have a lot of time to spend grooming a cat, consider a shorthair cat. There are many varieties to choose from, such as British Shorthairs or the Siamese and Burmese. For those who like something different, there is the curly coated Rex. You might choose an American Wirehair or a hairless one, if you find them attractive. The Scottish Fold, with its curious buttoned-down ears, the tailless Manx and the Japanese Bobtail are also fascinating. The newly developed Snowshoe, a Siamese with white feet and muzzle, may appeal to you. You may prefer the elegance of one of the pure Oriental Shorthairs or the affectionate Tonkinese, a hybrid Siamese-Burmese, or a sleek Bombay with its glossy coat and copper eyes. The quiet Russian Blue or Korat may suit your temperament. You may like the independent nature of the Abyssinian. You are sure to find a shorthair breed to suit you.

The language used to describe cats is almost as complex as the cats themselves. British Shorthairs are not Foreign Shorthairs. These are descriptions of body type more than origin. *Foreign* is a generic reference to cats that are long, svelte and slender, usually derived from the Siamese breed. These are often called *Oriental*. In the United States, a breed called Oriental Shorthair is recognized, so *Foreign Shorthair* refers to Siamese, Colorpoint Shorthair, Oriental Shorthair, Korat and sometimes other breeds.

British body type refers to husky cats with big bones and round heads, such as the British Shorthair, Manx and Scottish Fold. Some breeds do not fall into either category. The American Shorthair, for example, traces its roots to the British Shorthair, but has a style of its own.

The British call solid-color Oriental Shorthairs *Foreign Shorthairs*. They are in the process of phasing out the word Foreign as a breed name, because of the confusion it has caused, in preference to the more universally accepted term, Oriental. In some contexts, Oriental and Foreign are used interchangeably.

The inquisitive gaze of a Blue Oriental Shorthair.

AMERICAN SHORTHAIR

Advantages
- **Hardy**
- **Companionable**
- **Well-balanced**
- **Good mouser**
- **Easy to groom**

Disadvantages
- **No drawbacks known**

This hardy cat is independent and makes an excellent pet. In the house, it hunts, chasing and pouncing with velvet paws on whatever moves.

The American Shorthair is active and curious. A robust natural breed, it is a trouble-free pet with an affectionate, companionable nature. It is also an excellent mouser.

GROOMING
The coat is easily maintained. Comb it regularly to prevent formation of fur balls. Check eyes and ears regularly.

ORIGIN AND HISTORY
These cats came to the United States with settlers from Europe. They were brought as companions and rodent hunters on ships. Every ship had one or more cats to protect the ship's stores. Many left ship in the New World. These cats mated freely. After years of separation from European stock, they developed their own characteristics. Although still similar to the British Shorthair, the American Shorthair is larger, with a less-round head and longer nose. Years of free ranging ancestry have made this a hardy, fearless, intelligent breed. It was neglected as a pedigree variety until American breeders decided to breed it selectively to maintain its natural characteristics.

BREEDING
American Shorthairs are good breeders and make sensible mothers. They have a lot of patience.

KITTENS
Kittens are confident, courageous and healthy.

SHOW REQUIREMENTS
The American Shorthair is strong and well-built. It has the body of an athlete, built for an active life.
Coat—Thick, short, even and hard in texture. Heavier and thicker in winter.
Body—Large to medium size, lean and hard, athletic and powerful. Well-developed chest and shoulders. Legs sturdy and medium length, built for jumping and hunting. Paws full and round, with heavy pads. Excessive cobbiness or ranginess are faults.

Tail—Medium length, wide at the base, tapering slightly to a blunt tip. No kinks.
Head—Large and full-cheeked. Face bright and alert. Neck medium long, thick and muscular. An oval face, slightly longer than wide. Square muzzle, firm chin. Nose medium length and uniform width. Gentle curve from forehead to nose tip. Ears set wide apart. Not too wide at the base, with slightly rounded tips.
Eyes—Large, round and awake. Slightly higher on the outer edge. Set wide apart.

COLORS
White—White. Noseleather and paw pads pink. Eyes blue or gold, or one blue and one gold in odd-eye whites.
Black—Black, with no rusty tinge. Noseleather black. Paw pads black or brown. Eyes gold.
Blue—Even blue. Lighter shades preferred. Noseleather and paw pads blue. Eyes gold.
Red—Clear red without shading or tabby markings. Lips and chin red. Noseleather and paw pads brick-red. Eyes gold.
Cream—Buff-cream, without markings. Lighter shades preferred. Noseleather and paw pads pink. Eyes gold.
Bicolor—White, with unbrindled patches of black, blue, red or cream. Noseleather and paw pads in keeping with solid color or pink. Eyes gold.
Chinchilla—Undercoat white. Coat on back, flanks, head and tail tipped with black to give sparkling silver appearance. Eyerims, lips and nose outlined with black. Some tipping allowed on the legs. Chin, ear tufts, stomach and chest white. Noseleather brick-red. Paw pads black. Eyes green or blue-green.
Shaded Silver—Undercoat white with mantle of black tipping shading down from the sides, face and tail. From dark on the ridge to white on the chin, chest, stomach and under the tail. Legs the same tone as the face. Darker than the Chinchilla. Eyerims, lips and nose outlined with black. Noseleather brick-red. Paw pads black. Eyes green or blue-green.
Shell Cameo—Undercoat white. Coat on the back, flanks, head and tail tipped with red to give a sparkling appearance. Face and legs may be slightly shaded with tipping. Chin, ear tufts, stomach and chest white. Eyerims rose. Noseleather and paw pads rose. Eyes gold.

Shaded Cameo—Undercoat white with a mantle of red tipping and shading down sides, face and tail. From dark on the ridge to white on the chin, chest, stomach and under the tail. Legs same tone as face. General effect is redder than Shell Cameo.
Black Smoke—Undercoat white, deeply tipped with black. Appears black in repose. Points and mask black with narrow band of white at the base of the hairs, seen only when fur is parted. Noseleather and paw pads black. Eyes gold.
Blue Smoke—Undercoat white, deeply tipped with blue. In repose appears blue. Noseleather and paw pads blue. Eyes gold.
Cameo Smoke—Undercoat white, deeply tipped with red. In repose appears red. Noseleather and paw pads rose. Eyes gold.
Tortoiseshell Smoke—Undercoat white, deeply tipped with black. Clearly defined patches of red-and-cream tipped hairs in the tortoiseshell pattern. Appears tortoiseshell in repose. Facial blaze of red or cream tipping is desirable. Noseleather and paw pads red, black, or brick-red and black. Eyes gold.
Tortoiseshell—Black with unbrindled patches of red and cream. Clearly defined and broken on body, legs and tail. A facial blaze of red or cream desirable. Noseleather and paw pads brick-red, black, or brick-red and black. Eyes gold.
Calico—White with unbrindled patches of black and red. White predominant on underparts. Noseleather and paw pads pink. Eyes gold.
Dilute Calico—White with unbrindled patches of blue and cream. White predominant on underparts. Noseleather and paw pads pink. Eyes gold.
Blue-Cream—Blue with patches of solid cream, clearly defined and broken on body, legs and tail. Noseleather and paw pads blue, pink, or blue and pink. Eyes gold.
Van Colors—Mostly white with color on head, legs and tail. Noseleather and paw pads pink or in keeping with color patches. Eyes gold.

Van Bicolor—Black, blue, red or cream patches on head, legs and tail. White elsewhere.
Van Calico—Patches of black and red on head, legs and tail. White elsewhere.
Van Blue-Cream—Patches of blue and cream on head, legs and tail.
Classic-Tabby Pattern—Markings dense and clearly defined from ground color. Legs evenly barred. Tail ringed. Several unbroken necklaces on neck and upper chest. Frown marks form letter *M* on forehead. Unbroken line runs back from outer corner of eye. Swirls on cheeks. Vertical lines over back of head extend to shoulder markings resembling a butterfly. Three parallel lines run down the spine from the butterfly to the tail. Stripes are separated by the ground color. Large solid blotch on each side circled by one or more unbroken rings. Side markings symmetrical. Double row of buttons on chest and stomach.
Mackerel-Tabby Pattern—Markings dense, clearly defined with narrow pencilings. Legs and tail evenly barred. Distinct necklaces on neck and upper chest. Forehead has characteristic *M*. Unbroken lines run backward from the eyes. Lines run down the head to meet the shoulders. Spine lines run together to form narrow saddle. Narrow pencilings run around the body.
Brown Tabby—Ground color copper-brown. Markings dense black. Lips, chin and rings around eyes paler. Backs of leg black from paw to heel. Noseleather brick-red. Paw pads black or brown. Eyes gold.
Red Tabby—Ground color red. Markings deep red. Lips and chin red. Noseleather and paw pads brick-red. Eyes gold.
Silver Tabby—Ground color, lips and chin pale, clear silver. Markings black. Noseleather brick-red. Paw pads black. Eyes green or hazel.
Blue Tabby—Ground color, lips and chin pale blue-ivory. Markings deep blue. Noseleather and paw pads rose. Eyes gold.
Cream Tabby—Ground color, lips and chin pale cream. Markings buff-cream, darker than ground color for contrast, but not dark. Noseleather and paw pads rose. Eyes gold.
Cameo Tabby—Ground color, lips and chin off-white. Markings red. Noseleather and paw pads rose. Eyes gold.
Patched Tabby—Silver, Brown or Blue classic or mackerel tabby with patches of red, cream, or red and cream.

*Shaded Silver
American Shorthair*

*Silver Classic-Tabby
American Shorthair*

*Blue-Cream
American Shorthair*

American Shorthair

BRITISH SHORTHAIR

Advantages
- **Strong**
- **Sturdy**
- **Healthy**
- **Good mouser**
- **Affectionate**
- **Good with children**
- **Good with dogs**
- **Quiet**
- **Easy to groom**

Disadvantages
- **No drawbacks known**

The British Shorthair is a natural breed. It is healthy and sound, not susceptible to illnesses. Even-tempered, it is an excellent pet for children and older people. The most popular color is Blue, followed by Silver Tabby and spotted varieties. It is a strong, sturdy shorthair cat, active, graceful, intelligent and curious.

Only a few American breeders work with this animal. If you want to buy one, you may have to spend time on a waiting list and pay a higher price for the cat of your choice.

GROOMING
Daily grooming is necessary to remove dead hairs. Weekly combing keeps it looking neat and trim.

ORIGIN AND HISTORY
This cat is known from history, literature and art. It has been around for centuries. British Shorthairs were shown in the first cat shows in Great Britain. They are native to the British Isles, although some strains may have been imported by Romans. All earliest-known cats were shorthair.

British Shorthairs were imported to North America by early English immigrants. They took them to America as pets and mouse catchers. These cats mated with other shorthair cats brought from other parts of the world. This was the ancestor of the American Shorthair. Both British and American Shorthairs are recognized by American associations.

An orange-eye British White Shorthair.

SHOW REQUIREMENTS
The British Shorthair is medium-to-large, strong and sturdy on short legs. It has a short, thick coat. Males are larger than females.
Coat—Short, resilient and dense without being double or woolly.
Body—Hard and muscular, with a full, broad chest. Strong, short legs and a level back. Straight forelegs are the same length as hind legs. Paws are neat, round and firm.
Tail—Short and thick at the base. Tapers to a round tip.
Head—Broad and round on a short neck. Nose is straight, broad and short without a stop. Ears are set apart so the inner ear and eye corners are perpendicular to each other. Ears are small and round.
Eyes—Large, round and level. Wide awake and full of expression. There should be the width of an eye between the eyes.

COLORS
Seventeen colors are recognized, but every known color is possible and may appear.

British Black

Black cats have a long history. In the middle ages, they were often regarded with suspicion and were persecuted. At other times, they were considered lucky.

GROOMING
Preparing a Black for showing requires little work. Comb the coat daily. Use bay rum to clean the coat and enhance the shine a few days before the show. The coat may be bleached by strong sunlight, so black cats are best shown in the winter months.

BREEDING
Black cats can be obtained by mating two Blacks. They also appear in Tortoiseshell litters. Blacks are valuable in producing Tortoiseshells, Calicos and Bicolors. Type can be improved by mating Blacks to Blue or Black Persians. Longhair kittens must not be used again for breeding. They are neutered and sold as pets.

KITTENS
Black kittens may look rusty when young, but the red tinge disappears as the cat approaches adulthood. Look for a coat that is solid black down to the roots. No white hairs are permissible. Eyes are copper with no tinge of green when changing from baby blue.

SHOW REQUIREMENTS
The dense coat is a glossy, even black from root to tip, with no white hairs. Noseleather and paw pads black. Eyes copper or orange with no green tinge.

British White

There are three types of pedigree shorthair White cat: blue-eye, orange-eye and odd-eye. Non-pedigree white cats usually have green eyes. White cats were once highly prized in Japan, where they were regarded as symbols of purity and perfection. Despite their popularity, British Whites are rare.

GROOMING
A British White needs daily grooming to remove dead hairs. Give it careful attention if destined for a show career. A show cat must have an immaculate coat, with no yellow or gray. If necessary, shampoo the cat a week before the show. When dry, baby powder can be shaken on the coat and brushed out. All signs of powder must be removed before the show. Smooth the coat with a silk handkerchief.

BREEDING
Blue-eye white cats are often deaf, which may contribute to their rarity. Generally, deaf cats are not used for breeding. Orange-eye British Whites have helped solve the deafness problem, but in the process of their development, odd-eye Whites also appeared. These animals may have perfect hearing or may be deaf on the blue-eye side.

Whites can be mated to Whites or to Blacks, Reds, Creams and Blues to produce Bicolors. Mated to Tortoiseshells, they produce Calicos.

KITTENS
The average White litter contains 3 or 4 kittens. All kittens are born with blue eyes. Those destined to have orange eyes begin to change color at about 2 weeks. Odd-eyes are readily distinguished. There is a difference in the depth of the blue color in the eyes from the beginning.

It is believed a single black hair in the coat of a blue-eye kitten means the cat has good hearing, at least in one ear. White kittens of any eye color are always sought after.

SHOW REQUIREMENTS
Coat is white with no yellow tinge. Noseleather and paw pads pink. Eyes gold; orange or copper; sapphire blue; or one gold or copper and one blue.

British
Shorthair

British Odd-Eye
White Shorthair

British Black Shorthair

British Blue

The British Blue, with its light blue coat, is a popular cat. The Blue is known for its quiet, even temperament.

During World War II, there were few studs available. After the war, outcrosses to other breeds were made that resulted in loss of type. Outcrosses were then made to longhair Blues, which improved type. They produced coats that were too long. Selective breeding during the 1950s saw re-establishment of the shorthair Blue. Blue kittens are always in demand.

GROOMING
Daily combing to remove dead hairs keeps the coat looking good. It is usually unnecessary to shampoo a Blue. Bay rum rubbed into the coat the day before the show removes any greasiness that could mar the color.

BREEDING
Outcrossing to longhair Blues or shorthair Blacks helps maintain type and color. Some of the resulting kittens have undesirable features, such as overlong fur. These are not suitable for showing, but make excellent pets. Litters usually contain 3 or 4 kittens. Blues are useful for producing Blue-Creams when mated to Creams.

KITTENS
Blue kittens are pretty. They are usually born with faint tabby markings, but these disappear within the first few months as the coat grows.

SHOW REQUIREMENTS
Coat is light to medium blue, sound from root to tip with no white hairs or tabby markings. Noseleather and paw pads blue. Eyes copper or orange.

British Cream

The British Cream Shorthair is an attractive, rare variety. The coat is pale cream with no tabby markings. This is difficult to achieve.

Pedigree Cream Shorthairs have never been numerous. In the early days of pedigree cat breeding, no one knew how to produce these cats. They appeared occasionally in Tortoiseshell litters and were usually regarded as freaks. They were not recognized for competition until the late 1920s.

GROOMING
Preparing a Cream Shorthair for show may require a shampoo a few days before the show. Grease or dirt in the coat mars the color. Daily combing removes dead hairs.

BREEDING
Breeding good Cream Shorthairs is not easy. The color is sex linked and produces more males than females. They can be bred from Tortoiseshells and Blue-Creams. The Blue-Cream with Blue or Cream sires produce the best Creams. It seems these matings benefit Blues and Creams.

KITTENS
Cream female kittens are obtained by mating a Blue-Cream to a Cream sire. Cream males are obtained by mating a Blue-Cream to a Blue sire. Creams are attractive as kittens, but few possess the desired pale coat. Many have tabby markings or are too dark to be shown.

SHOW REQUIREMENTS
Coat is a light, even cream all over without white hairs or markings of any kind. Noseleather and paw pads pink. Eyes copper or orange.

British Smoke

This cat is the shorthair equivalent of a Persian Smoke. It has a similar breeding history. Hair is one color, but near the roots it is white or silver. The coat appears to be a solid color until the fur is parted or the cat moves.

GROOMING
Daily combing and grooming are required. Show cats need powdering to remove grease. Shampoo a few days before a show if dirty. Powder must be completely brushed out.

BREEDING
It is necessary to mate Silver Tabby Shorthairs to solid-color shorthairs of the required color. Smokes are then mated to Smokes and occasionally to Blue Shorthairs for type.

KITTENS
At birth, Smoke kittens look like solid-color kittens. The smoke effect is seen only as the adult coat develops.

SHOW REQUIREMENTS
Black Smoke—Undercoat pale white. Topcoat heavily tipped almost to the roots with black. Long white hairs or tabby markings are faults. Noseleather black. Paw pads black or dark brown. Eyes yellow to copper.
Blue Smoke—Undercoat pale white. Topcoat heavily tipped almost to the roots with blue. No white hairs. Noseleather and paw pads blue. Eyes yellow to orange.

British Tipped

This is the shorthair equivalent of the longhair Chinchilla, Cameo, Shaded Silver and Shaded Cameo. The cat has a similar history. It is striking with a white undercoat tipped lightly with a contrasting color. Tipping can be of any color. Different colors do not have separate classes at shows.

GROOMING
These cats need daily combing. Before a show, powder the undercoat or shampoo it if it is dirty.

BREEDING
Breeders report unexpected crosses such as Siamese to Chinchilla have produced British Tipped Shorthair kittens. The most common is Silver Tabby Shorthair to Chinchilla and back to Chinchilla Shorthairs. With Chocolate and Lilac Tipped, matings would be Chocolate and Lilac Shorthairs to Chinchilla Shorthairs. These colors were probably developed from breeding Longhair Chocolate and Lilac Kashmirs to British Shorthairs.

KITTENS
Because of outcrossing to longhairs in the past, kittens have longer coats at birth. This disappears with the adult coat.

SHOW REQUIREMENTS
Undercoat as white as possible. Topcoat tipped with a contrasting color to give a sparkling effect on the back, flanks, head, ears, legs and tail. The chin, stomach, chest and underside of the tail white. Tabby markings are faults. Noseleather and paw pads in keeping with the color tipping. Eyes green in black-tipped cats. Eyerims, nose and lips outlined in black. Eyes orange or copper in other colors. Eyerims and lips deep rose.

British Bicolor

Bicolor cats have been common for centuries, and were seen at the earliest cat shows. They did not achieve official recognition as a variety until recently, when they were found to be essential in the breeding of Calicos and Dilute Calicos.

The Bicolor is attractive when the standard is met. The necessary symmetrical distribution of color patches and white is hard to achieve. This may account for their scarcity on the showbench. Bicolors may be black and white, blue and white, red and white, or cream and white.

GROOMING
Bicolors are easy to groom and only need a daily combing. Paler colors may require a shampoo a few days before a show. Do not use powder on black parts or it may deaden the color.

BREEDING
Bicolors appear in mixed litters of solid-color and Calico kittens. They result from matings between a solid-color male and a Calico female, two Bicolors or a solid-color and a White.

Bicolor queens make excellent mothers. They have kittens of various colors, according to the sire and both parents' genetic backgrounds.

KITTENS
Bicolor kittens are colorful. They mature early and are independent, intelligent, healthy and hardy.

SHOW REQUIREMENTS
The show Bicolor must have a certain percentage of white and color on the body. Patches must be distinct, not intermingled. The coat pattern is similar to a Dutch rabbit, with symmetrical patches of color, either black, blue, red or cream, evenly distributed on the head, body and tail. White predominantly on the feet, legs, face, chest and underparts. The coat cannot be more than two-thirds colored or more than half white. A white facial blaze is desirable. Markings must be as symmetrical as possible. Tabby markings or white hairs in the color patches are faults. Noseleather and paw pads according to the main color or pink. Eyes copper or orange.

British Red-And-White
Bicolor Shorthair

British
Shorthair

British Blue Shorthair

British Cream Shorthair

British Tipped Shorthair

British Tortoiseshell

Cats with the tortoiseshell pattern, a patched coat of black, red or cream, have been known for centuries. They have appeared on the show bench since cats were first exhibited. In the Tortoiseshell Shorthairs, patches show up distinctly, and are attractive and colorful. Tortoiseshell cats are affectionate and gentle. They are a female-only variety, although an occasional male has occurred. One is even recorded as having sired a litter. It is not known what factor makes 99.9% of Tortoiseshell cats female.

GROOMING
Daily combing is necessary. Bay rum rubbed into the coat before a show adds sheen.

BREEDING
Because this is a female-only variety, to produce Tortoiseshell kittens a Tortoiseshell female must be mated to a Black, Red or Cream male. Even then, there is no guarantee there will be Torties in the litters. Bicolors are not usually used as sires because it often produces Calico kittens.

KITTENS
Tortoiseshell kittens appear in litters with Black, Red and Cream kittens. Tortoiseshell kittens are rare. Kittens are pretty and develop early. They are usually strong, healthy and resistant to diseases and illnesses. The markings on a kitten may not be bright. They may be blue, pale red and dirty cream when young. When the adult coat begins to grow, the blue turns to jet black and the red and cream become clear.

SHOW REQUIREMENTS
The coat is evenly patched with black, red and cream, without intermingling colors or any white hairs. Color patches evenly distributed on legs and face, and a facial blaze of red or cream is desirable. Noseleather and paw pads pink, black or a combination of the two. Eyes copper or orange.

British Blue-Cream

A dilute form of the Tortoiseshell, the Blue-Cream is a female-only variety. It was not officially recognized until 1956. Blue-Cream kittens had appeared for many years in litters of Blue and Cream matings and in Tortoiseshell litters, when both parents carried a gene for blue. The palest shades of blue and cream are preferred, with no touch of red.

GROOMING
Preparation for a show is easy for a Blue-Cream. Comb it daily to remove dead hairs. Clean the coat with bay rum a few days before the show. Hand grooming makes the coat glossy.

BREEDING
Blue-Creams can be produced by mating a Blue with a Cream shorthair or from Tortoiseshells. When a Blue-Cream female is mated to a Cream sire, it is not possible to get Blue female kittens. Kittens of all other colors and both sexes result. When mated to a Blue sire, there will be no Cream female kittens, but all other possibilities. No Blue-Cream males have grown to adulthood or are known to have sired any kittens. If any appear, they are sterile.

KITTENS
When kittens are born, it is not immediately apparent which is a Blue-Cream. Some of the best Blue-Creams may look more like pale Blues at first.

SHOW REQUIREMENTS
Coat color is blue and cream, softly intermingled over the body. No facial blaze. Tabby markings and white hairs or patches are faults. Noseleather blue. Paw pads blue, pink, or blue and pink. Eyes copper or orange.

British Calico
British Tortoiseshell-And-White

The Calico coat pattern, like the Tortoiseshell, has been seen for centuries among alley cats. The Calico Shorthair is found in many countries and is prized for its brilliant coloring. This is a female-only variety; the occasional male is sterile. Hardy and robust, it makes an excellent mouser. It was formerly known as the *Chintz* or *Spanish Cat.*

GROOMING
A daily comb is necessary. Bay rum rubbed into the color patches before a show enhances their brilliance.

BREEDING
The best sires for this variety are Bicolors, particularly those from a Calico mother. When mated with a Calico, Black-And-White or Red-And-White males are the most likely sires to produce Calico kittens.

KITTENS
Kittens are even-tempered, happy and healthy. They develop early but coat patches may not be bright at first. The coat develops fully at about 9 months.

SHOW REQUIREMENTS
Coat is boldly patched with black, cream and red with white. Patches are equally balanced. White must not predominate. Tricolor patchings cover the top of the head, ears, cheeks, back, tail and part of the flanks. Patches are clearly defined. A white facial blaze is desirable. Noseleather and paw pads pink, black or a combination of the two. Eyes copper or orange.

Dilute Calico
Blue Tortoiseshell-And-White

There is a dilute form of the Calico cat. In the coat color, blue replaces black and cream replaces red. Paw pads and noseleather are pink, slate-blue or a combination of the two. Eyes gold.

An orange-eye Calico British Shorthair.

British Tabby

Shorthair Tabbies occur in brown, red and silver colors. They are also found in several coat patterns, such as the classic, mackerel and spotted. In some countries, Blue and Cream tabbies are also recognized.

The name *tabby* comes from the similarity of the coat pattern to tabby or plain woven watered silk or taffeta. This type of weaving produces a striped or ridged effect on the cloth. It is known as *tabbisilk.*

The tabby pattern is common among domestic cats. Non-pedigree shorthairs are usually varieties of Brown Tabbies or Ginger Toms. Judging from the marking of many wild felines, the original domestic tabbies were probably striped or spotted cats. Many cats depicted on Egyptian scrolls are spotted coats. Spotted Tabbies were shown at the first cat shows, but at the beginning of the 19th century they almost disappeared from the show bench—possibly because the classic tabby pattern was preferred by the breeders of the time. They began to make a comeback in 1965 and are now bred in five colors for competition: Brown, Silver, Red, Blue Tabby and Cream.

British Calico Shorthair

British
Shorthair

British Tortoiseshell
Shorthair

British Blue-Cream Shorthair

The classic or blotched pattern, the most common tabby pattern in pedigree cats, is a mutation from the striped form. This appeared in Europe among domestic and wild cats and was common by the middle of the 17th century.

Of the tabby colors, the Silver Classic Tabby is the most popular variety. Since World War II, breeding lines have been improved as a result of crossing with Silver Tabbies from France.

Brown Tabbies are not common on the show bench. It is difficult to breed a cat to the required color standard. The name Red Tabby is often associated with the ginger alley cat. The pedigree Red Tabby, with its striking red coat, does not resemble the ginger tom.

GROOMING
Tabbies need daily combing to remove dead hairs. Bay rum rubbed into the coat a few days before a show gives a gloss to the coat to show off markings.

BREEDING
Mating two Tabbies of the required color together gives several generations of good type. Breeders sometimes mate to other solid-color shorthairs or longhairs to improve type. Usually this is to Blues but can also be to the solid color in the coat pattern. Breeders mate Brown Tabby to a Black, Red Tabby to a Tortoiseshell, Silver Tabby to a Chinchilla, Blue Tabby to a Blue, and Cream Tabby to a Cream British Shorthair.

KITTENS
Tabby kittens are born with obvious markings. Usually the best-marked kittens at birth become the best-marked adults. Soon after birth, markings may fade and then take up to 6 months to develop fully. Imperfectly marked kittens with white hairs, patches or incorrect coat pattern are not suitable for showing.

COLORS
Classic-Tabby Pattern—All markings clearly defined from the ground color. The characteristic head marking is a letter *M* resembling frown marks on the forehead. Unbroken lines run from the outer corners of the eyes toward the back of the head, with pencilings on the cheeks. Lines extend back from the top of the head to the shoulder markings, which are shaped like a butterfly. Three unbroken lines run parallel to each other down the spine from the shoulder markings to the base of the tail. A large blotch on each flank is circled by one or more unbroken rings. These markings are symmetrical on either side of the body. There should be several unbroken necklaces on the neck and upper chest. A double row of

buttons runs from chest to stomach. Legs evenly barred with narrow bracelets. Tail is evenly ringed.

Mackerel-Tabby Pattern—Head is marked with an *M*. There is an unbroken line running from the outer corner of the eye toward the back of the head, with other pencilings on the cheeks. A narrow unbroken line runs from the back of the head to the base of the tail. The rest of the body is marked with narrow unbroken lines running vertically from the spine line. These lines are narrow, numerous and clearly defined from the ground color. There should be several unbroken necklaces on the neck and upper chest. A double row of buttons runs from chest to stomach. Legs evenly barred with narrow bracelets. Tail is evenly ringed.

Spotted-Tabby Pattern—All markings are dense and clearly defined from the ground color. Head is marked with an *M*. There is an unbroken line running from the outer corner of the eye toward the back of the head, with other fine pencilings on the cheeks. All the stripes in the tabby coat are broken into spots, which may be round, oval or rosette-shape. They are numerous and distinct from the ground color. A dorsal stripe runs the length of the back, but is broken into spots. A double row of buttons run from chest to stomach. Spots or broken rings appear on the legs and tail.

Brown Tabby—Ground color sable or copper-brown. Markings in classic, mackerel or spotted tabby patterns are dense black. Hind legs black from paw to heel. Noseleather brick-red. Paw pads black. Eyes orange, hazel or deep yellow.

Red Tabby—Ground color red. Markings, lips, chin and sides of feet dark red. Noseleather brick-red. Paw pads deep red. Eyes deep copper.

Silver Tabby—Ground color clear silver with no white hairs or tinge of brown on the nose. Chin and lips silver. Markings in classic, mackerel and spotted patterns dense black. Noseleather brick-red or black. Paw pads black. Eyes gold, orange or hazel.

Blue Tabby—Ground color pale blue-white. Markings in classic, mackerel and spotted patterns are dark slate-blue. Noseleather rose-pink. Paw pads rose. Eyes gold.

Cream Tabby—Ground color pale cream. Markings in classic, mackerel and spotted patterns are dark cream, but not too red. Noseleather and paw pads pink. Eyes gold.

CHARTREUX
Chartreuse
The Chartreux is a shorthair blue cat similar to the British Blue. The breed was developed in France in the Carthusian monastery which made the liqueur *Chartreuse*. The monks originally brought the cats from South Africa.

The Chartreux has a long history in France. In the 16th century, the French poet Joachim du Bellay was fond of a cat with a blue-gray coat that could have been a Chartreux.

It is a large cat with a blue-gray coat. World War II forced some co-mingling of Chartreux and British Blue bloodlines in Europe, but a pure strain acquired from a French island is flourishing. The Chartreux is distinguishable by a strong, broad jaw, dense plush coat and tiny, kittenlike voice, which it seldom uses.

The Chartreux is a French breed closely resembling the British Blue Shorthair.

A British Blue Classic-Tabby Shorthair kitten, full of curiosity.

British Shorthair

British Silver
Spotted-Tabby Shorthair

British Silver
Classic-Tabby Shorthair
kitten

British Brown
Mackerel-Tabby Shorthair

British Red
Classic-Tabby Shorthair

British Tabby   55

EXOTIC SHORTHAIR

Advantages
- *Intelligent*
- *Quiet*
- *Even-tempered*
- *Playful*
- *Responsive*
- *Loving*
- *Good with children*
- *Good with animals*

Disadvantages
- *No drawbacks known*

If you like a docile cat, this may be the breed for you. The Exotic Shorthair is a hybrid, produced by crossing a Persian with an American Shorthair. It is a Persian type with short hair. The cat resembles a Persian with its short, snub nose and side cheeks, cobby body and short tail, but its coat is more manageable. It combines the best characteristics of both breeds, with its quiet, gentle nature and an even-tempered, sweet disposition. It is alert, playful, responsive and not as destructive as some of the more energetic breeds. It is an ideal pet, willing to please its owner.

GROOMING
Although the Exotic Shorthair is easy to groom, the coat must be combed daily to remove dead hairs. If too many hairs are swallowed, a fur ball could form in the stomach. The coat is short and plush, so a medium-tooth comb is best. Occasionally use a rubber-spiked brush for massage.

ORIGIN AND HISTORY
The Exotic Shorthair was bred to satisfy the desire of some breeders to have a Persian-type cat with a short coat. Persians were first mated to American Shorthairs and Burmese. Now the cross is restricted to American Shorthairs. In 1966, these hybrids became known as Exotic Shorthairs at American shows. Earlier American Shorthairs, similar to the Exotic in type, were allowed to be re-registered as Exotics and to keep any wins they had gained as American Shorthairs.

The Exotic Shorthair is healthy, affectionate and easy to care for. It is becoming more popular. Its docile nature makes it easy to handle in the show ring.

BREEDING
To be registered as an Exotic Shorthair, a cat must have one Persian parent and one American Shorthair parent, two Exotic Shorthair parents or one Persian and one Exotic Shorthair parent. All colors and patterns are allowed. Queens are robust and have kittens that are healthy and strong.

KITTENS
Exotic kittens are playful and quiet. They love other animals and people. They respond to gentle handling and affection.

SHOW REQUIREMENTS
The Exotic Shorthair conforms to the standard set for the Persian, but has a short, plush coat.
Coat—Medium length, dense, soft, glossy and resilient. Not close lying, but stands out from the body.
Body—Medium to large, cobby and low on the legs. Deep in the chest, massive across the shoulders and rump, with a short, round middle. Back level. Legs short, thick and sturdy. Forelegs straight. Paws large, round and firm.
Tail—Short, thick, straight and carried low. Round at the tip. No kinks.
Head—Wide, round and massive with a sweet expression. A round face sits on a short, thick neck. Short, broad snub nose with a nose break. Cheeks full and chin developed. Ears small, set wide apart and low on the head, fitting into the curve of the head. Ears have round tips and tilt forward on the head.
Eyes—Large, round and full. Set wide apart.

COLORS
All colors and patterns of the American Shorthair and Persian allowed. These include white, with blue, orange or odd eyes; black; blue; red; cream; chinchilla; shaded silver; chinchilla golden; shell cameo; shaded golden; shaded cameo; shell tortoiseshell; smoke in either black, blue or tortoiseshell; classic and mackerel tabby in silver, red, brown, blue, cream and cameo; shaded tortoiseshell; patched tabby in brown, blue and silver; tortoiseshell; calico; dilute calico; blue-cream; bicolor; van-bicolor; van-calico; van blue-cream, and white.

A Blue-Cream Exotic Shorthair. It is a Persian type, with a shorter, more manageable coat.

SCOTTISH FOLD

Advantages
- *Distinctive personality*
- *Gentle*
- *Loves people*
- *Good with animals*
- *Good with children*

Disadvantages
- *No drawbacks known*

A Scottish Fold is distinctive in appearance. It wears its ears like a hat! The cat is charming, sensible and good with other animals, children and strangers. It makes a good pet, does not suffer ill effects from its folded ears and has lots of personality. The Scottish Fold has been bred to preserve the distinctive ears. This breed has attracted criticism in some countries.

GROOMING
No special attention to the ears is necessary, except that they must be kept clean. Check the teeth weekly. Daily brushing and combing keeps the coat neat.

ORIGIN AND HISTORY
The Scottish Fold appeared as a natural mutation of the British Shorthair in a Scottish litter of farm cats in 1961. The first was a white cat, but the folded ear is not restricted to color. Folds can have any coat color or pattern. The *Universal Magazine of Knowledge and Pleasure,* published in China in 1796, refers to a cat with folded ears. It was also known in China in 1938. This proves the gene producing folded ears has been present in the domestic cat for centuries.

An orange-eye white Scottish Fold.

BREEDING
Folds mated to shorthair domestics produce litters containing 50% kittens with normal ears and 50% with ears folded downward and forward. Breeders recommend Folds be mated only to normal-ear cats. Fold-to-Fold matings produce skeletal deformities.

KITTENS
The ears of Scottish Fold kittens may be only slightly folded. The definite forward folding may not become fully apparent until the kittens are 9 months old.

SHOW REQUIREMENTS
The Scottish Fold is a domestic shorthair, with distinctive ears folded forward and downward.
Coat—Thick, short and dense. Soft and resilient.
Body—Medium size, short, round and cobby. The same width across shoulders and rump. Full, broad chest. Powerful and compact build. Medium length legs with neat, round paws.
Tail—Medium length, thick at the base. Kinks, broad, thick or short tails are faults.
Head—Massive and round. Well-rounded whisker pads. Short, thick neck. Cheeks full, chin round, jaw broad. Ears wide apart. Distinguished by a definite fold line. The front of the ear completely covers the ear opening. Small neat ears are preferred. Round at the tips. Nose short and broad, with a gentle curve.
Eyes—Large, round, set wide apart.

COLORS
Almost all colors and coat patterns are recognized, including solid white, black, blue, red, cream; chinchilla, shaded silver, shell cameo, shaded cameo; smoke in either black, tortoiseshell, cameo or blue; tortoiseshell, calico, dilute calico, blue-cream; bicolor; classic and mackerel tabby patterns in silver, brown, blue, cream and cameo tabby. Eye color in keeping with coat color.

Blue Classic-Tabby
Scottish Fold kitten

Scottish Fold

Calico
Scottish Fold

Exotic Shorthair

Exotic Shaded Cameo
Shorthair

MANX

Advantages
- **Intelligent**
- **Courageous**
- **Good with children**
- **Good with dogs**
- **Affectionate**
- **Good mouser**

Disadvantages
- **Requires a lot of attention**
- **Does not like to be ignored**
- **Needs daily grooming**

The Manx has a unique appearance. It has no tail. Hind legs are longer than forelegs and the back is short. This gives it a rabbit look and gait, and a round rump. The show Manx has a definite hollow where the tail should be. This does not affect its balance. The powerful hind legs are capable of strong, high springs. It can also run fast and makes a good mouser.

The Manx is a loyal, affectionate pet. It is curious, intelligent, amusing and likes to be part of the family. It may resent being ignored or being left alone.

GROOMING
Its short, thick undercoat and soft medium-length topcoat require daily grooming. Use a medium-bristle brush and a medium-tooth comb to remove dead hairs. Ears, eyes and teeth need regular attention.

ORIGIN AND HISTORY
Tailless cats have been known for centuries. Charles Darwin reported seeing them in Malaysia. They were also seen in Russia and China. It is possible they were brought to the Isle of Man by ships from the Far East. Once there, they were geographically isolated and the taillessness was perpetuated. A book written in 1780 refers to the tailless cats of the island. They were considered lucky, and their likeness appeared on jewelry, in paintings and on coins.

A state cat farm on the island now breeds Manx cats with some success. Vacationers can buy them to take home. They are also being exported to other countries. The cats were first imported to the United States in the 1930s, where they continue to be popular.

BREEDING
Manx cats are difficult to breed because like-to-like mating does not necessarily produce tailless kittens. Tailed, tailless and stump-tail kittens may result. Continuous like-to-like Manx matings result in the majority of kittens dying before or just after birth. The tailless gene seems to be connected with other skeletal defects such as vertebrae being fused together, producing deformed kittens with *spina bifida*.

Frequent outcrossings to tailed Manx or to normal-tail Shorthairs must be made.

Manx litters may contain a completely tailless Manx, also called a *rumpy*. It may also contain a *riser*, which has a small number of vertebrae, usually immobile; a *stubby*, which has a short tail, often knobbly or kinked; and a *longy*, with a medium-length tail. For showing, the Manx tail must be totally absent. There must be a hollow where the tail would normally be. The other types of Manx make excellent pets and can be used for breeding.

KITTENS
Many kittens of other breeds regard mother's tail as a toy, but Manx kittens still seem to find plenty to play with.

SHOW REQUIREMENTS
The principal feature of a show-standard Manx cat is the complete absence of any tail. There should be a hollow in the rump where the tail normally is. It also has the round, rabbit look of a short-back cat, with hind legs longer than forelegs and a deep flank.

Coat—Short, glossy double coat. Undercoat is thick and cottony, the topcoat longer, but not too long. Soft and open.

Body—Solid, with round rump, strong hindquarters, deep flanks and a short back. Hind legs are longer than forelegs, with muscular thighs. The back arches from shoulder to rump. Feet are neat and round.

Tail—Entirely missing, with a hollow where the tail would normally be. A residual tail is a fault.

Head—Large and round with prominent cheeks. Short, thick neck and strong chin. Nose medium long, with a gentle nose dip. Round whisker pads and a definite whisker break. Ears large, wide at base, tapering to round tips. Set on top of head.

Eyes—Large, round and expressive. Set at an angle to the nose. Outer corners higher than inner corners.

COLORS
Almost all colors and coat patterns or combination of colors and coat patterns permitted. Chocolate, lavender and Himalayan colors and patterns, or colors with white are not allowed. Color in a Manx is a secondary consideration after taillessness, shortness of back, depth of flank and round rump. Eye color in keeping with the coat color. White Manx may be blue-eye; orange-eye; or odd-eye, one eye blue, one eye orange.

JAPANESE BOBTAIL

Advantages
- **Does not shed**
- **Intelligent**
- **Friendly**
- **Easy to groom**

Disadvantages
- **No drawbacks known**

The Japanese Bobtail is native to Japan, where it is called the *Mi-Ke* (mee-kay) cat. Its most distinctive feature is its short, bobbed tail. It is intelligent, loyal and friendly, loves swimming and can retrieve like a dog. It is vocal without being noisy and has a large vocabulary of chirps and meows.

The Bobtail sometimes stands with one front paw lifted in welcome. Store windows and counters in Japan often display china models of the cat with its paw lifted to welcome shoppers and passersby. These cats are called *Maneki-neko* or welcoming cats. The cat mixes well with other cats but prefers members of its own breed.

GROOMING
The Japanese Bobtail is easy to groom. It has a non-shedding coat. A light brushing and combing with a medium-tooth comb and pure-bristle brush keeps the coat in condition.

ORIGIN AND HISTORY
The Japanese Bobtail is a natural breed, native to the Far East. It is most often found in Japan, China and Korea. Its likeness has appeared in Japanese prints and paintings for centuries, and decorates a Tokyo temple, called the Gotokuji. The cats shown have one paw lifted in greeting. They were first imported to the United States in 1968, but are still rare.

BREEDING
The Bobtail gene is recessive. A Bobtail mated to an ordinary-tail shorthair produces only normal-tail kittens. Bobtail-to-Bobtail mating produces 100% Bobtail kittens. No outcrossing to other breeds is necessary or permitted. Bicolor males are the best to produce the red, black and predominantly white females.

KITTENS
Japanese Bobtail kittens are lively and healthy. There are usually 4 in a litter. There is no lethal factor with Bobtails, as in the Manx.

SHOW REQUIREMENTS
The Japanese Bobtail is medium size, slender and shapely, with a distinctive bobbed tail and almond-shape eyes.

Coat—Soft and silky, single and non-shedding. Medium length but shorter on the face, ears and paws. Longer and thicker on the tail than elsewhere, camouflaging tail conformation.

Body—Medium size. Long and slender, but sturdy and muscular. Not fragile or dainty, like other Orientals. Not cobby either. Same width across the shoulders as the rump. Legs long and slender but not fragile or dainty. Hind legs longer than forelegs. Hind legs bent in stance when relaxed. One foreleg often raised. Paws oval.

Tail—Tail vertebrae are set at angles to each other. The furthest extension of the tail bone from the body is 2 to 3 inches (5 to 7.5cm) even though if straightened out to its full length the tail might be 4 to 5 inches (10 to 12.5cm) long. The tail is normally carried upright when the cat is relaxed. Hair on the tail grows outward in all directions, producing a fluffy, pompon effect that camouflages underlying bone structure.

Head—Forms an equilateral triangle, curving gently at the sides of the face. High cheekbones give way to a distinct whisker break. Muzzle is broad and round, not square or pointed.

Eyes—Large and oval. Slanted and wide apart with an alert expression.

COLORS
Preferred color is tricolor black, red and white, with patches large and distinct. White predominates. Colors not allowed are the Himalayan pattern and the unpatterned Agouti or Abyssinian. The more brilliant and bizarre the colors, the better. White; black, free from rust; deep red; black and white; red and white; a tricolor black, red and white or calico; tortoiseshell, black, red and cream. Other Japanese Bobtail colors include any other color, pattern or combination, with or without a solid color. Other solid colors are blue or cream. Patterned self colors: red, black, blue, cream, silver or brown. Other bicolors: blue and white, cream and white. Patterned bicolors: red, black, blue, cream, silver or brown combined with white. Patterned tortoiseshell. Blue-cream. Patterned blue-cream. Dilute tricolors: blue, cream and white. Patterned dilute tricolors. Patterned tricolor.

Red Tabby-And-White Manx

Manx

Black Manx kitten

Mi-Ke
Japanese Bobtail
and kitten

Japanese Bobtail

SIAMESE

Advantages
- **Intelligent**
- **Resourceful**
- **Likes company**
- **Good with children**
- **Walks on a harness and leash**

Disadvantages
- **Demanding**
- **Active**
- **Dislikes being left alone**
- **Dislikes being caged**
- **Likes to cry**
- **Needs warmth**

The Siamese is one of the most popular breeds. It is loving, enchanting and delightful, but also exasperating, demanding and boisterous. Some Siamese seem to cry all the time. A Siamese queen can be annoying. Be sure everyone in the family wants a cat with a boisterous temperament before purchasing a Siamese.

A Siamese enjoys walks on harness and leash, but rarely walks to heel. It performs tricks and plays games. It dislikes being ignored and can be wary and jealous of strangers and other animals.

With its personality and affectionate nature, the Siamese has a large following. It becomes more popular every year.

GROOMING
This cat is easy to groom. A Siamese needs a twice-weekly brushing and combing with a fine-tooth comb to remove dead hairs. A rub with a chamois leather gives a shine to the coat.

HEALTH CARE
The Siamese may not be more prone than other cats to feline diseases, but when ill it needs a lot of attention and affection. If not cared for, it gives up and dies. To guard against illness, inoculate it early, between 8 and 12 weeks of age.

Spectacle marks around the eyes or white hairs in the points are signs of illness or distress.

ORIGIN AND HISTORY
Siamese cats are believed to have existed in Siam (Thailand) for 200 years before they made their way to Europe and then America in the 19th century. They are of Eastern origin, although their early history has been lost. Two came to England as a gift to the British Consul from the King of Siam. They were shown in London in 1885. The first Siamese had round faces and darker coats than those seen today. Tail kinks and eye squints were also permitted at early shows. Such faults have now been bred out and the modern Siamese does not look like its earlier counterpart.

BREEDING
Siamese are prolific breeders, often having two litters a year with an average of 5 to 6 kittens in a litter. Litters of 11 and 13 have been recorded. Siamese make good mothers, though high-strung ones are unlikely to properly care for their kittens. Do not use a nervous or bad-tempered queen for breeding.

KITTENS
Siamese kittens develop early. They have individual personalities soon after birth and are precocious and self-assured. They are white when born. Point color develops gradually. In the Seal-points and Blue-points, a blob of color appears on the nose after about 10 days. It may be 3 months before chocolate and lilac points become apparent. In all colors, points may not fully develop until a year old.

Do not take kittens from their mother until they are at least 12 weeks old. If left together for at least part of the day until this age, they seem to be more well-adjusted as adults.

SHOW REQUIREMENTS
The Siamese is medium size, long, slim, lithe and muscular. It has the characteristic Himalayan coat pattern of pale body color and darker contrasting points.
Coat—Short, fine and close lying with a natural sheen.
Body—Medium size, dainty, long and svelte. Fine boned but strong and muscular. Not fat or flabby. Hind legs slightly longer than forelegs. Paws small, neat and oval.
Tail—Whiplike, long, thin and tapering to a point. No kinks.
Head—Long, narrow, tapering wedge with flat width between the ears. Profile straight, although there may be a slight change of angle above the nose. No nose break. Strong chin, jaws not undershot. No whisker break. Ears large and pointed, open at the base.
Eyes—Almond shape, medium size and slanted toward the nose. The width of an eye between the eyes. No squints.

COLORS
The first recorded Siamese cat was a Seal-point. Blue-point, Chocolate-point and Lilac-point followed. All appeared naturally within the breed and are genetic dilutions of the Seal-point. At present, these are the only colors recognized as Siamese in the Cat Fancier Association. Most other U.S. associations also classify Colorpoint Shorthairs as Siamese.
Coat Pattern—Body an even pale color, with the main contrasting color confined to the points—mask, ears, legs and tail. Mask covers the face, but not the top of the head. It is connected to the ears by tracings, except in kittens. Paler coats are easier to achieve in warmer climates. Most Siamese coats darken with age.
Seal-Point—Body an even, warm cream. Slightly darker on the back. Lighter on the stomach and chest. Points deep seal-brown. Noseleather and paw pads seal-brown. Eyes deep blue.
Chocolate-Point—Body ivory. Points warm milk-chocolate. Noseleather and paw pads cinnamon-pink. Eyes deep blue.
Blue-Point—Body blue-white, shading to a warmer white on chest and stomach. Points slate-blue. Noseleather and paw pads slate-blue. Eyes deep blue.
Lilac-Point—Body white. Points gray with a pink-lilac tone. Noseleather and paw pads lavender-pink. Eyes deep blue.

Seal-point Siamese kittens in an alert mood. Vivacious as kittens, Siamese are extroverted adults.

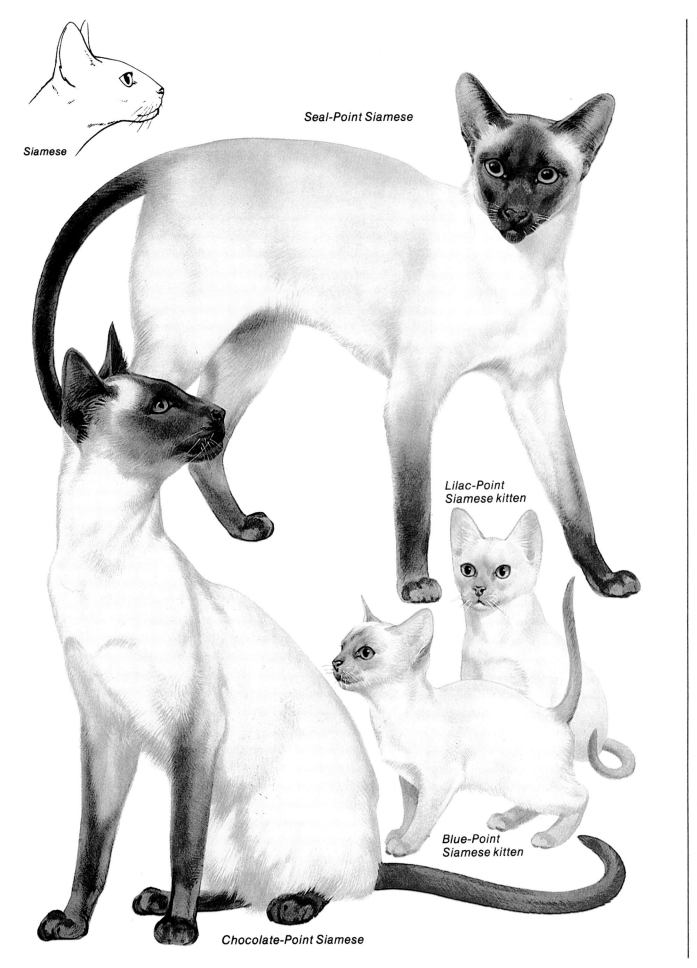

Siamese

Seal-Point Siamese

Lilac-Point
Siamese kitten

Blue-Point
Siamese kitten

Chocolate-Point Siamese

COLORPOINT SHORTHAIR

This is a Siamese cat with point colors other than seal, chocolate, blue or lilac. It resulted from outcrossing Siamese to shorthair cats to introduce other colors into the points.

It is regarded as Siamese in some countries. It is classified in the United States as a Colorpoint Shorthair by the Cat Fanciers Association. Colors recognized include red, cream and tortoiseshell points and tabby points in all recognized point colors.

COLORS

Coat Pattern—Body is pale, with the main contrasting color confined to the points—mask, ears, legs and tail. Mask covers the whole face, but not the top of the head. Connected to the ears by tracings, except in kittens.

Red-Point—Body white with any shading in the same tone as the points. Points bright apricot to deep red, deeper shades preferred, without barring. Noseleather and paw pads flesh-pink or coral-pink. Eyes blue.

Cream-Point—Body white with any shading in the same tone as the points. Points pale buff-cream to light pink-cream without barring. Noseleather and paw pads flesh-pink or coral-pink. Eyes blue.

Seal-Tortie-Point—Body pale fawn to cream, shading to lighter color on the stomach and chest. Points seal-brown, uniformly mottled with red and cream. Blaze desirable. Noseleather seal-brown or flesh-pink where there is a blaze. Paw pads seal-brown or flesh-pink. Eyes blue.

Chocolate-Tortie-Point—Body ivory. Points warm milk-chocolate, uniformly mottled with red, cream, or red and cream. Blaze desirable. Noseleather and paw pads cinnamon or flesh-pink. Eyes blue.

Blue-Cream-Point—Body blue-white to platinum-gray, shading to lighter color on the stomach and chest. Points deep blue-gray uniformly mottled with cream. Blaze desirable. Noseleather and paw pads slate-blue or flesh-pink. Eyes blue.

Lilac-Cream-Point—Body white. Points gray with pink tone, uniformly mottled with pale cream. Blaze desirable. Noseleather and paw pads lavender-pink or flesh-pink. Eyes blue.

Seal-Lynx-Point—Body cream or pale fawn, shading to lighter color on the stomach and chest. Body shading may take the form of ghost striping. Points seal-brown bars, distinct and separated by lighter background color. Ears seal-brown with paler thumbprint in the center. Noseleather seal-brown or pink, edged in seal-brown. Paw pads seal-brown. Eyes blue.

Chocolate-Lynx-Point—Body ivory. Body shading may take the form of ghost striping. Points warm milk-chocolate bars, distinct and separated by lighter background color. Ears warm milk-chocolate with paler thumbprint in center. Noseleather cinnamon-pink or pink, edged in cinnamon. Paw pads cinnamon. Eyes blue.

Blue-Lynx-Point—Body blue-white to platinum-gray, shading to lighter color on the stomach and chest. Body shading may take the form of ghost striping. Points deep blue-gray bars, distinct and separated by lighter background color. Ears blue-gray with paler thumbprint in center. Noseleather slate or pink, edged in slate. Paw pads slate. Eyes blue.

Lilac-Lynx-Point—Body white. Body shading may take the form of ghost striping. Points gray with pink tone distinct and separated by lighter background color. Ears gray with pink tone. Paler thumbprint in center. Noseleather lavender-pink or pink edged in lavender. Paw pads lavender-pink. Eyes blue.

Red-Lynx-Point—Body white. Body shading may take the form of

Seal Tortie-point Colorpoint Shorthair.

ghost striping. Points deep red bars, distinct and separated by lighter background color. Ears deep red, paler thumbprint in center. Noseleather and paw pads flesh-pink or coral-pink. Eyes blue.

Cream-Lynx-Point—Body white, shading to palest cream on the back. Points deeper buff-cream bars on white background. Ears cream with paler thumbprint in center. Noseleather and paw pads pink. Eyes blue.

Torbie-Point—Colors and point markings as for Tabby-points, with patches of red, cream, or red and cream irregularly distributed over the tabby pattern on the points. Red, cream, or red and cream mottling on the ears and tail permissible. Noseleather and paw pads as appropriate to the basic point color or mottled with pink. Eyes blue.

SNOWSHOE

Advantages
- **Good-natured**
- **Easy to groom**
- **Good with children**

Disadvantages
- **Vocal**
- **Dislikes being left alone**

The Snowshoe is a hybrid breed, produced by mating Siamese with bicolor American Shorthairs. It has characteristics of both breeds. It is not usually as noisy as a Siamese, but is not as quiet as most shorthair cats. It is calm, but alert, and is an ideal pet. Do not leave it alone for long periods.

Because of its origin, the Snowshoe has a modified Oriental body type, usually larger and heavier than a Siamese, with less-extreme features. It has a rounder head and a distinct nose break, which distinguishes it from other Siamese-derived breeds.

GROOMING
The Snowshoe needs minimal grooming with a brush or comb to remove dead hairs.

ORIGIN AND HISTORY
The Snowshoe is a new breed and looks like a shorthair Birman. It has the Himalayan coat pattern with white feet but, unlike the Birman, it also has a white muzzle.

There are many unregistered Snowshoe cats as a result of Siamese queens mating with bicolor alley cats. The variety was considered so attractive, devotees selectively bred these cats. A show standard is now being developed. Snowshoes are experimental and it may be some time before widespread official recognition is granted.

At present, only seal and white, and blue and white are being bred.

Other Siamese-point colors may be available in the Snowshoe in the future.

BREEDING
Any solid color Himalayan-pattern cat without white, that results from the breeding of Snowshoe with Snowshoe or Snowshoe with Siamese, can be used for breeding. However, it is not eligible for competition. It is hoped such breeding will build up foundation stock.

KITTENS
Snowshoe kittens are lively, healthy and respond to affection. There may be 3 to 7 in a litter. Kittens without correct markings are available at reasonable prices and make excellent pets. They cannot be shown.

SHOW REQUIREMENTS
The Snowshoe is a modified Oriental-type shorthair cat with white and colored points.

Coat—Medium coarse in texture, short, glossy and close lying.

Body—Medium to large, muscular and powerful. Long back. Heavy build. Males larger than females. Legs long and solid with round paws. Sleek, dainty, Oriental type is a fault.

Tail—Medium length, thick at the base, tapering slightly to the tip. Whip or long tail is a fault.

Head—Triangular wedge. Obvious nose break. Round or long head is a fault. Neck medium length, not thin. Ears large, alert and pointed, broad at the base. Small or large ears are faults.

Eyes—Large and almond shape, slanted upward from nose to ear.

COLORS
Coat pattern—Mask, ears, legs and tail clearly defined from the body color. Mask covers the face, connected to the ears by tracings. Slightly darker shading of body color is allowed across shoulders, back and top of hips. Chest and stomach are paler. Forefeet white and symmetrical. White ends in an even line around the ankle. Hind feet white, with symmetrical white marking extending up the leg to the heel. Muzzle white. Nose may be white or point color. No other white hairs or patches allowed.

Seal-Point—Body color an even fawn, shading gradually to a lighter tone on the stomach and chest. Points, except feet and muzzle, deep seal-brown. Noseleather pink if nose is white or black if nose is seal. Paw pads pink, seal-brown or a combination. Eyes blue.

Blue-Point—Body color even blue-white, shading gradually to a lighter color on the chest and stomach. Points, except feet and muzzle, a deep gray-blue. Noseleather pink if nose is white or gray if nose is blue. Paw pads pink, gray, or pink and gray. Eyes blue.

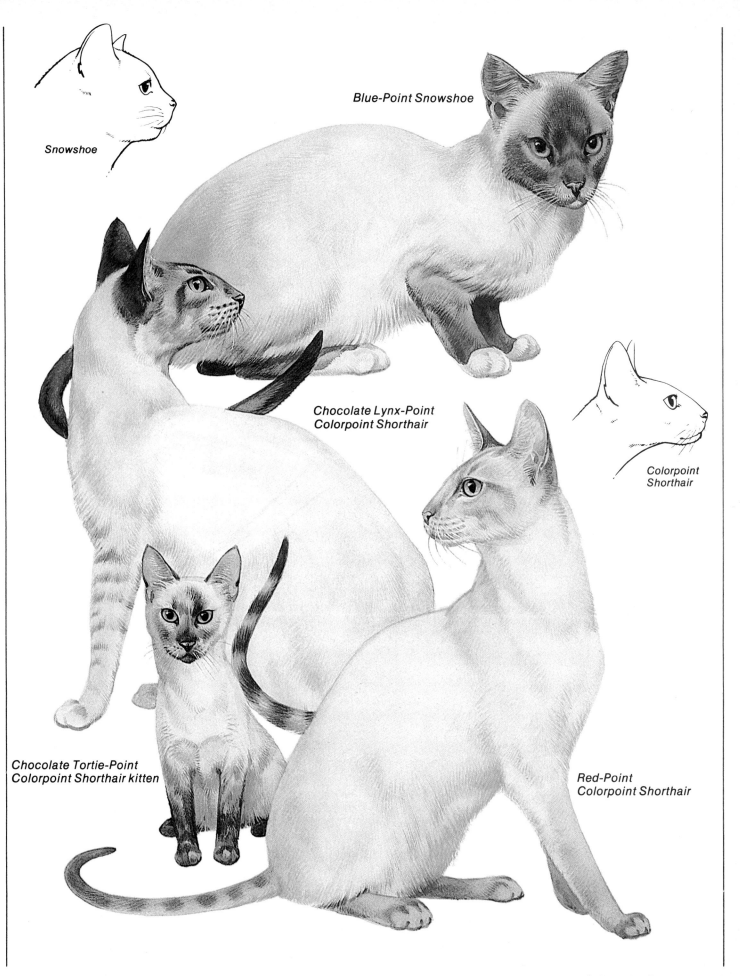

Snowshoe

Blue-Point Snowshoe

Chocolate Lynx-Point
Colorpoint Shorthair

Colorpoint
Shorthair

Chocolate Tortie-Point
Colorpoint Shorthair kitten

Red-Point
Colorpoint Shorthair

AMERICAN HAVANA BROWN

Advantages
- *Agile*
- *Intelligent*
- *Active*
- *Hardy*
- *Playful*
- *Affectionate*

Disadvantages
- *Needs human companionship*

The American Havana Brown is an active, intelligent cat. It loves people and needs human companionship and affection. It enjoys playing, hunting and doing other things with the family. It is gentle by nature and makes a hardy, attractive pet.

GROOMING
This cat is easy to groom. A daily combing with a fine-tooth comb and polishing with a chamois leather before a show will keep it in condition.

ORIGIN AND HISTORY
The breed is named *Havana* after its similarity in coat color to the tobacco of a Havana cigar. The American Havana Brown has developed differently from the British Havana, although both had the same origins. Both were developed from a Seal-point Siamese mated to a domestic shorthair. American Havanas were not allowed to mate back to Siamese, so a less-Oriental, more-rounded type developed. The American Oriental Self-Brown is almost the equivalent of the British Havana. British Havanas were bred back to Siamese to preserve the Oriental type.

BREEDING
Havana queens call loudly, clearly and frequently. They usually have 4 to 6 kittens in a litter and make good mothers. American breeders do not mate Havanas back to Siamese. They do not want to perpetuate the Oriental type.

KITTENS
Kittens are playful and agile. They are born the same color as their parents, but coats are a dull brown. They do not have the gloss of adults. White hairs found frequently in a kitten's coats disappear when the adult coat is grown.

SHOW REQUIREMENTS
The overall impression is medium size, rich, solid color and firm muscle tone.
Coat—Medium length, smooth and lustrous.
Body—Medium size and muscular. Medium length neck and legs. Oval paws.
Tail—Medium length, tapering to a point. No kinks.

Head—Slightly longer than wide. Distinct nose break and whisker break form a unique muzzle. Chin strong. Ears large and tilted forward, with round tips.
Eyes—Oval, no squints.
Color—Mahogany-brown all over. Solid from tip to root with no tabby markings or white patches. Noseleather and paw pads rose-pink. Eyes chartreuse to green. Greener shades preferred.

COLOR
Mahogany-brown all over. Solid from tip to root with no tabby markings or white patches. Noseleather and paw pads rose-pink. Eyes chartreuse to green. Greener shades preferred.

ORIENTAL SHORTHAIR

Advantages
- *Affectionate*
- *Active*
- *Intelligent*
- *Good with children*
- *Good with dogs*
- *Easy to groom*

Disadvantages
- *Needs exercise*
- *Needs companionship*
- *Needs warmth*

This long-legged, sleek, svelte cat is the tomboy of the feline world, always into everything. With boundless energy, it takes an interest in all the family's activities and loves walks on a harness and leash. Do not expect it to obey commands or walk to heel. Because it is energetic and has an inquisitive nature, it may stray from home. Restrict freedom for its own safety. A large wire run, leading from inside the house, is ideal.

This cat may become morose if left alone for long periods. You may want to have more than one, or another pet, for companionship.

GROOMING
Comb daily to remove dead hairs. Rub the coat with a chamois leather or silk cloth. Hand stroking burnishes the coat. Check ears and teeth regularly.

HEALTH CARE
Have kittens inoculated before they are 2 months old.

ORIGIN AND HISTORY
The original Oriental Shorthair cats came from arranged matings between Siamese for type, and other shorthair cats for color. Later, Siamese were mated to longhair Chinchillas to produce Oriental cats with tipped coats. This has allowed for breeding solid

caramel, apricot and beige colors, tipped tabbies, torbies and shaded, tipped and smoke tortoiseshells.

All cats of this type are known as Oriental Shorthairs. In Great Britain, solid-color cats are known as Foreign Shorthairs. The name Foreign is being replaced by Oriental.

BREEDING
Oriental queens are prolific and can have 2 litters a year, often of 5 or 6 kittens each.

KITTENS
Kittens are born the same color as the adults. This is unlike the Siamese from which this breed was originally derived, whose kittens are paler at birth.

SHOW REQUIREMENTS
Oriental Shorthairs have long, svelte, lithe and muscular bodies, with long, thin, tapering tails.
Coat—Short, fine, glossy and close lying.
Body—Medium size and fine boned. Shoulders and hindquarters same width. Legs long and slim. Hind legs longer than forelegs. Paws small, dainty and oval.
Tail—Long and tapering to a point. Thin at the base. No kinks.
Head—Long wedge with no whisker break or nose break. Flat skull. Fine muzzle. Strong chin. Neck long and slender. Ears large and pointed, wide at the base.
Eyes—Clear, almond shape, medium size, slanted toward the nose. No squints.

COLOR
Breeding programs have produced the following selection of colors and patterns within this breed.

Chestnut Oriental

The first all-brown shorthair cat was a cross between a Black Domestic Shorthair and a Seal-point Siamese. It resulted from an accidental mating. The line was not perpetuated at that time.

The type was deliberately bred in the 1950s. A Chocolate-point Siamese and a Domestic Shorthair of Oriental type were bred. The name has been altered. Originally it was called Havana because the coat was the color of Havana tobacco. The name changed and the variety was registered as Chestnut-Brown Foreign. Exported to the United States, these cats became Havana Browns. In 1970, British and European governing bodies also readopted the name Havana. This caused confusion because the varieties developed differently in the United States and Europe.

In Europe, the Oriental type was encouraged and the cats were outcrossed to Siamese. The American Havana Brown is a cat of

less-extreme type. Outcrossing to Siamese is not permitted. The British Havana is identical to the American Chestnut Oriental. American Havana Browns were not used in the development of the Oriental Shorthair in Great Britain.

SHOW REQUIREMENTS
Coat warm chestnut-brown from root to tip. Tabby or other markings, white hairs or patches are faults. Noseleather brown. Paw pads pink-brown. Eyes green.

Lilac Oriental
Lavender Oriental
Foreign Lilac

These cats were developed in Great Britain in the 1960s, during the Havana breeding program. Mating two Self-Brown Havanas produces Lilac kittens if the parents were produced from a cross between a Russian Blue and a Seal-point Siamese. Soon there will be sufficient Lilac studs so outcrosses will be unnecessary.

SHOW REQUIREMENTS
The Oriental Lilac has a pink-gray coat with a gray tone, not too blue or too fawn. White hairs, patches or tabby markings are faults. Noseleather and paw pads lavender. Eyes green.

Cinnamon Oriental

This cat was originally developed from a Seal-point Siamese carrying genetic factors for Chocolate, mated to a Red Abyssinian. It is a lighter color than the Havana, but is similar. It is becoming popular in Europe.

SHOW REQUIREMENTS
Coat a warm milk-chocolate brown, from root to tip. No white hairs or tabby markings. Eyes green.

The Cinnamon Oriental is a striking variety.

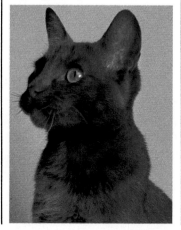

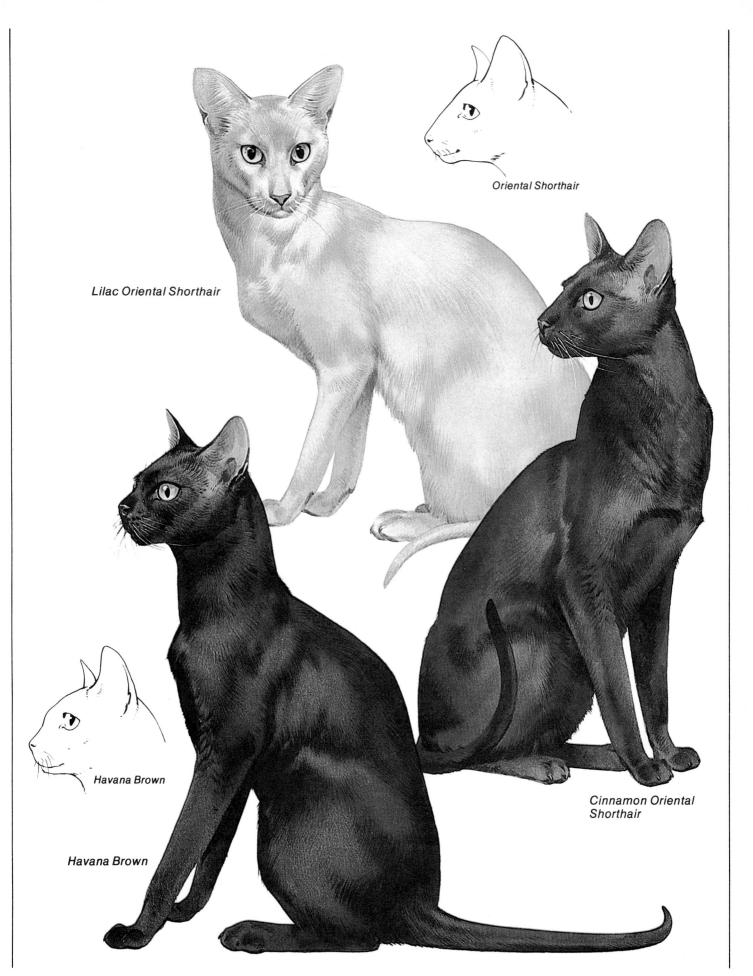

Oriental Shorthair

Lilac Oriental Shorthair

Havana Brown

Havana Brown

Cinnamon Oriental
Shorthair

White Oriental
Foreign White

A striking variety, the White Oriental looks like porcelain, with a smooth white coat and blue eyes. It was developed in the 1960s and 1970s by mating White Domestic Shorthairs to Siamese. The white coat is dominant genetically to other coat colors. It obscured the Himalayan coat pattern. Later, White Oriental were outcrossed to Siamese to improve eye color. In the early stages, green-eye, yellow-eye and odd-eye kittens were born. Now blue is the preferred eye color and selectively bred. Blue-eye White Oriental Shorthairs are not deaf.

COLOR

Coat white throughout with no black hairs. Noseleather pale pink. Paw pads dark pink. Eyes green or blue. Odd-eyes are not allowed on the show bench.

Ebony Oriental
Foreign Black

This is a long, svelte, black cat with emerald-green eyes and an alert, intelligent expression. Interest in it began in the 1970s, when many Ebony Shorthairs had been bred experimentally or accidentally, but were sold as pets. There was no official show standard for them.

They were originally obtained from mating Self-Browns to Seal-point Siamese. Today there are sufficient Ebony Oriental studs available so crossing to Siamese is no longer necessary.

COLOR

Coat black from root to tip. A rusty tinge to the fur is considered a fault. Noseleather black. Paw pads black or brown. Eyes emerald green.

Blue Oriental
Foreign Blue

The Blue Oriental appears naturally in litters of Self-Brown Havanas and Lilacs. It is appearing on the show bench. Its striking Siamese type makes it easily distinguishable from other blue cats with green eyes—the Korat and the Russian blue.

COLOR

Coat light to medium-blue all over, sound from root to tip. A lighter shade of blue is preferred. White hairs or patches, especially on the chin and stomach, are faults. Noseleather and paw pads blue. Eyes green.

Red Oriental
Foreign Red

This cat was developed from the Red-point Siamese breeding program, when Red Tabby British Shorthairs were mated to Siamese to introduce red into the Oriental type. It was a natural product of these matings. Today it results from mating Oriental Blacks to Red-point Siamese. The Red Oriental is difficult to breed without tabby markings. Use breeding stock without tabby ancestry or markings may persist into adulthood. It is now possible to use Red Burmese. Burmese breeders have succeeded in breeding out markings in the coat of the Red Burmese.

COLOR

Coat clear red, without shading or markings. Lips and chin red. Noseleather and paw pads brick-red. Eyes copper to green. Green preferred.

Cream Oriental
Foreign Cream

The Cream Oriental is a by-product of a breeding program to produce Oriental Blue and Lilac Tortoiseshells. In these programs, Tortoiseshell Domestic Shorthairs were mated to Siamese. All solid colors appeared in the mixture. Genetically, the Cream is a dilute of the Red, and makes an elegant cat of Oriental type.

COLOR

Coat buff-cream without markings, an even color from root to tip. Noseleather and paw pads pink. Green eyes preferred.

Other Solid Colors

In order to produce the Shaded Oriental Shorthairs, Chinchilla American Shorthairs were used. Their offspring were mated to Red-point Siamese to introduce all the other colors simultaneously. In the process, other solid-color cats were produced, including Caramel Oriental, a cafe-au-lait color; Apricot Oriental, a Red bred from a Caramel; and Beige Oriental, a Cream bred from a Caramel. All have pale green eyes. These are still experimental colors and cannot be produced reliably.

Shaded Oriental

The Shaded Oriental Shorthair was developed from the Siamese-Chinchilla Persian mating. Their offspring were mated back to Siamese, Oriental Blacks and British Havanas. Afterward, selective breeding took place to preserve the amount of tipping required. Any color tipping is possible and all colors are allowed, including silver, cameo, cameo tabby, blue, chestnut, lilac, and tortoiseshell in brown, blue, chestnut and lilac. The shaded color class includes only ebony-silver, blue-silver, chestnut-silver, lavender-silver and cameo.

COLORS

Undercoat white, sufficiently tipped on the back, flanks, head and tail with a contrasting color to give the effect of a mantle overlying the white undercoat. Noseleather and paw pads according to tipping color. Color of eyes according to tipping color. Green preferred.

Tipped Oriental

A revolution occurred with Orientals when a Siamese was mated to a Chinchilla Persian to produce an Oriental-type cat with a tipped coat. Resulting kittens were mated back to Siamese for type. Now Oriental tipped coats are mated only to Oriental tipped, to preserve the coat pattern.

The Tipped Oriental does not have a separate class. Similarly marked cats are designated as Shaded or Smoke, depending on the amount of coloration. American Orientals have such short hair, there is hardly room for 3 distinct degrees of shading.

COLORS

Undercoat white. Topcoat lightly tipped on the back, flanks, head and tail with a contrasting color to give a sparkling sheen to the coat. Chest and underparts white. Noseleather and paw pads appropriate to the tipping color. Eyes according to tipping color. Green preferred.

Smoke Oriental

A by-product of the Siamese-Chinchilla Persian mating was the first Smoke Oriental, produced by mating a Shaded Silver to a Red-point Siamese. Today, the best Smoke Orientals are mated back to Siamese, Black Orientals and British Havanas to preserve type. Tipping is heavy, giving the appearance of a solid-color cat, except when fur is parted to reveal a narrow band of white hair.

Like Tipped and Shaded Oriental Shorthairs, any color Smoke is possible. Most are now allowed for competition. These include ebony, blue, red and cream, chestnut, lavender and tortoiseshell in brown, blue, chocolate and lilac.

COLORS

Undercoat white. Topcoat heavily tipped with a contrasting color so the cat in repose appears that color. Noseleather and paw pads in keeping with tipping color. Eyes green.

Tortie Oriental
Oriental Particolor

The Tortie Oriental is a female-only variety derived from the Red and Cream Oriental Shorthairs. It was originally produced by mating Black Orientals with Red-point Siamese or Havanas with Red-point Siamese. Today, Tortie Orientals are mated to Siamese or other solid-color Oriental Shorthairs.

COLORS

Brown Tortie—Coat black with unbrindled patches of red and cream, clearly defined and broken on body, head, legs and tail. A facial blaze of red or cream is desirable. Noseleather and paw pads black, pink, or black and pink. Eyes green.
Blue Tortie—Coat blue with patches of solid cream, clearly defined and broken on body, head, legs and tail. Noseleather and paw pad blue, pink, or blue and pink. Eyes green.
Chestnut Tortie—Coat chestnut-brown with unbrindled patches of red and cream, clearly defined and broken on body, head, legs and tail. A facial blaze of red or cream is desirable. Noseleather and paw pads dark or light pink. Eyes green.
Lilac-Cream Tortie—Coat lilac-gray with patches of solid cream, clearly defined and broken on body, head, legs and tail. Noseleather and paw pads pink. Eyes green.

White Oriental
Shorthair

Ebony Oriental
Shorthair

Oriental
Shorthair

Red-Tipped Oriental
Shorthair

Torbie Oriental

The Torbie Oriental, or patched tabby, appeared during the breeding program to obtain the Tipped Oriental. It resulted from matings between Shaded Silver Orientals and Red-point Siamese.

COLORS
Brown Tabby with patches of red or silver, Chocolate Tabby with patches of red, blue, or Lilac Tabby with patches of cream. Noseleather and paw pads patched with appropriate solid colors. Green eyes preferred.

Cats with such markings must be shown as patched tabbies. This standard may be amended in the future to reclassify these cats as Torbie Orientals.

Tabby Oriental

Using shorthair tabbies and Siamese, the Tabby Oriental Shorthair was produced during the breeding program for Tabby-point Siamese. Later, British Havanas were mated to Tabby-point Siamese. All colors and tabby patterns have been developed.

COLORS
Classic-Tabby Pattern—All markings dense and clearly defined. Frown lines on the forehead form the characteristic letter *M*. Unbroken lines run from the outer corners of the eyes toward the back of the head. Other pencil lines on the face form swirls on cheeks. Lines extend from the top of the head to shoulder markings, which are shaped in a butterfly pattern. Three unbroken lines run parallel to each other down the spine from the shoulder markings to the base of the tail. A large blotch on each flank is circled by one or more unbroken rings. These markings are symmetrical on either side of the body. There should be several unbroken necklaces on the neck and upper chest. A double row of buttons runs from chest to stomach. Legs and tail evenly ringed.

Mackerel-Tabby Pattern—Head is marked with the characteristic *M*. An unbroken line runs from the outer corner of the eyes toward the back of the head. Fine pencil markings occur on the cheeks. A narrow unbroken line runs from the back of the head to the base of the tail. The rest of the body is marked with narrow, unbroken lines running vertically from the spine line. There should be several unbroken necklaces on the neck and upper chest. A double row of buttons runs from chest to stomach. Legs evenly barred with narrow bracelets and tail evenly ringed.

Spotted-Tabby Pattern—Head markings the same as the Classic Tabby. Body markings broken into numerous spots, which may be round, oval or rosette-shape. Dorsal stripe along the spine broken into spots. A double row of spots runs from chest to stomach. Spots or broken rings on legs and tail.

Ticked-Tabby Pattern—Body hairs ticked with various shades of marking color and ground color. When viewed from above, body free from noticeable spots, stripes or blotches, except for darker dorsal shading. Lighter underside may show tabby markings. Face, legs and tail must show distinct tabby striping. At least one distinct necklace on neck or upper chest.

Brown Tabby—Ground color copper-brown. Markings black. Eyes rimmed with black. Noseleather black or brick-red rimmed with black. Paw pads black or brown. Green eyes preferred.

Blue Tabby—Ground color pale blue-ivory. Markings deep blue. May have warm fawn highlights. Eyes rimmed with blue. Noseleather blue or rose rimmed with blue. Paw pads rose. Green eyes preferred.

Chocolate Tabby—Ground color warm fawn. Markings chestnut-brown. Eyes rimmed with chestnut. Noseleather chestnut or pink rimmed with chestnut. Paw pads cinnamon-pink or chestnut. Green eyes preferred.

Lilac Tabby—Ground color pale lavender. Markings deep lilac-gray. Eyes rimmed with lilac. Noseleather lilac or pink rimmed with lilac-gray. Paw pads lavender-pink. Green eyes preferred.

Red Tabby—Ground color red-apricot. Markings deep rich red. Eyes rimmed with pink or red. Noseleather brick-red or pink rimmed with red. Green eyes preferred.

Cream Tabby—Ground color pale cream. Markings deep cream. Eyes rimmed with pink or cream. Noseleather pink or pink rimmed with cream. Paw pads pink. Green eyes preferred.

Silver Tabby—Ground color silver. Markings black. Eyes rimmed with black. Noseleather black or brick-red rimmed with black. Paw pads black. Green eyes.

Cameo Tabby—Ground color off-white. Markings red. Noseleather and paw pads rose. Green eyes.

OCICAT

The Ocicat is another Siamese-derived spotted breed that has been produced recently. It was achieved by crossing a Chocolate-point Siamese male with a half-Siamese, half-Abyssinian female. This cat is unknown outside the United States. Except for color, it closely resembles the Spotted Tabby Oriental. These cats may attain championship status in the future, but currently they are considered experimental.

COLORS
Dark Chestnut—Ground color pale cream. Dark chestnut tabby spots and markings on the chest, legs and tail. Eyes gold.

Light Chestnut—Ground color pale cream. Milk-chocolate tabby spots and markings on the chest, legs and tail. Eyes gold.

EGYPTIAN MAU

Advantages
- Agile
- Playful
- Friendly
- Quiet
- Easy to groom
- Good with children

Disadvantages
- Does not like to be caged

The Egyptian Mau is the only natural breed of spotted Oriental-type cat. It originated in Egypt and is a descendant of the cat worshipped by Ancient Egyptians. It is shy, loving and has a good memory. Strong and muscular, it can easily be trained to perform tricks. It enjoys walking on a harness and leash.

Do not confine this active cat. If you cannot take the cat for walks, build a pen in the yard with a roof and access to the house or a shelter. It adores people and should not be shut up on its own.

GROOMING
Little grooming is required for this cat. The Mau benefits from daily combing to remove dead hairs. Before a show, use bay rum. Do not use powder because it mars the spots on the coat.

ORIGIN AND HISTORY
The Egyptian Mau may be the original domestic cat. Spotted cats are depicted in early Egyptian art and symbolized in the gods Ra and Bast, both personified as cats. *Mau* is the Egyptian word for cat.

The Egyptian Mau has been developed principally in the United States. Similar spotted cats, formerly called Egyptian Maus in Great Britain, are now known as Spotted Oriental Shorthairs. They are a Siamese-derived breed.

The first Egyptian Maus were seen in Europe at a mid-1950s cat show in Rome. They were taken to the United States in 1956 and shown at the Empire Cat Show in in New York in 1957, attracting great interest.

BREEDING
Because the Mau is a natural breed, outcrossing to other breeds is not permitted. Queens make excellent mothers. They are even-tempered, quiet and devoted. The gestation period for Egyptian Maus is 63 to 73 days.

KITTENS
Egyptian Mau kittens are born with obvious spots and are active and playful. There are usually 4 in a litter.

SHOW REQUIREMENTS
The Egyptian Mau looks like a cross between the svelte Oriental-type and the cobby Domestic Shorthair. Egyptian Maus are alert, balanced, muscular and colorful.

Coat—Fur is dense, resilient and lustrous. Medium long, silky, fine.

Body—A modified Oriental-type. Medium length, graceful and muscular, especially the males. Hind legs are longer than forelegs and give the appearance the cat is standing on tiptoe. Paws are small and dainty, round to oval.

Tail—Medium long. Wide at the base, tapering slightly. A whip tail is considered a fault.

Eyes—Large and almond shape. Small, round or Oriental eyes are considered a fault.

COLORS
Coat Pattern—Contrast between the pale ground color and spots. Each hair carries two bands of color. The pigmentation of spots and stripes is seen in the fur and on the skin. The forehead is marked with the characteristic *M*. Other marks form lines between the ears that continue down the back of the neck, breaking into elongated spots along the spine. As the spinal lines reach the hindquarters, spots merge to form a dorsal stripe that continues along to the tail tip. Two darker lines cross the cheeks. One starts at the outer eye corner and extends to below the ear, the second starts at the center of the cheek and curves upward, almost meeting the first. The upper chest has one or more necklaces, preferably broken in the center. Shoulder markings may be stripes or spots. Front legs are heavily barred. Markings on the body

Egyptian Mau

Egyptian
Mau Smoke

Silver Spotted-Tabby
Oriental Shorthair

Chocolate Tabby
Oriental Shorthair

Oriental Shorthair

spotted. Spots vary in size and shape. Round, even spots are preferred. The spotting pattern on each side of the body need not be symmetrical, but spots should not run together in a broken, mackerel pattern. Hindquarters and upper hind legs carry spots and stripes, bars on the thighs and back, and spots on the lower leg. A row of buttons runs from chest to stomach.

Four colors have developed:

Silver—Ground color light silver, lighter on the undersides. Markings charcoal-gray. Backs of ears gray-pink, tipped in black. Toes black, color extending up the backs of the hind legs. Nose, lips and eyes rimmed in black. Noseleather brick-red. Paw pads black. Eyes green.

Bronze—Ground color honey-bronze, shading to pale ivory on undersides. Markings dark brown. Backs of ears pink edged with dark brown. Paws dark brown with dark color extending up backs of the hind legs. Nose, lips and eyes rimmed with black or dark brown. Bridge of the nose ocher. Noseleather brick-red. Paw pads black or dark brown. Eyes green.

Smoke—Ground color charcoal-gray with silver-white undercoat. Markings black. Paws black, with black extending between the toes and up the backs of the hind legs. Nose, lips and eyes rimmed with black. Noseleather and paw pads black. Eyes green.

Pewter—Ground color pale fawn. Each hair on the back and flanks ticked or banded with silver and beige, tipped with black, shading to pale cream on the undersides. Markings charcoal-gray to dark brown. Nose, lips and eyes rimmed with charcoal to dark brown. Noseleather brick-red. Paw pads charcoal to dark brown. Eyes green.

BURMESE

The Burmese is an excellent pet. It has a sleek, shorthair coat that is easy to groom. It is more intelligent and affectionate than many cats. It has a fantastic personality, loves people and is wonderful with children. But it does not like to be left alone. If you are gone all day, it is better to have two cats. They will be company for each other.

The Burmese is tomboyish by nature. Many fanciers consider the beautiful coat and yellow eyes elegant. This cat welcomes a stranger. The time and affection devoted to this cat more than repay the owner in loyalty and affection. A Burmese loves to sleep with family members if it gets the chance.

GROOMING
The Burmese is one of the easiest cats to groom. A fine-tooth comb used once or twice a week removes dead hairs. For shows, a bran bath a few days before absorbs any excess grease in the coat. The glossy Burmese coat is obtained by using a chamois cloth. A healthy Brown Burmese looks like polished mahogany.

ORIGIN AND HISTORY
Cats resembling the Burmese have been recorded in books from Thailand dating back to the 15th century. The breed was developed in the United States in 1930. A brown female cat of Oriental type, named Wong Mau, was imported to the West Coast from Burma. She was mated to a Siamese because there were no similar cats. All her kittens were hybrids, but when mated back to their mother, brown kittens resembling the mother were produced. The personality of these cats was admired. They were affectionate and intelligent, and less vocal and less destructive than the Siamese. The breed soon became popular.

In some American associations the Blue, Brown and Lilac Burmese colors are considered a separate breed known as the *Malayan*. They were bred from other-colored shorthairs.

BREEDING
The Burmese is a prolific cat. A queen usually has large litters, sometimes up to 10 kittens. Four or five is the average number. The Burmese makes an excellent mother and demands strict obedience from her kittens.

KITTENS
Kittens are active and playful. They are born with paler coats than adults. In the Brown Burmese, mother and kittens look like plain and milk-chocolate together. It is often difficult to determine the shade of a paler-coated Burmese at birth, because final coat color takes weeks to develop, as does eye color. Due to increasing demand, you may have to wait for a Burmese.

SHOW REQUIREMENTS
The Burmese is a medium size, modified-Oriental type with a muscular frame and heavier build than looks suggest. The American Burmese is long and has slender legs.

Coat—Fine, sleek and glossy. Short and close-lying.
Body—Medium size, hard and muscular. Chest round and back straight. Legs long and slender. Hind legs slightly longer than forelegs. Paws neat and round.
Tail—Medium length, tapering slightly to a round tip. Not whiplike or kinked.
Head—Slightly round on top between the ears. Ears wide apart. High, wide cheekbones taper to a short, developed muzzle. A jaw pinch is a fault. Ears round at the tips and open at the base, with a slight forward tilt in profile. Nose is medium length with a distinct break in profile. Face should have a sweet expression.
Eyes—Oriental shape along the top line. Round. Large and lustrous, set apart.

COLORS
Brown was the first color to be bred and recognized. It is often considered the most attractive. Brown Burmese have been exported to many countries. Selective breeding has produced several color varieties, but only Brown, Blue, Champagne and Platinum are recognized for competition.

Brown—Adults an even dark chocolate or sable-brown, shading slightly to a lighter tone on underparts. Noseleather and paw pads brown. Eyes deep yellow to gold with no tinge of green.

A Blue Burmese kitten is always in demand as a pet.

Blue—Adults soft silver-gray, shading to a paler tone on the underparts. Ears, face and feet have a silver sheen. Noseleather dark gray. Paw pads gray. Eyes deep to golden yellow preferred, although a green tinge is acceptable.
Chocolate—Adults a warm milk-chocolate all over, with slightly darker shading on the points permitted. Noseleather warm chocolate-brown. Paw pads brick-red to chocolate-brown. Eyes gold.
Lilac—Adults a delicate dove-gray with a pink tinge. Ears and mask slightly darker. Noseleather and paw pads lavender-pink. Eyes gold.
Red—Adults light tangerine. Ears slightly darker. Noseleather and paw pads pink. Eyes gold.
Cream—Adults a rich cream. Ears slightly darker. Noseleather and paw pads pink. Eyes gold.
Brown Tortie—Adults brown and red patches without barring. Noseleather and paw pads plain or blotched brown and pink. Eyes gold.
Blue Tortie—Adults have patches of blue and cream without barring. Noseleather and paw pads plain or blotched blue and pink. Eyes gold.
Chocolate Tortie—Adults chocolate and red blotches without barring. Noseleather and paw pads plain or blotched chocolate and pink. Eyes gold.
Lilac Tortie—Adults lilac and cream blotches, without barring. Noseleather and paw pads plain or blotched lilac and pink. Eyes gold.

Brown Burmese

Red Burmese

Lilac Tortie
Burmese

Burmese

TONKINESE
Tonkanese

Advantages
- *Friendly*
- *Affectionate*
- *Easy to groom*
- *Good with children*
- *Active*
- *Loves people*
- *Walks on a harness and leash*

Disadvantages
- *Gets lost easily*
- *Not afraid of traffic*

The Tonkinese is a hybrid breed, a cross between the Siamese and the Burmese. It has characteristics of each. It is still awaiting full endorsement by all American associations.

Restrict its freedom, but do not confine a Tonkinese to a room or cage. A large wire run with a roof and shelves at different heights is ideal. The cat amuses itself for hours, running up and down, jumping from one shelf to another. Some shelter should also be provided against rain or sun.

GROOMING
The Tonkinese is easy to groom. Use a fine-tooth comb and a rubber brush. A bran bath just before a show removes excess grease from the coat. A silk cloth or chamois leather gives it a polish. Inspect ears regularly for mites.

ORIGIN AND HISTORY
This breed was developed in the 1960s and 1970s. Breeders of Siamese and Burmese got attractive crossbred kittens and considered perpetuating them. The Tonkinese was accepted as a breed in 1975 by some cat associations. Europeans do not consider it a breed.

BREEDING
Tonkinese, or Tonks as they are known, are bred only to Tonks, producing 50% Tonks, 25% Siamese and 25% Burmese kittens. The first cross of Siamese to Burmese gives 100% Tonkinese. Non-Tonk kittens from matings cannot be shown because their pedigrees are not pure, but they make excellent pets.

KITTENS
Tonkinese kittens are born paler in color than their parents. Adult color develops gradually.

SHOW REQUIREMENTS
The Tonkinese is an Oriental-type cat, medium size, lithe and muscular. Its bulk is more substantial than current show-quality Siamese.
Coat—Soft and close-lying with a natural sheen.
Body—Medium size, muscular, with long legs. Hind legs slightly longer than forelegs. Slim legs

terminate in small, dainty, oval paws.
Tail—Long and tapering from a thick base to a thin tip. No kinks.
Head—A modified wedge with a square muzzle. In profile there is a slight nose break. Medium-long neck, but not as long as a Siamese. Ears medium size, pricked forward and round.
Eyes—Almond shape, set wide apart.

COLORS
Four colors are accepted. The adult coat is a solid color, shading to a slightly lighter tone on the underparts, with clearly defined points.
Natural Mink—Warm brown with dark chocolate points. Noseleather and paw pads brown. Eyes blue-green.
Honey Mink—Warm, ruddy-brown, with chocolate points. Noseleather and paw pads brown. Eyes blue-green.
Champagne Mink—Soft beige, with light-brown points. Noseleather and paw pads cinnamon-pink. Eyes blue-green.
Blue Mink—Soft blue to blue-gray with light-blue to slate-blue points. Noseleather and paw pads blue-gray. Eyes blue-green.
Platinum Mink—Soft silver body with metallic silver points. Noseleather lilac and paw pads pink. Eyes blue-green.

A Honey-Mink Tonkinese. Tonks make affectionate pets, but like to wander.

BOMBAY

Advantages
- *Even-tempered*
- *Quiet*
- *Good with children*
- *Good with animals*
- *Easy to groom*

Disadvantages
- *Needs attention*

The Bombay has been described as a *mini black panther* with a patent-leather coat and copper-penny eyes. It has an ideal temperament and personality. It is hardy, affectionate and contented. It seems to be always purring.

The Bombay is easy to groom because of its sleek coat. It is an ideal pet in many ways. It is good with children and mixes with other animals. It loves people and activity. Have more than one if you must be out all day. It does not like to be ignored and should not be left alone for too long.

GROOMING
The close-lying coat needs daily combing with a fine-tooth comb to remove dead hairs. A show animal can be polished with a silk cloth or chamois leather. Give the cat a bran bath occasionally. Inspect ears and eyes regularly.

ORIGIN AND HISTORY
The Bombay was produced by crossing Brown Burmese with Black American Shorthairs. The cat has the black color and hardiness of the American Shorthair and the coat, physique, intelligence and affection of the Burmese.

BREEDING
The Bombay, although developed as a hybrid, breeds true. Bombay with Bombay produces 100% Bombay kittens. In the original crosses, black was the dominant color. With the first cross, all kittens can be registered as Bombay. Type, color and eye color have been maintained by carefully controlled breeding programs that include frequent use of purebred Burmese. Queens make sensible mothers and mature early.

KITTENS
Kittens are lively, full of energy, affectionate and trusting. They need companionship and should not be neglected. Kitten coats may be a rusty color at first, maturing to pure black.

SHOW REQUIREMENTS
More show points are given to the coat condition and color in this breed than in any other. Coat is considered more important than type.
Coat—Short and close-lying with a patent-leather sheen or satin finish. It resembles the Burmese coat.
Body—Medium size and muscular. Not cobby or rangy. Males larger than females. Legs medium length.
Tail—Medium long, straight, no kinks.
Head—Round, without any flat planes. Face wide, with width between the eyes. Short, developed muzzle. Nose broad with a distinct nose break. Ears round, medium size and alert. Broad at base, set wide apart on curve of head, tilted forward.
Eyes—Round and set wide apart.

COLOR
Black to the roots without white hairs or patches. Noseleather and paw pads black. Eyes bright copper. Gold eyes sometimes accepted, but not green.

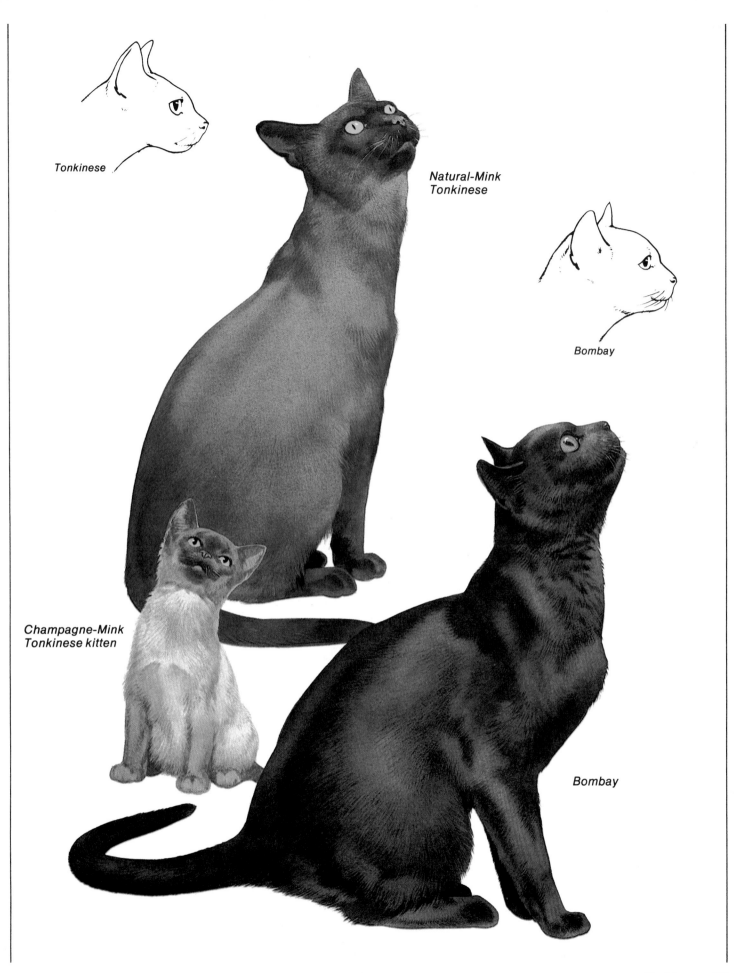

Tonkinese

Natural-Mink
Tonkinese

Bombay

Champagne-Mink
Tonkinese kitten

Bombay

RUSSIAN BLUE
Maltese

Advantages
- Good-natured
- Quiet
- Gentle
- Likes company
- Easy to groom
- Suitable for an apartment
- Walks on a harness and leash

Disadvantages
- Difficult to hear its voice

The outstanding feature of the Russian Blue is its quiet sweetness. It is shy and gentle, and makes a loving, agreeable companion. It becomes attached to its owner, is eager to please and likes living in an apartment. It prefers an indoor life. Its blue coat is different from any other breed. Guard hairs are tipped with silver, which gives a silver sheen that enhances the cat's look.

The cat's voice is often so quiet you may find it difficult to hear. If shut up somewhere, this quietness may prevent the cat from being found. It does not usually roam away from home.

GROOMING
This cat is easy to groom. Fur is short and plush. It needs only an occasional brushing and combing with a fine-tooth comb. Polish it with a chamois leather. Give it a bran bath before a show to absorb excess grease from the coat.

ORIGIN AND HISTORY
The original Russian Blue probably came from Archangel, Russia. It was brought to England by British sailors visiting the port. Before 1900, it was known as the Archangel Blue, but also as Maltese and Spanish cats. There was confusion as to what was or was not a Russian Blue.

It was shown in Great Britain at the end of the 19th century. Because there were few cats of the same breed to mate with, it was outcrossed to British Blues and Blue-point Siamese. This was nearly the death of the breed and produced undesirable results, particularly the loss of the distinctive coat. After World War II, efforts were made to reinstate this breed. Today better specimens are appearing.

BREEDING
The Russian Blue usually has one or two litters a year, with an average of 4 or 5 kittens in each. Finding appropriate breeding stock is still a problem. It is difficult to breed a cat with good type and coat.

KITTENS
Russian Blue kittens are born with fluffy coats. They may have faint tabby markings until the adult coat develops.

SHOW REQUIREMENTS
The Russian Blue is a medium-to-large Oriental type, lithe and graceful with a short, dense, plush coat.
Coat—Short and dense. Plush, silky and soft, resembling sealskin.
Body—Long, lithe and graceful. Medium-strong bones. Long legs with small round paws. Hind legs longer than forelegs.
Tail—Long and tapering. Thicker at the base.
Head—Wedge shape, shorter than a Siamese's. A receding forehead. Straight nose and forehead, with a change of angle above the nose. Flat, narrow skull. Prominent whisker pads. Strong chin. Neck long and slender but appears shorter because it is covered with thick, short, plush fur. Ears pointed, large and wide at the base. Set vertical on the head. Almost transparent and without ear tufts.
Eyes—Almond shape and set wide apart. Slanting to the nose.

COLORS
A clear blue all over, without shading or white hairs. Silver-tipped guard hairs give the coat a silvery sheen. A paler blue color is preferred. Black Russians and White Russians are now being bred, particularly in New Zealand. Noseleather and paw pads lavender-pink. Eyes bright green.

KORAT

Advantages
- Quiet
- Gentle
- Intelligent
- Not destructive
- Good with animals

Disadvantages
- Does not like loud noises
- Not good with children

The Korat has been described as having busy charm. It loves to be petted, is smart and likes energetic games. It dislikes loud noises and is best suited to a quiet household. It is not the best choice for a family with children.

The Korat likes quiet, gentle people and becomes attached to its owner. It gets along with other cats, but prefers its own breed. It settles happily with a docile dog, if it is introduced gently. The Korat is not talkative, except when calling. It makes an ideal pet for someone wanting a sweet, loving, quiet companion.

A charming Korat kitten with amber-green eyes.

The Korat is still a rare breed and you may have to wait for a kitten. There are more kittens in the United States than elsewhere, but they are now being bred in Great Britain, Canada, South Africa, Australia and New Zealand. The Korat is becoming popular.

GROOMING
The Korat's single coat is easy to keep in condition. It needs a daily combing to remove dead hairs and a polish with a chamois leather or silk cloth.

ORIGIN AND HISTORY
Korats have been known for hundreds of years in Thailand. In a book of cat poems from the Ayudhya period of the 14th century, three cats are referred to: the Seal-point Siamese; a copper-color cat, probably Burmese; and the Korat. These cats have spread to all parts of the world where pedigree cats are bred and shown.

In the town of Korat, these cats are known as Si-Sawat, which means *good fortune*. It is often called "the cloud-colored cat with eyes the color of young rice" in Thailand. A Thailand travel poster shows a girl in native Thai costume holding a Blue Korat. The cat is prized in its homeland. A pair given to a bride means a fortunate, prosperous and happy marriage. The male Korat is a fearless fighter.

The Korat is a natural breed, native to the Korat plateau in Thailand. Since 1959, several have been imported to the United States. One was shown in England as early as 1896, at the National Cat Show. It was thought to be a Blue Siamese but later was recognized as a Korat.

BREEDING
When a kitten is sold, the new owner must promise to neuter it at six months or mate it only to another Korat. This is to keep the breed pure, without contamination from other breeds. Korat queens make good mothers and are meticulous and clean. The average Korat litter contains 3 or 4 kittens.

KITTENS
Kittens are born the same color as adults. The beautiful silver-gray coat is present from birth. Kittens often have amber eyes. Adult eye color may take from 2 to 4 years to develop fully.

SHOW REQUIREMENTS
The Korat is medium size, strong and muscular. Males are more powerful than females.
Coat—Single, short and glossy. Fine and close-lying. Short and fine on the back of the ears, nose and paws.
Body—Medium size, strong and muscular. Semicobby with a round back, lying low on the legs. Forelegs slightly shorter than hind legs. Paws oval.
Tail—Medium long, tapering to a round tip.
Head—Heart-shape head and face with a semipointed muzzle. Strong chin and jaw. A large flat forehead. Nose is short with a downward curve above the tip of the nose. Gentle nose break. Ears alert with round tips, medium large, set high on head. Open at the base.
Eyes—Prominent, overlarge and luminous. Set wide apart. Round when open, with slight slant when closed.

COLOR
Silver-blue, tipped with silver to give a sheen. Intense on backs of the ears, nose and paws. No white hairs, spots or tabby markings. Noseleather dark blue or lavender. Paw pads dark blue or lavender with a pink tinge. Eyes brilliant green. Amber tinge permitted in kittens.

Korat

Korat

Russian Blue
kitten

Russian Blue

Russian
Blue

ABYSSINIAN

Advantages
- *Affectionate*
- *Playful*
- *Quiet*
- *Gentle*
- *Good with children*
- *Easy to groom*

Disadvantages
- *Independent*
- *Active*
- *Does not like to be caged*

The Abyssinian is an intelligent cat. It is capable of obedience, which is rare in cats. It responds to affection and likes to be part of the family. It can be trained to do tricks and to retrieve.

An Abyssinian looks like a wildcat. This appearance, along with its responsive personality, makes the cat appealing to some who often do not like cats.

Because of its active nature, the Abyssinian needs plenty of room and dislikes being confined to a small area or caged. Do not have an Abyssinian unless you have lots of room.

Generally strong and healthy, feline leukemia has taken its toll of the breed in the past. Obtain a leukemia-free kitten. There is no cure for this virus.

GROOMING
An Abyssinian is easy to groom. Brush it daily to remove dead hairs. A short, soft-bristle or rubber brush is ideal. A fine-tooth comb removes hair and can be used as a flea comb. For show cats, apply bay rum and rub with a chamois cloth to show the coat to advantage. Regularly check teeth and ears.

ORIGIN AND HISTORY
Early cats that looked like Abyssinians were known as *rabbit cats* because of the similarity of their ticked coats. A good Abyssinian will have two or three bands of darker color on each hair, with the pale color next to the skin.

It has a likeness to pictures of Ancient Egyptian cats. The Abyssinian may originate from the sacred cats of Egypt, but it is more likely breeders decided to perpetuate these features by careful breeding. The Romans took cats from Egypt to England. The genes necessary to produce the Egyptian look could have been introduced in this way. American Abyssinians can trace their origins to British imports after 1907.

Abyssinians were first recorded in Britain in 1882. By 1970, all countries in the world recognized the Abyssinian as a true breed. It is one of the most popular shorthair breeds. The cat is represented in competitive classes at shows and takes high honors in shorthair and all-breed championships.

BREEDING
Abyssinians have never been numerous. They usually have only 3 or 4 kittens in a litter. They produce mostly males. Queens are usually attentive mothers.

SHOW REQUIREMENTS
The Abyssinian is a medium size, modified Oriental type, firm, lithe and muscular, with a distinctive ticked coat.

Coat—Short, fine and close-lying. Lustrous and resilient.

Body—Medium size, slender and lithe. Solid and muscular. Oriental type, though not as extreme as a Siamese. Medium length, slim, fine-boned legs with small oval paws. Stands as if on tiptoe.

Tail—Medium long, broad at the base and tapering. Not whiplike. No kinks.

Head—Medium broad, slightly round wedge on an elegant arched neck. Muzzle not sharply pointed. Ears wide apart, broad at the base, cupped and tufted. Chin firm. Slight nose break in profile.

Eyes—Set wide apart and expressive. Slightly slanted in setting. Almond shape.

COLORS
Originally only two color varieties were recognized for this breed, the ruddy and the red. The blue color occurs naturally within the breed and was recognized in 1975. Now, several colors are appearing in assessment classes, including lilac, chocolate, silver, tortie, red and cream. These are all the result of outcrossing to other shorthair cats for colors.

Ruddy—Coat red, ticked with two or three bands of black or dark brown, with a paler orange-brown undercoat. Darker shading along the spine, tail tipped with black, without rings. Black between toes, with color extending up the back of the hind legs. Tips and edges of ears black or dark brown. Noseleather brick-red. Paw pads black. Eyes green, yellow or hazel rimmed, with black or dark brown, circled by a paler area.

Red—Body copper-red, ticked with dark red or chocolate-brown. Paler apricot undercoat. Darker spine and tail tip. Chocolate between toes extends up the back of the hind legs. Noseleather and paw pads pink. Tips and edges of ears chocolate-brown. White allowed only on lips and chin. Eyes green, yellow or hazel, the more brilliant and deep the color the better. Pale eyes are a fault.

Blue—Body warm blue-gray, ticked with a darker steel-blue. Base hair is cream or oatmeal. Spine, tail tip and back of hind legs dark steel-blue. Tips and edges of ears slate-blue. Noseleather dark pink. Paw pads mauve-blue. Eyes green, yellow or hazel. Pale eyes are considered a fault.

A Blue Abyssinian kitten. At 5 weeks it shows the assertive nature of the breed.

SINGAPURA
Drain Cat

Advantages
- *Responsive*
- *Quiet*
- *Loves people*
- *Good with children*
- *Easy to groom*

Disadvantages
- *No drawbacks known*

The Singapura is known as the *drain cat* of Singapore. In its native country, some people regard cats with suspicion. Native cats must fend for themselves and are reserved and suspicious by nature. Foreigners living in the area have befriended some cats. Once the cats know no harm is intended, they become less shy, more trusting and responsive.

Several cats were brought to the United States and are becoming established as a new breed. The Singapura is an affectionate cat, though quiet and demure. It is smaller than other domestic cats, possibly because of its deprived ancestry. In Singapore, the cats are many different colors and patterns. Those imported have ticked ivory and brown coats, and gold eyes.

The breed in now receiving publicity and there is a waiting list for kittens, both as pets and for breeding.

GROOMING
A Singapura needs little grooming. A daily combing and attention to ears and eyes are all that are necessary.

ORIGIN AND HISTORY
The Singapura is a natural breed from Southeast Asia. Most native cats have ticked coats resembling Abyssinians. It is a smaller breed, with different features. Free-roaming, taking shelter in the drains of Singapore, Singapuras have been adopted by foreigners living on the island. It has been given a standard for competition in Singapore and the United States. It was first shown in 1977, but is still rare. It has not been granted recognition by all American registries.

KITTENS
Singapura kittens mature slowly and often do not come out of the nesting box until they are five weeks old.

SHOW REQUIREMENTS
The Singapura is small, alert and healthy with noticeably large, cupped ears and large eyes.

Coat—Fine, short, silky and close-lying. A little longer in kittens.

Body—Smaller than average. Females: 4 pounds (1.8kg) or less. Males: 6 pounds (2.7kg) or less. Medium-long body, moderately stocky, dense and muscular. Back slightly arched. Medium-long legs and small, tight paws. Body and legs form a square with the floor. Neck short and thick with high shoulder blades.

Tail—Medium long, tapering to a blunt tip. No kinks.

Head—Round, narrowing to a blunt. Medium-short muzzle with a definite whisker break. Full chin. In profile, a slight break down the bridge of the nose. Ears large. Slightly pointed, wide open at the base, possessing a deep cup. Small ears are a fault.

Eyes—Large, almond shape, wide open and slanted.

COLOR
Each hair on the back, flanks and top of the head must have at least two bands of dark brown ticking separated by bands of lighter, warm, old-ivory ticking. The tip of each hair is dark and the base light. A darker line along the spine is permitted, ending in a dark tail tip. Legs without barring preferred. Toes dark brown. Color extends up the back of the hind legs. Muzzle, chin, chest and stomach a warm pale fawn. Ruddier tones allowed on ears and bridge of the nose. White lockets or white hairs are faults. Eyes, nose and lips rimmed in dark brown. Noseleather red, paw pads dark brown. Eyes hazel, green or gold.

Singapura

Singapura

Abyssinian

Ruddy Abyssinian kitten

Sorrel Abyssinian

REX

Advantages
- *Intelligent*
- *Hardy*
- *Agile*
- *Quiet*
- *Loves people*
- *Walks on a harness and leash*
- *Easy to groom*

Disadvantages
- *Tendency to obesity*

The Rex does not seem to feel the cold, even with its short coat. It does not need coddling and is hardy even in the coldest weather. It is an unusual-looking cat with its curly coat and curly whiskers and eyebrows. The coat feels warm to the touch because the hair is fine and short.

There are two types of Rex—the Cornish and the Devon. They are similar in many ways. The Devon Rex is playful and its pixielike face betrays a sense of mischief. It wags its tail like a dog when pleased. Intelligent and enterprising, either Rex makes an excellent family pet.

The Rex tends to overeat and can easily get fat. Avoid overfeeding because a fat Rex is unhealthy and unattractive.

GROOMING
The Rex is easy to groom. Use a silk cloth or a chamois to polish the coat. Before a show, give it a bran bath to remove grease in the coat. Grease upsets the flow of the waves and curls. If the coat is dirty and requires a wet bath, do this a couple of weeks before a show. Curl goes limp immediately after a bath.

ORIGIN AND HISTORY
The two strains of these curly coated cats appeared as natural mutations in the United States, the United Kingdom, Germany and Canada. The Cornish Rex first appeared in Cornwall in 1950, in a normal litter of farm cats. It was named after the Rex rabbit, which also has a curly coat. The curly kitten was mated back to its mother. This produced more curly coated kittens. When mated together, they appeared to be compatible and produced all curly coated kittens.

The second strain of curly coated cats appeared in a litter of kittens in Devon, England in 1960. When mated to the Cornish Rex, they were incompatible. They produced all straight-coated kittens.

Today, two separate varieties of Rex are recognized. They should not be intermated because they are genetically different. The Rex was first recognized as a breed in 1967. The first all-Rex cat show was held in Kentucky, November, 1980. The Rex is now accepted in many countries and has been imported to Australia and New Zealand. New Zealand breeders have introduced the Rex gene into Manx stock.

BREEDING
Mating two Cornish Rexes together and two Devon Rexes together produces 100% Rex-coated kittens. By mating a Rex to a Siamese, the Himalayan coat pattern is introduced and the Si-Rex is obtained. Rex queens make good mothers.

KITTENS
Kittens are robust and healthy. They are active, precocious and mischievous.

Cornish Rex

SHOW REQUIREMENTS
Although the original curly coated kittens were British Shorthair type produced from farm stock, a more streamline type is now preferred on the show bench. The cat is fine boned and elegant, with a longer wedge-shape face and whip tail.
Coat—Short, thin hair, but dense, plush and close-lying. No guard hairs. The hair curls, waves or ripples, especially on the back and tail, but preferably all over, even on paws. Whiskers and eyebrows also curly. Too short or shaggy a coat or hairless patches are faults.
Body—Hard and muscular. Medium size but slender, not cobby. Stands high on long, straight legs. Back arched. Paws small, dainty and oval.
Tail—Long, thin and tapering.
Head—Medium-length wedge. Flat skull and straight profile with no nose break. Ears large and set high on the head. Ears wide at the base, round at the tips. Covered in fine, short fur.
Eyes—Oval and medium size.

A Dilute-Calico Cornish Rex. The curly coat, which gives this breed its distinctive appearance, originally appeared as a mutation.

Devon Rex

SHOW REQUIREMENTS
The Devon Rex has a coarser coat than the Cornish Rex. They are similar in build—muscular yet dainty—but have different faces. A firm medium-size cat with a long tail and huge ears.
Coat—Short, fine, wavy and soft. Not shaggy, but coarse, due to the presence of minute guard hairs. Short curly whiskers and eyebrows, which are brittle.
Body—Medium size, slender, hard and muscular. Broad in the chest, with long, slim legs. Hind legs generally longer than forelegs. Feet small and oval.
Tail—Long, fine and tapering. Covered with short, curly fur. No kinks.

Head—Round wedge with a flat top. Set on a slender neck. Round cheeks with a whisker break and definite nose break in profile. Ears set low on the head, large, with or without ear muffs and tufts. Wide at the base, round at the tips. Covered in fine, soft fur.
Eyes—Wide set, oval and slightly slanted.

CORNISH REX AND DEVON REX COLORS
Most colors and coat patterns are acceptable for competition, including the Himalayan coat pattern. Chocolate, Lilac and Si-Rex are not acceptable, but most other colors and combinations of colors and patterns are currently recognized. Colorpoint Cornish Rex are showable in some U.S. associations.

Eye color in keeping with the coat color or pale green, yellow or gold. White Rex may have gold, blue or odd-eyes, one gold, one blue. Colorpoint eyes must be blue.

A Cream-Tabby Devon Rex. Its brittle whiskers have broken off at the ends.

Black Devon Rex

Devon Rex

Devon Si-Rex kitten

Cornish Rex

Blue-Cream Cornish Rex

AMERICAN WIREHAIR

Advantages
- *Sturdy*
- *Robust*
- *Even-tempered*
- *Affectionate*
- *Adaptable*
- *Agile*
- *Intelligent*

Disadvantages
- *No drawbacks known*

The American Wirehair has a distinctive wiry coat, hard and springy to the touch, like sheep's wool in texture. It is bred in all colors and is a sturdy breed. However, it is rare.

It takes an interest in its surroundings and is intelligent, active and agile. Naturally sweet and affectionate, it is an ideal pet.

GROOMING
Almost no grooming is necessary. Brushing with a soft-bristle brush once or twice a week removes loose hairs. It is essential to shampoo the cat. This can be done just before a show, as the hair springs quickly back into place.

ORIGIN AND HISTORY
The American Wirehair is a natural mutation that occurred in a normal domestic shorthair litter. The first was recorded in New York in 1966. Kittens with identical coats were seen at London bomb sites after World War II. That strain seems to have died out. Kittens from American matings have been exported to Canada and Germany.

BREEDING
Wirehair cats mated to normal-coat shorthair cats product 50% wirehair kittens. The gene is not linked to color. All coat patterns are possible.

KITTENS
Wirehair kittens are born with tight curly coats. They are healthy, playful and robust. An average litter contains 4 or 5 kittens.

SHOW REQUIREMENTS
The overall impression of the American Wirehair is medium size, round and woolly.
Coat—Medium length and tightly curled. All the hairs are crimped and hooked at the ends, even in the ears. Hair forms ringlets rather than waves in some places, particularly on the head. Whiskers are crimped or wavy and untidy. The coat is formed by a change in the structure of the guard hairs of the topcoat. These are normally smooth and tapering, but in the Wirehair are crimped along the shaft, hooked at the ends and thinner. This produces a woolly coat that is thick, coarse, resilient and springy to the touch. Hair on the chin, chest and stomach is slightly less coarse.
Body—Medium to large. Muscular, with shoulders and haunches the same width. Back level. Legs medium long, paws oval and compact.
Tail—Moderately full, tapering to a round tip.
Head—Round with prominent cheekbones. Well-developed muzzle and chin. Slight whisker break. Nose is concave in profile. Ears medium size and set wide apart with round tips.
Eyes—Large, round, bright and clear. Set apart at an angle.

COLORS
Nearly all colors and coat patterns are permissible. They include white, black, blue, red and cream; chinchilla, shaded silver, shell cameo, black smoke, blue smoke, cameo smoke; calico, tortoiseshell, dilute calico, blue-cream; bicolor; classic and mackerel tabby patterns in silver, brown, red, blue and cream; and any other color or pattern, or combination of colors and patterns and white. The Himalayan pattern, or chocolate and lilac are not acceptable. Eye color appropriate to coat.

A Silver Tabby American Wirehair. The hard, springy fur appeared as a natural mutation.

SPHYNX
Moon Cat; Canadian Hairless

Advantages
- *Hardy*
- *Affectionate*
- *Needs little grooming*

Disadvantages
- *Needs regular sponging*
- *Needs warmth*

The hairless cat is an unusual animal. It may not be to everyone's taste. The body feels hot and smooth to the touch because there is little fur to act as a temperature barrier or to insulate the body warmth. Unlike other cats, the Sphynx perspires, leaving residue on the skin that must be sponged off periodically.

This is an affectionate, good-natured, loyal cat. Few Sphynx exist. Most cat fanciers regard it more as a curiosity than as a serious candidate for pet or show purposes.

GROOMING
No brushing or combing is required. Residue that accumulates on the skin should be sponged away daily with warm water.

ORIGIN AND HISTORY
Hairless kittens have appeared in litters of ordinary cats in matings with the Devon Rex. Since 1966, Canadians have taken an interest in this breed and have developed a breeding program to perpetuate it. This began in Ontario, when a hairless male kitten was born to a Black-And-White Domestic Shorthair.

The Aztecs may have had hairless cats. Some were recorded in Mexico at the end of the 19th century. They were known as Mexican Hairless and grew fine winter hair that was shed in summer. The Mexican Hairless is now thought to be extinct.

BREEDING
Hairless cats breed true to type. They can also be produced from normal-coat cats carrying the gene for hairlessness. Outcrosses to Domestic Shorthairs are used from time to time to improve stamina. They do not seem to affect the Sphynx body type.

KITTENS
Sphynx kittens are born with a fine covering of soft, short hair. Most of it is lost as they approach adulthood, when hair is confined to the face, paws, tail tip and testicles in males. Kittens are usually bowlegged and have wrinkled, loose skin that appears too big for them.

SHOW REQUIREMENTS
The Sphynx is medium size, fine-boned but powerful, without hair on most of its body.
Coat—A short velvet pile covers face and ears. Hair is longest and heaviest on the nose and sides of the mouth. Paws are covered with fine hair to the ankles. The end of the tail is covered with fine hair. There is a ridge of hair on the back. Testicles are covered in long, close-lying hair. Too much hair is a fault.
Body—Long, fine boned and muscular. Skin is taut without wrinkles, except on the head. Legs are long and slim with small, round paws. Hind legs are slightly longer than forelegs.
Tail—Long, thin and hard. No kinks.
Head—Not round or wedge shape. Flat between the eyes. The neck is long and the chin square. The short nose is covered with velvetlike fur. There is a decided nose break. Ears are large, wide at the base and round at the tips. They stick out from the head at the lobes.
Eyes—Deep set and slanted.

COLORS
All colors and coat patterns are allowed, excluding the Himalayan pattern, chocolate, lilac or any of these colors with white.

A pink locket at the neck is acceptable. White is allowed only around the nipples and navel. Particolor patterns arranged symmetrically. Eyes gold, green or hazel or in keeping with the coat color.

Black Smoke American
Wirehair

American Wirehair

Sphynx

Sphynx

PRACTICAL GUIDE

Essential information for cat owners.

Decisions must be made before you buy a cat. Your cat may be with you for 20 years. You must decide what kind of cat you want and whether you want a kitten or a full-grown cat. The Practical Guide gives you information on buying, owning and caring for a cat.

Chapter 1 explains what you should know about choosing a cat, from appearance and temperament to grooming requirements. Chapter 2 deals with the new kitten, such as what a kitten eats, and its requirements for sleep and play.

Understanding your cat is the subject of Chapter 3. It discusses psychology of cats and how you can build a relationship with your cat.

Chapters 4, 5 and 6 deal with feeding, grooming and health care. They will help you keep your cat in the best condition. They discuss food, vitamins and table manners, how to shampoo and groom your cat, and how to nurse a sick cat. Sections on illnesses and parasites, and what to do about them, are also included.

Chapter 7 gives you information on breeding and raising cats. Chapter 8 provides you with information on the history of cats and gives you the knowledge necessary to breed champion cats or create new breeds and colors.

If you want to show your cat, you will find necessary information in Chapter 9. It explains how to enter your first show and what to do.

Chapter 10 gives details on carriers and methods of travel available to cat owners. Chapter 11 discusses your legal rights and responsibilities as a cat owner, and cats' rights.

This Practical Section was written to help make life with your cat more enjoyable.

This white American Shorthair is relaxing in the sun. You can tell she is alert by the way her ears are cocked.

1

CHOOSING A CAT

When you decide to get a cat, plan ahead. Is it to be a show or pet cat? Male or female? Longhair or shorthair? What color? Pedigree or mix breed?

SHOW OR PET CAT?

If you have never been to a cat show, you might not consider the possibility of showing your cat. If you choose your kitten at a cat show, the breeder may persuade you to show it. You may like showing. It is possible to show a non-pedigree housecat, but only in pet-cat classes. If you do not want a cat to have kittens, you can have a pedigree cat neutered. You can then show it, but only in neuter classes.

A tabby and white household cat is a good choice for a family. Its short coat is easy to groom.

This little girl is playing with her pedigree Siamese kitten.

MALE OR FEMALE?

If you want to breed kittens, buy a female. If you plan to sell the kittens, you must breed a pedigree female with a pedigree male of the same breed when she matures. Breeding cats will not make you much money. It is a labor of love.

If you do not want to breed kittens, have your cat spayed. Do this at around 6 to 8 months old, depending on the breed.

Your first cat should not be an unaltered male. It is difficult to keep a male happy without females to mate with. Do not let him run free. He will fight with neighboring males. An adult male is impossible to keep indoors as a family pet because of his strong urine, which he sprays around the house to attract females. Choose a male

Once you decide what kind of cat you want, consider how much you want to pay. Good show specimens can cost a lot of money. Do not pay a high purchase price unless you intend to show your cat. Often a pedigree cat with less-perfect features than a champion's can be purchased for less money than a champion. It makes a wonderful pet. It is a waste of money to buy a top show kitten and have it neutered without breeding or showing it.

You may find pedigree kittens in a pet shop. Often they are advertised there and kept at the home of the breeder. He pays the pet shop a commission for introducing buyers. Pedigree kittens are also advertised in newspapers.

Visit the breeder's home and inspect the surroundings. It is best if the kitten has been reared in the house with humans, even if it is put in a pen in the yard during the day. Kittens grow used to a household.

Watch the whole litter for an hour or so if the breeder lets you. Do not make an instant decision. By watching the kittens, you can choose one with the right personality for you. Some kittens are shy, some boisterous, some bullies, some loving. Studying the litter can give clues to physical condition. Be suspicious of a kitten sitting quietly at the back while others play. It may be sick. Do not choose the smallest or weakest of the litter. It may look sweet, but could spend a lot of time at the vet's. Instead, select one of the outgoing, lively ones.

A healthy kitten has bright eyes, a shiny coat and lots of energy. A sign of sickness may be a visible third eyelid. If there is any sign of illness, do not touch any from that litter. The mother cat should also look healthy and well-fed. The breeder's home should be clean, not dirty or smelling of cat.

A very inexpensive pedigree kitten is usually a bad investment. Choose the best one you can afford.

kitten only if you have him neutered by the time he is 6 months old.

Some people think neutered animals suffer a sense of loss or deprivation. This is untrue because mating is purely instinctive. Once the mating desire is removed, cats grow up losing the temperamental behavior that accompanies mating. A pet cat should be neutered. Neuters of both sexes are lovable. Neutering a female is a major operation and costs more than neutering a male.

LONGHAIR OR SHORTHAIR?

This depends on how much time you can spend grooming the cat. A longhair cat is lovely, but daily brushing, combing and untangling knots may be necessary.

A longhair cat may cause asthma in some people. Other people are allergic to cats. Before choosing a cat, visit friends who have them. You can find out if cats affect anyone in your family.

WHAT COLOR?

Cats are bred in all colors except green. You can find black, white, brown, cream, red, blue and gray. There are also many coat patterns, such as tabby, spotted and pointed.

With care and grooming, this beautiful Chinchilla kitten could become a champion.

There are mixtures of all colors and patterns. Many people develop a loyalty to the color or breed of their first cat, replacing that pet when it dies with another much like it.

Your preferred breed may not be available. You must either be patient in acquiring your cat or choose from what is available in your area.

CATS WITHOUT PEDIGREES

If you cannot afford to buy a pedigree kitten, it is easy to find a non-pedigree one. Often a pet shop will have inexpensive non-pedigree kittens, for a smaller cost. Your local newspaper probably carries advertisements for cats or kittens offered for free. Local humane societies usually have cats and kittens looking for good homes. Addresses and telephone numbers are listed in the telephone directory. They may require payment in exchange for the cat or kitten.

Consider adopting an adult cat if you have no other cat at home. Adult cats are more difficult to place than kittens. If you have one adult cat, do not bring home another adult. They will be jealous of each other. An adult cat is set in its ways. It needs more patience and understanding than a kitten.

If you get a mongrel kitten, you will not have information about its background. You probably will not know about its parents or the care it has had. When you buy a pedigree cat from a breeder, you can learn a lot about the cat's heredity and environment. You may have a healthier kitten and fewer vet bills if you buy from a breeder.

This black and white household pet loves the close attention of a devoted owner.

Two kittens are fun! Here, a Tabby-point and Seal-point Siamese play happily together.

IS IT OLD ENOUGH?

Your cat should be old enough to leave its mother. You can often check by examination. The kitten should have a full set of teeth or be at least 8 weeks old. Pedigree kittens are usually 12 weeks old before the breeder lets them go. It is not just a question of being able to eat solid food, but a matter of finishing their education with their mother. She teaches them how to eat and wash, and how to use a litter box and scratching post. She shows them how to play, making the moves they would need to know in the wild for fighting. She teaches them how to hunt for food, to lie in wait, pounce and growl over prey. She shows each kitten how to keep other cats away from prey. A mother teaches her kittens using toy spiders and mice. If kittens are removed from their mothers too soon, they miss needed instruction.

ONE CAT OR TWO?

Often two kittens in a litter seem inseparable. They play and sleep together, and seem to have more affinity for each other than for the rest of the litter. The breeder hopes to sell both to one buyer who has decided two are better than one. Two cats keep each other company. Cats may settle down better if they go to their new home together. If you can afford it, get two at the same time.

PARTING WITH A CAT

Unforeseen circumstances sometimes require that people part with their pet. If this happens, try to find your cat a good home. If a home cannot be found, you may have to put your cat to sleep rather than abandon it.

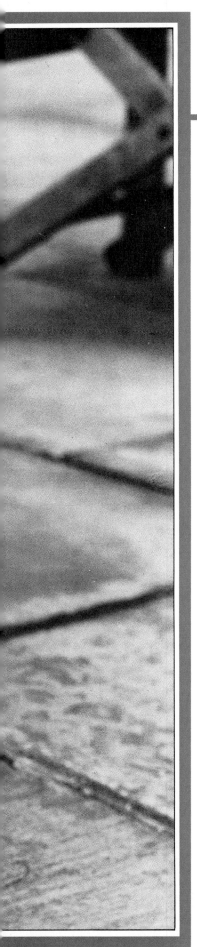

2

THE NEW KITTEN

You have chosen a kitten for its health, looks and temperament. Now it is time to think of what things you need before your kitten arrives.

FEEDING DISHES AND WATER BOWL

Your kitten needs its own feeding dishes and water bowl. Stainless steel or plastic bowls are best. Wash the cat's bowl and dishes separately from family dishes. Each meal should be served in a clean dish or on a disposable paper plate.

Always place the food and water containers in the same place. If you are gone all day, use an automatic feeder.

This cat owner is introducing her new Persian kitten to the litter tray. Usually, housetraining kittens is not difficult.

Every cat should have its own place to sleep. There is room in this basket bed for this kitten to grow.

FOOD

Buy a supply of food before you bring the kitten home. For the first few days, limit the kitten to foods it is used to. After that, begin to introduce other interesting varieties. Your kitten may prefer some commercial foods to others. Cats require a balanced diet.

If your cat is not allowed outside, provide it with a supply of grass. Cats eat grass to give their digestive system roughage. A free-roaming cat will choose coarse grass. You can grow grass in a pot for a confined cat. The grass takes about 6 weeks to grow. You can also buy instant grass in packets. It is ideal for apartment cats. Add water and the grass is ready to eat in 7 to 10 days. Cats love it.

BOWLS AND AUTOMATIC FEEDERS

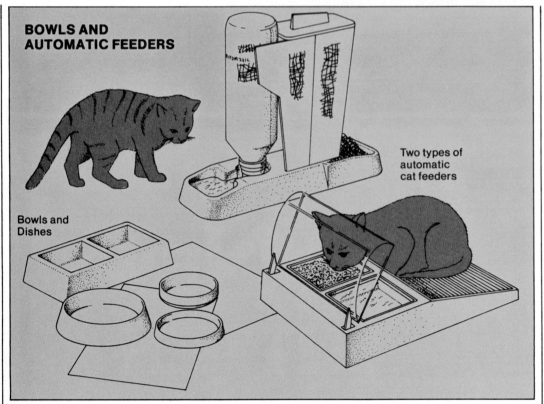

Two types of automatic cat feeders

Bowls and Dishes

These feeding bowls are suitable for food, milk or water. A placemat underneath keeps the floor clean. Keep these bowls for the cat's use only. Do not share them with humans.

The dish at top is a hopper feeder for dry foods and water. The other dish keeps the food free from dust and flies. Both are ideal if you are away from home during the day.

Below: A covered litter tray gives the cat privacy.

Below right: This Chocolate-point Siamese can retire to its own place for peace and quiet.

Two types of perforated litter scoops. One has a disposable bag to collect debris.

LITTER BOX

Do not let your kitten out of the house until it is used to its new home. Your kitten needs a litter box. The best litter to use is what the breeder uses. Gradually change to another material if necessary. The most efficient and convenient type is clay cat litter sold in most pet shops. Some have a built-in deodorant. It is often less expensive to buy cat litter in large bags. Use a plastic scoop to ladle litter from bag to box. Do not use shredded newspaper in a litter tray because the cat may get used to it and use newspaper anywhere in the house.

Housetraining kittens is not difficult. A kitten that has grown up with its mother will be housetrained by the time you get it. Most cats are clean. A stray kitten placed on a litter tray will instinctively use the litter. As its paws sink into the soft soil, the kitten digs a hole and sits down in it. Accidents happen only when there is no litter tray available.

There are many types of litter trays on the market. There are giant trays for breeders or people with more than one cat. There are covered ones for people who like their cats to have privacy. These trays may be expensive, but they help hide a used litter pan. A cover also prevents the cat from throwing litter all over the floor. The top of the covered litter tray is removable for cleaning. Some tops have built-in deodorizers.

Some cats will not use litter once they have soiled it, forcing you to change it completely or clean it once a day. Many pet stores sell plastic spoons for this purpose. Baking soda added to the litter acts as a deodorant. This is effective only if it makes up one-third of the bulk of the cat litter. Do not use disinfectants and deodorants sold for other purposes. Some contain chemical substances poisonous to cats.

If you keep your kitten inside, it needs access to a litter tray. Keep the tray clean. Empty and clean it regularly with hot soapy water and bleach.

LITTER SCOOPS

BED AND BLANKET

Make the cat's bed in a quiet, warm, draft-free area. A cat will sleep on your bed or with a child, if permitted, but it should have its own bed for security.

SCRATCHING POST

Many people combine scratching post and bed in a piece of cat's furniture called a *cat tree*. This is useful if you have room for it. The cat will love it. It will feel safe away from strangers, dogs and children.

A scratching post is necessary to prevent cats from damaging furniture. Posts are made of cardboard, carpet on a pole or carpet in plastic. There is one made of bark, which is the most natural material for a cat to use. In a yard, a cat uses tree trunks to sharpen nails. The cat keeps its claws sharp for tearing prey apart to eat. The mother shows her young how to use a scratching post. A kitten from a breeder should be trained to use one. Cats learn by imitation.

If you invest in a cat tree, let the cat use it for sleeping, scratching and retreat only. Do not feed the cat there. Make it come down for food in its usual place.

CARRYING BOX

Buy a carrying box when you get your first kitten. Take the kitten home in it and use it afterward. The box should last the life of the animal, so buy a good one. Cardboard carriers serve for one or two journeys. For long-term use, get something more substantial.

Many airlines do not allow cats in the passenger section of planes. They travel in a carrying box in the cargo section. If allowed in the passenger section, the carrier must fit under the seat.

EXERCISE, TOYS AND PLAY

A cat that roams free exercises itself by chasing, climbing and running. When it comes indoors, it is usually to rest. A cat confined in the house has less chance to exercise. Encourage it to exercise by providing toys. Playing with your cat is a good way to establish your relationship.

Two Siamese cats use a cardboard scratching pad. It may prevent your cat from scratching the furniture.

Deluxe scratching posts combine a carpet-covered base and toys to bat with paws, as this cat demonstrates.

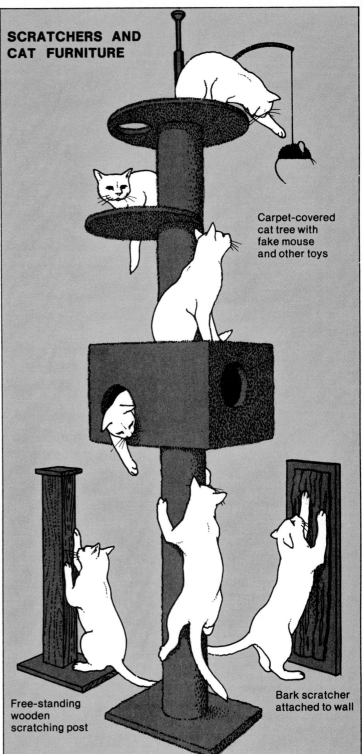

SCRATCHERS AND CAT FURNITURE

Carpet-covered cat tree with fake mouse and other toys

Free-standing wooden scratching post

Bark scratcher attached to wall

Cats are attracted to bark as a natural scratching material. Free-standing posts are convenient for the home. All types will be well-used.

A cat tree is fun for a cat if you have the space and more than one cat.

Cats love to chase small, movable objects. Sometimes spider shapes excite a cat. They are also fascinated with mouse-shape things, whether made of fur or cloth. They like to hold them in their paws, throw them in the air and pounce on them. You can also hang toys by elastic from refrigerator and other door handles, so they bounce around easily. Buy cloth toys filled with dried catnip.

Catnip is an aromatic herb that can be grown in most gardens. The herb has a psychological effect on cats. Cats enjoy catnip and it has no known ill-effects. You may find your cat likes catnip more when it matures. Adult cats roll in it, eat it, sniff it and play with it.

Many pet shops sell a variety of cats' toys or you can make your own. Empty thread spools hanging on string will keep a cat entertained.

RESTRAINT

Do not give your cat the run of the house while you are out. Confine it to one room that contains food, water, a litter tray, a warm place to sleep and some toys.

FRESH AIR

You may need an outdoor run for your cat. The cat will be happier there than sitting indoors. The run can extend from the house or be a separate unit in the yard. It should have a sheltered area. Cats in an outdoor run must have a wire roof to keep them from escaping.

ARRIVAL OF THE NEW KITTEN

Introduce your new kitten to one room at a time. Start where the litter tray, food dishes and other items are going to be kept. If it has just had a long journey, the kitten will probably want to use the litter tray. When it discovers the litter tray, it may perform at once.

Shut all doors and windows before the carrier is opened. Let the kitten come out when it is ready. Open the lid or door

Cats kept indoors will eat grass you grow from seed. After planting the seeds, the grass is ready to eat in 7 to 10 days. Packages of instant grass are also available.

Safety is combined with fresh air in this large run, complete with shelter and space for exercise.

and wait. It will jump out and begin to investigate. Do not pick it up before it has finished smelling everything and getting its bearings.

The kitten will probably not be hungry. Once it sits down to wash, it has made itself at home. Try offering food then. Water should always be

Indoor Grass

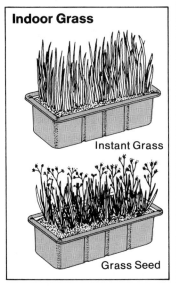

Instant Grass

Grass Seed

available and changed frequently. Establish regular feeding times and serve all meals in the same place. Remove all food not eaten in 20 minutes. Do not offer more until the next meal.

Once the kitten has grown used to one room, introduce it to others. Allow constant access to its room to avoid accidents. Or put a cat door in the door to its room. The cat can then go from room to room freely. Do not allow your new kitten out of the house for several days. You may decide to let your pet have full freedom and insert a cat door in an outer door of the house so your cat can come and go as it pleases.

FIRST NIGHT

Your kitten will miss its mother and litter mates its first night in its new home. Comfort the kitten by holding, stroking and talking to it softly. Build its confidence and you will start to develop a loving relationship.

The first night is the time to decide where your pet will sleep. Put it firmly down in its own bed. Turn out the light and shut the door. It will probably cry, but the second night will be better. Left to the kitten, the choice would be to sleep with one of the family. If you allow it into your room, a smart cat will soon be in the bed, not just on it. Once you allow it in for one night, it will be difficult to persuade it to sleep alone.

The outdoors awaits this tiny Persian kitten. It is taking an immediate interest in all its surroundings.

It may be as long as two weeks before it realizes it must sleep alone. During that time it will spend the nights crying for you to come and get it.

HANDLING

Use both hands to pick up a kitten. Place one hand under the body behind the front paws to lift it. Use the other hand to support the hindquarters. The kitten will feel secure and not struggle. If children are shown the correct way to handle a kitten, they will not get scratched. When a kitten feels it is about to fall or lose its footing, it struggles to get a foothold and may scratch someone. Always support a kitten's hind feet so it feels secure.

If destined for a show career, a cat can begin being handled at an early age. Hold it up high to examine it from all angles. Position it on a table as it will be handled in the show ring.

GROOMING

For a very young kitten, brushing and combing often turn into a game, with the kitten biting the brush and comb. Later, it learns to appreciate and enjoy grooming. Cats love routine; regular grooming helps liven up the day.

Handling a kitten the correct way keeps you from getting scratched. This silver tabby kitten feels secure because its hind end is well-supported by one hand.

Many kittens can be trained to do tricks. This Chinchilla Persian kitten is learning to sit up.

TRICKS

Some cats can be taught to retrieve, shake hands and other tricks. Many cats sit and beg before a meal if you hold the plate of food above their head. If you also ask "What do you say?" or a similar phrase each time, the cat will meow. You can reward it and reinforce the behavior by giving food. Most cats like the taste of yeast tablets and learn to associate the sound of shaking the tablets with giving treats. A cat may enjoy sitting up on its hind legs on command, before being rewarded with a tablet. Repeat this the same time every day.

When routines are established, a cat will present itself at the right time in the right place for all activities. People will be amazed when your cat is well-behaved.

THE CAT'S NAME

Your cat learns its name as you repeat it each time you call it for food, grooming and play. It is important for it to have a name it responds to. When you name your cat, be sure you choose a name you can use when it strays and you want to call it. It is easier to shout vowels rather than consonants, and two syllables rather than one. If your cat is a pedigree, its pet name will probably be shorter and simpler than the official name under which it is registered.

INOCULATIONS

Once a kitten settles down in its new home, have it checked and inoculated by a vet. The breeder should supply a certificate showing what injections the kitten has had. There should be a note saying what other care the cat needs. The vet will want to see the certificates before he treats the cat.

SPAYING

If you do not plan to breed or show your kitten, have it spayed or neutered when it is 6 to 8 months old. This may be done earlier if the cat is a Foreign Shorthair. Foreign Shorthair females sometimes call, and males spray, as early as four months. These are normal functions for adult cats, but it is advisable to spay or neuter before these habits are established in a kitten kept as a pet. If a male is not spraying, it can be left until 10 to 12 months old.

RELATIONSHIPS

The kitten will probably develop different relationships with different members of the family. Children may represent playtime for the kitten and time for teaching tricks with rewards. As it hears the children come in, the kitten will bound toward them. The grooming session may involve another member of the family who has a different relationship with the cat.

DISCIPLINE

Punishing a cat is pointless. It does not associate the punishment with the crime and thinks you are being cruel. The best way to show displeasure is a loud "No!" If your usual voice is soft, a harsh command should be enough to make the animal stop whatever it is doing, at least while you are there. Many people use a water pistol; it is very effective. Aim it at the body, never the eyes.

Keep the list of forbidden activities short, but discipline firmly. You will not be able to make your cat behave like a child. It can act only as an animal, using instinct and intelligence. Do not punish it for being a cat. Thoughtful owners study cat nature and realize what can and cannot be expected from a cat. If you or your family cannot tolerate normal cat behavior, do not have one as a pet.

UNDERSTANDING YOUR CAT

To enjoy your cat, you must discover its needs, desires and instincts. A cat is not a dog and cannot be expected to act like one. Some cats trained by dog owners act like dogs, retrieving, going for walks and performing tricks. But a cat behaves like this only when it is in its own interest and does not conflict with something it would rather be doing. A cat never learns complete obedience. This is because it has inborn, instinctive and unalterable behavior characteristics.

INSTINCTS

Feeding, scratching, hunting, playing, loving, curiosity, mating and sleeping are instincts that play important parts in a cat's life.

A cat likes to chase and jump at moving toys. Encourage this play to keep your pet amused and exercised.

Hunting is natural for cats. Outdoors they find many things to stalk and chase to keep fit.

Scratching—Your cat scratches instinctively. Provide a suitable place for this or provide a scratching post as soon as you bring your cat home.

Hunting—Do not scold a cat for hunting. Cats are programmed to hunt. Some owners object to their cat bringing home prey. Do not commend your cat for killing rats and mice, then scold it for killing birds.

Playing—This is associated with hunting. The cat is the only animal that plays with its prey before killing it. It is an instinct that must be indulged at home. Toys for the indoor cat keep it exercised and amused for hours. Outside, cats chase anything that moves, and chase and pounce on imaginary prey. When two cats play, they embrace, bat paws, bite, chase,

pounce, stalk, leap, catch, roll, kick and hug. All are good exercise. The wise owner makes sure the cat can enjoy some of these activities during the day.

Loving—Cats are naturally affectionate and need physical contact with other cats, animals and humans. They respond to affection, hand stroking and cuddling.

Curiosity—Cats are curious. They will help you pack or unpack a package. They love the noise of paper and take a great interest in what you are doing with it. Because of their curiosity they walk through any open door. If you are often out and let your cat outside, you may find it has two homes. While you are away it spends its time in its second home, returning to you when you come back.

Mating—This natural instinct accounts for thousands of unwanted kittens and cats. Having a cat sterilized is not cruel; it settles the cat down to domestic life.

Sleeping—Cats sleep for approximately 65% of their life and should be allowed to do so. Prevent children from waking cats to play with them. Protect the cat from other harassments.

The family should realize a cat needs to sleep somewhere quiet, dark and comfortable. A cat loves to sleep in secret places. Even as a kitten it may disappear for a quiet nap.

The dreaming cat often relives a hunt or other activity. On waking, cats invariably stretch, pushing one leg at a time away from them. They often wash to wake themselves up.

CATS' SENSES

Cats are generally reputed to have nine senses: touch, smell, taste, sight, hearing, temperature, balance, place and time.

Touch—A kitten gains awareness of touch from early contact with its mother. Her tongue washes the kitten and she moves it toward her in the nest with her paws. The kitten learns to associate its mother's tongue with affection. Later in life, stroking by a human hand becomes a substitute for licking by the mother. Grooming reduces tension by slowing down the heartbeat. This is one reason a cat may start to wash when in doubt or after a scare.

Sometimes a cat's curious nature gets it into trouble. This kitten is meeting a goat for the first time.

Cats take a lively interest in everything. Here a Seal-point Siamese watches the world from a motor-home window.

Touch also is important when a cat chooses its sleeping place. Cats seem to be able to sense texture though their paws. They like warm, soft fabrics and often refuse to stay on the lap of someone wearing a material that is cold or slippery.

Smell—This sense develops early in the nest. If kittens are moved from a familiar nest into a new one, they shriek or cry and the mother comes running. They know the smell has changed. When the mother rejoins them in the new nest and reassures them with her own smell, they settle down again. Older kittens can see and smell their litter mates, so they are less perturbed when moved into a clean bed. Kittens seem to attach themselves to one particular teat when breastfeeding in a litter. It is probably the sense of smell that guides each kitten to its proper place. Because of their acute sense of smell, cats closely scrutinize every new object they encounter.

When a cat rubs up against a piece of furniture or a human leg, it leaves a scent mark on it. Two cats rubbing heads together leave their scent on each other, so they recognize each other the next time they meet. If one cat goes off to be mated, she will be rejected

when she returns by the cats who stayed home. She carries the stud-cat's smell, which is unacceptable to them. She has to wash them before they realize it is her. Your cat knows when you have been to a house where there are other cats. The cats you met would have known you were a cat owner. The scent a cat emits may tell other cats more than we realize about its sex, age and health.

It is probably the smell of a strange place that makes some cats detest moving. They feel secure with remembered smells. Some find moving so traumatic they stop eating and wander about crying. Some cats even become aggressive. Love and attention is the remedy. Most cats eventually settle down in their new home. Keep them inside a few days to make sure they do not take off, forget where they live and get lost. Emotionally stable and confident cats adapt faster than others.

Cats instinctively like pleasant smells. They try to cover up the smell of their own excreta.

The scents of certain plants fascinate many cats. Catnip seems to give them a high. Cats roll in a bed of catnip, play with toys tuffed with catnip or play with dried catnip leaves and flowers. Some cats are more susceptible than others and

A kitten's introduction to touch is its mother's tongue. She grooms the kitten from head to toe and makes a game of it.

The calm and composed Silver Tabby has slit pupils. Cats on the attack also have slit pupils.

adult cats like catnip more than kittens. Valerian is another plant cats like.

Cats sometimes smell flowers. This is not always to determine who has been in the yard that day. Cats like nice-smelling things.

Taste—Taste is linked to smell. A cat that cannot smell often refuses to eat. Occasionally you see your cat smelling something with its mouth open. This is known as *flehmening*. The purpose is to let scent particles reach the *vomeronasal organ,* so the cat discovers more than it would learn merely by using its nostrils. Catnip, a stranger or a sexual stimulus often triggers this reaction, which involves a combination of taste and smell.

Sight—Cats have acute eyesight, but are able to see moving objects better than still ones. This is why a cat freezes when it sees another cat. A mouse also freezes, hoping to be overlooked by an approaching cat. In poor light, cats can see better than humans. But they can see nothing in total darkness. Their pupils dilate to enable them to see more clearly when the light is dim. The pupils form narrow slits in broad daylight. A cat's pupils also dilate when it is on the defensive and contract when it attacks. Cats are not color blind as many people believe.

Many cats take an interest in cats on television or home movies. They may even try to get on the screen. Other cats seem to enjoy watching television. They may find its flickering images fascinating.

Hearing—Cats have acute hearing and can detect sounds too faint for people to register. This explains how your cat can tell someone is approaching the door before you hear a knock. The cat picks up faint vibrations you cannot detect.

White cats with blue eyes may be deaf. But even deaf cats hear with other parts of the body. They may be able to sense sound vibrations as they pass through solid objects.

Cats like certain sounds and dislike others. Some like music. One boarding place plays music during the day to reassure the cats and make them feel at home. Most cats dislike loud noises. Cats make themselves scarce if any building is in progress. If there is going to be much noise in your house, put your cat in a room as far from the noise as possible.

This Siamese cat is complaining loudly about something it is unhappy with.

COMMUNICATION

Cats can communicate with one another, other animals and humans in two ways: vocally and by body language.

Vocal Language—Cats make whatever noise appears appropriate to an occasion. An owner who listens and talks to pets comes to understand the different meanings of sounds they produce. Many people say their cats understand each other. When you start to pay attention to what your cat is saying, you soon learn its basic vocabulary. Always respond to a vocal greeting from your cat. Some cats always speak when spoken to and appear to possess a vocabulary of small talk.

Your cat is sensitive to the tone of your voice. This helps you control its behavior. Cats dislike shouting, so a shouted command may make your pet stop some activity you dislike. Cats enjoy responding to the sound of their name and usually come when called.

Cats love to have you whisper to them and purr in response to whispering. What you say is not as important as the tone of your voice.

Temperature—Some cats like hot weather and some like cold weather. Foreign, shortcoat cats like heat and sunbathe on a hot day. In cold climates, cats prefer to sleep in a warm place inside. If a cat is too hot, it will find a cool draft to sit in.

Balance—Cats have an extraordinary sense of balance when climbing trees, roof tops, ledges and window sills. This sense of balance helps a cat reach places that are out of the reach of enemies, dogs and other animals.

If a cat falls from low or medium heights, its sense of balance makes it twist its body in the air and land securely on its feet. This helps prevent injury. But from a great height a cat can fall to its death.

Place—Numerous stories tell of cats traveling hundreds of miles to places where they used to live. Like homing pigeons, cats have an instinctive direction-finding ability.

Time—Cats like routine. They like the same things to happen at the same time. They expect food at fixed times. Cats enjoy being groomed regularly, too.

These nine highly developed senses may contribute to the myth that cats have nine lives.

A Tortoiseshell British Shorthair uses its sense of balance to climb a tree.

This Burmese, which is on the defensive, has dilated pupils.

A cat pleased to see its owner moves forward with its tail held high in the air.

A Burmese on the defensive. Back arched and tail fluffed out, it spits and wails.

Sounds include purring, when the cat is relaxed; hissing, when uncertain; growling, when you intrude into its affairs or possessions; and various other sounds for hunger, going out, play and companionship. The complaining voice is different from that expressing anger or indignation.

A cat also has a silent meow. This is a soundless vocalization when the cat opens its mouth but no audible sound comes out. It may be a sound other animals can hear.

Most vocal sounds are for communicating with humans. Exceptions are mothers talking to kittens and mating vocalizations. The mother bleats if her kittens run from her when she wants them nearby. She has other sounds which they understand. They learn to growl as she does over a live mouse. This warning helps to keep their prey from being taken by other cats.

Toms or females in heat sometimes wail. When a young queen starts to roll on the floor and push her head along the ground, with her rear in the air, she is calling for a mate. If she will not be mated, have her spayed.

Body Language— Apart from sexual vocalizing, adult cats communicate with each other by body language. This can involve movement of the tail, ears, paws, whiskers, eyes, head or body.

The tail is very expressive. It may be held upright for pleasure and greeting or hung low and curled under before a fight. Cats show anger by lashing the tail from side to side.

Cats usually carry their ears upright on top of the head or projecting from the sides. A cat's ears can be swiveled around to receive noises. Often a cat may lie completely still but movements of its ears tell you the animal is listening. Ears flattened backward can mean an invitation to the owner or another cat to play. But ears flattened sideways usually mean anger or annoyance. A crouching attitude with eyes half closed and ears flattened is a submissive gesture.

A mother cat uses her paws to hold kittens down so she can wash them or keep them in one place. Cats use their paws to pin down an enemy in a fight. A hit with claws unsheathed indicates annoyance. A gentle tap on the cheek or the nose with the claws well-sheathed indicates affection.

This is an example of submissive, left, and aggressive behavior, right, between two Oriental Tabbies. They use such gestures to establish the pecking order.

Whiskers twitch in different directions to suit various moods. Eyes may be wide open showing interest or vacant and half-closed while the cat is being stroked. Cats sometimes seem to focus on something that is not there.

The head is used expressively for butting up to a person to gain attention or as a loving gesture. Cats butt each other in this friendly way. It is a signal of acceptance. Head butting is used extensively in courtship.

Disciplining a cat can be simple because your cat is more sensitive to your voice than to most other sounds. It responds to "No!" said in a sharp voice.

Scratching the furniture or carpet can be handled in the same way. Be sure your cat has its own cat tree or scratching post. Take the cat to it whenever it scratches elsewhere. It will learn to respect your wishes. Be patient.

Another habit you must deal with is biting. If you allow a cat to bite, it may become vicious. Instead of removing your hand, put it further into the animal's mouth. Your hand in its mouth prevents aggressive behavior and the cat backs off.

Training consists of lots of love and affection expressed in a soft voice, plus a firm "No!" whenever needed. Never hit a cat. A soft finger on its nose, like a mother's paw, is enough.

SOCIAL GATHERINGS

Cats often form groups and sit and watch each other. If there are many in one

This White Persian has lifted itself up to its owner's hand in the hope of being stroked and petted. This is one way cats show affection for owners.

A cat's body can tell you about its feelings. A cat turned sideways with arched back and fur fluffed up is on the defensive. A queen with kittens to protect may take this position. Aggression is signaled by a confident attack. The cat moves toward the intruder, expecting submission.

Sitting near a door with the head raised means the cat wants to go out. Sitting near a door but with head near the floor may mean there is something outside.

Sitting on a chair or window sill with paws tucked underneath it and tail wrapped around its body is an indication of a happy, relaxed, unthreatened cat. Sitting upright in a window shows a cat is interested in people, birds and other things outside.

If you chastise your cat and its feelings are hurt, it may show displeasure by grooming itself with its back to you. This is often followed by skittish behavior.

MOODS AND FEELINGS

When a cat gets to know you, it responds to your mood. If you are ill, it will sit on your bed all day, content to be with you. If you are happy, it will want to play. You should respond to the moods of your cat. Do not be too busy to pick it up for some attention. Make time for togetherness.

Cats can appear angry, possessive, jealous, hungry, tired, sick, resentful, rebellious, disgusted and disdainful. They can appear happy, playful, affectionate, loving, restful, friendly and thoughtful. Cats never seem to feel guilt. It is useless to punish a cat, because it never associates punishment with the crime. Cats can appear embarrassed, though. The cat's cure for embarrassment is compulsive self-grooming.

Anybody who has owned a cat is familiar with the phenomenon known as the *mad half hour.* Early evening is often the time when a cat fully wakes up from its rest. In the wild, this may be the time to think about hunting for the evening meal. Many pet cats unleash a burst of energy and rush all over the furniture and around in circles, leaping and pouncing on pretended prey. Make this a time for family fun and games, tricks and exercise. Harness the energy constructively. As they grow older, most cats are more settled but occasionally indulge in a mad half hour.

Cats like to play hide and seek. If you have more than one cat, they play hide and seek together. Cats suggest games that appeal to them. Be responsive. They love movement, so many games involve chasing moving objects. Try not to laugh at a cat. It will sense an affront to its dignity.

A cat is capable of bereavement when its owner or an animal friend dies or departs. It may seem entirely inconsolable. It goes off its food and wanders around the house mewing.

Cats need companionship, particularly some breeds. Some cats make friends with other animals, even those that would normally be their prey.

TRAINING

The way you train your kitten determines the kind of adult it will become. Do not allow a kitten to do things you would not want an adult cat to do. It is better not to encourage wrong behavior from the beginning.

If a cat is ignored it retreats into itself and become a loner. Treat your cat as one of the family. Choose a kitten from a breeder who has handled and played with the litter from an early age.

household, a hierarchy develops. It consists of dominant cats, less powerful ones and the weakest. Protect the weaker ones from the dominant ones.

If two queens run free in a house and have kittens at the same time, the kittens must be marked at birth. The dominant queen will steal the other queen's kittens if she can and mix them with hers. The submissive queen's kittens must be given back to her. Separate her so the dominant queen cannot get to them.

ABNORMAL BEHAVIOR PATTERNS

Cats left without the companionship of other animals or humans may grow bored. They groom all day, wear out their fur and even bite their own flesh. The more damage they do, the more they groom to put it right. Wool sucking is often reported. The oil in wool, which smells like a queen's nipple, may attract and soothe a young kitten if it has been removed from its mother when it was too young.

Bereaved cats may starve themselves and become susceptible to infection. Give them a companion for awhile. It may help them get over their sadness.

A sudden scare can shock a cat and cause it to sweat, shiver, salivate and sit with pupils dilated. If you suspect your cat has been frightened like this, sit with it quietly and talk soothingly or it could collapse and die.

Some cats drool while being petted. This is not a disorder, but it may mean their teeth or gums need veterinary attention.

Cats that are lonely, shut in, neglected and bored may defecate where they should not. If you have this problem and cannot spare time for the cat, find it another home where it will be loved. There also may be physical reasons for urinating or defecating in the wrong places. A vet can determine this, but the trouble may be be psychological.

This tabby cat is interested in something above it. Cats that take an interest in many things are usually happy and well-adjusted.

This Himalayan is sitting up for its food. Training can teach good manners and is an enjoyable routine for a cat. Daily performances with rewards add interest to a cat's life.

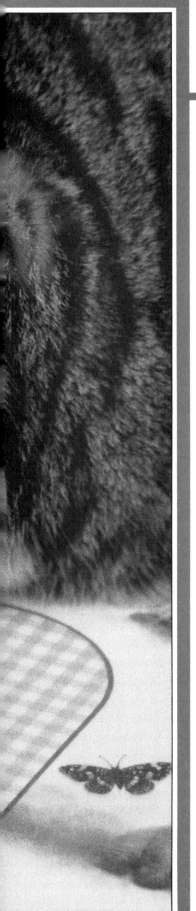

FEEDING YOUR CAT

Cats need a balanced diet containing proteins, carbohydrates, fats, vitamins and minerals. About 30% to 40% of the diet should be protein. The animal's condition is the best way to tell whether it is eating the correct diet. A satisfactory diet produces a shapely, healthy, lively animal with normal stools. An unbalanced diet may cause diarrhea, lethargy, shedding, scurf, dull eyes or obesity. These signs may also be due to some specific illness or infection.

A cat has no chewing teeth. It tears its food with large canines at the front and cuts it with sharp-edged cheek teeth.

This cat enjoys a bowl of semimoist cat food, one of many types of prepared cat food.

A CAT'S NATURAL DIET

Cats have canine teeth to penetrate and kill their prey, and tear its flesh apart. A cat tears pieces from the carcass and swallows them whole. It does not have teeth designed for chewing. Serve food in swallowable pieces or a large lump the cat must tear apart with its sharp teeth. A cat also eats minced animal flesh and liquidized foods. A combination of these forms of foods adds variety and interest to their diet. Some cats like dried foods. They help clean teeth. If feeding dried food to your cat, make sure water is available.

In the wild a cat eats small mammals such as rabbits, rats, mice, reptiles, amphibians, birds, spiders and insects. Some cats catch fish and eat them.

green vegetables, grass and seaweed. This vitamin can be manufactured in the cat's body.

Vitamin D—Sunshine is needed for its synthesis. It promotes healthy bones. Cats can synthesize it by sitting in sunshine or in ultraviolet light. Fish liver oil is extremely rich in vitamin D.

Vitamin E—Promotes fertility and virility. It is plentiful in wheat germ and lettuce.

CARBOHYDRATES

Carbohydrates are energy-rich foods. They are found in grains and root vegetables. They are essential in small quantities. Some cats like these more than others. If your cat likes milk, mix it with cereal. If it likes sardines and other oily fish, add cereals or breadcrumbs. If the cat dislikes carbohydrates, pureé them and mix them with minced fish. They are usually acceptable. Do not mix cereals with meat, because it could turn sour.

VEGETABLES, FRUITS, GRASS

Some cats get green vegetables from the stomachs of mice they kill and eat. Domestic cats may have traces added to their food. Fruits are not essential, but some cats like melons, grapes, olives, asparagus and avocados.

Grass is beneficial. It is eaten by most cats who are allowed to roam free. The cat cannot extract the carbohydrates in grass but uses it for roughage and as a source of vitamins. Vomiting up grass can be beneficial if it brings up furballs which could cause an obstruction.

FATS

Cats need small quantities of fats. They usually eat these in the form of butter, margarine, fish oils or meat fat from table scraps. Most cats eat butter mixed with yeast extract. This is beneficial occasionally.

PROTEIN

Protein provides the major part of a cat's food. It can be in the form of lean meat, fish, eggs, cheese, milk or vegetable protein, and prepared pet food. A diet of pure protein leaves a cat deficient in minerals and

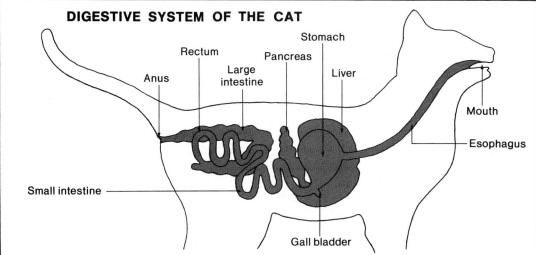

DIGESTIVE SYSTEM OF THE CAT

Stomach
Rectum
Pancreas
Anus
Large intestine
Liver
Mouth
Esophagus
Small intestine
Gall bladder

WATER

Fresh water should always be available in a clean bowl. Change it frequently, even when the cat does not appear to use it. A cat that does not drink indoors may drink from puddles. For lactating queens, add a sodium citrate tablet to the water. If your cat will not drink water from a bowl, add water to its food to prevent dehydration. The easiest way to add water is to serve some meals in pureéd form.

VITAMINS

Small amounts of vitamins are essential to healthy growth. Fish oils, liver, seaweed powder, wheat germ, yeast, milk and raw or lightly cooked vegetables are valuable sources of vitamins. Lack of vitamins or minerals results in medical problems and sometimes death. Prepared cat food contains all the essential vitamins.

Vitamin A—Promotes growth of body cells and aids resistance to infection. It helps the eyes

work well in light of varying intensity. Cats are unable to synthesize this vitamin, so it must be in its diet. It is found in egg yolks, fish liver oils, carrots, green vegetables, grass and seaweed.

The Vitamin B Complex—Includes vitamins for growth, healthy skin and eye function. It prevents various deficiency diseases. Milk, wheat germ, yeast and liver are rich in these vitamins.

Vitamin C—Prevents scurvy. It is found in malt extract,

This display shows types of cat food owners can feed their pets. Dry complete diets can be mixed with water.

vitamins, and can cause kidney disease. Protein should make up 30% to 40% of an adult cat's diet.

MEAT

All lean meats are suitable, with small quantities of fat. You can feed your cat beef, lamb, venison, cooked pork, kidney, heart, chicken and liver.

FISH

Wild cats often catch fish and eat it. Most cats like fish. Serve it cooked, although some cats prefer it raw. Remove scales if the skin is to be fed. All bones must be removed if the fish is cooked. Kittens prefer fine-grain fish, but coarse-grain fish is accepted by most adult cats.

Fish is a way to introduce fish oil, a small quantity of powdered seaweed and cereals, potatoes or breadcrumbs in small quantities. Fish oils are needed as a source of vitamin D in the winter when the cat is not in the sun.

Canned fish is excellent for cats and most seem to like it.

Most cats drink milk, which is a good source of valuable protein, calcium and minerals.

TYPES OF CAT FOOD

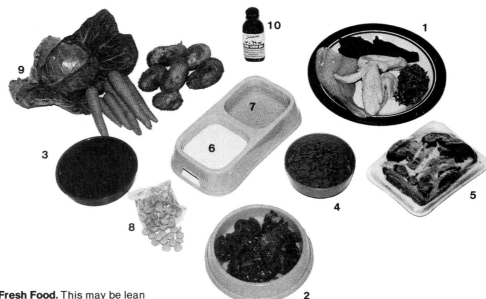

1. Fresh Food. This may be lean meat, liver, chicken or fish. It can be cut up, minced or left in one piece for the cat to tear up.
2. Canned Cat Food. This is convenient for today's busy owners. It comes in many varieties including meat, liver, chicken and fish. It is clean, healthy and usually accepted. Tuna fish for cats should have Vitamin E added.
3. Semimoist Cat Food. This is easy to use, especially when traveling. Some cats prefer this to dried or canned cat food. There are a variety of flavors to choose from.

4. Dried Cat Food. These combine cereals with meat, liver or fish. Cats like them for their crunchy texture. More water must be given with dried foods. They can be soaked overnight for a change in taste.
5. Frozen Cat Food. This may be available in some pet stores.
6. Milk. A valuable source of nutrition. It must not be diluted. Egg yolks can be added.
7. Water. It should always be available. Change water every day.

8. Cat Treats. These may be vitamin or yeast tablets, or chocolate drops. They make good rewards when training.
9. Vegetables And Cereals. These are necessary in small quantities. You can use soybean products, root vegetables, potatoes or green vegetables. You can liquify or mince them. Seaweed powder can be sprinkled on food for vitamins and valuable trace elements.
10. Fish Liver Oils. They are a ready source of vitamin A.

Offer sardines, mackerel or salmon. Many cats like jelly made of fish with chicken stock. Use canned tuna with Vitamin E added. Herring and some fatty types of canned fish may act as laxatives. Serve these if your cat is constipated.

EGG YOLKS

Egg yolks are rich in protein. You can add them to milk for a nutritious meal. Sugar added to the mixture gives energy.

CHEESE

Cheese is a rich source of protein. It does not make a complete meal, but is a good addition to a meal.

MILK

Milk is a valuable source of protein, as well as calcium and other minerals. Some cats cannot tolerate the lactose in cow's milk. Try goat's milk, milk substitutes, cream or a complete liquid food. Do not water down milk for kittens.

They need concentrated foods. If a pregnant queen cannot take milk, add calcium to her diet in some other form, such as crushed calcium tablets or bonemeal. Cats that normally dislike milk often instinctively drink milk when pregnant.

VEGETABLE PROTEIN

Protein-rich vegetable foods, such as soybeans, are often used in cat food because they are cheaper than animal protein. Most cats eat them if they are mixed with other protein. Because cats are flesh eaters, they are not usually satisfied with an all-vegetable-protein diet.

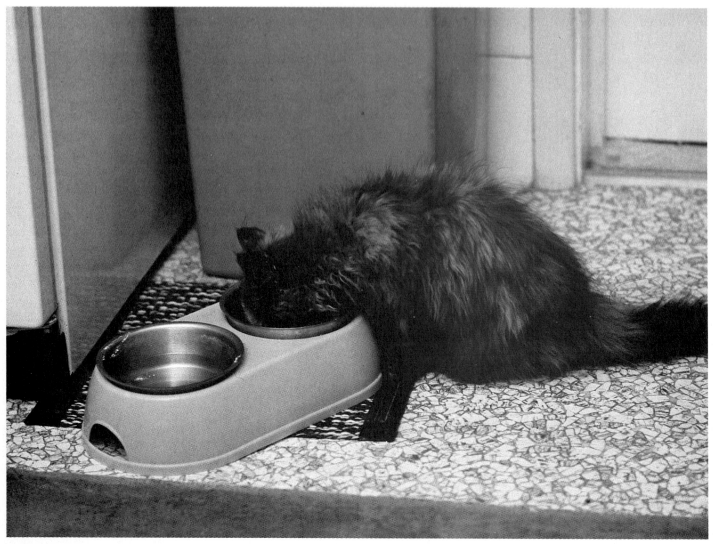

PREPARED CAT FOODS

Prepared cat foods are available in canned, dried or semimoist forms. Each type of food is convenient to use and provides variety. Each type of food has its advantages.

Dried foods can be left out for hours without spoiling or attracting flies. Semimoist foods are good for traveling or when you are in a hurry. Canned foods now come in a wide assortment of flavors and ingredients; there is something for every cat.

When prepared foods first appeared, some breeders were opposed to them. They felt the food would give kittens diarrhea. Pet food manufacturers have researched preferences to produce nutritious foods cats like.

Now almost every home uses prepared cat food. It is hygienic, safe to use and time saving. Some foods are more acceptable to your cat than others. If a prepared food has adverse effects on your cat, discontinue feeding it.

DIET SUPPLEMENTS AND TREATS

These include yeast tablets, chocolate drops and vitamin pills. They can be useful in small quantities as treats and for trick training. Do not give them too often.

TABLE MANNERS

Each cat in the household should have its own dish. The cat may remove some of the food to tear it up, so put a placemat under the bowl to keep the floor from getting messy. If your cat is greedy, feed it small, frequent meals. Otherwise it eats its food quickly, only to regurgitate it a few minutes later. When a small quantity of food has stayed down, give the cat more.

When you have more than one cat, be sure slower eaters get their share of food. Active cats may need extra food.

Twin feeding bowls are convenient for cat and owner. When offering complete dried foods, one bowl can be filled with water.

Kittens feed from a shallow bowl. Young kittens learning to eat solids should be given four small meals a day rather than fewer larger ones. Two meals should contain milk.

Some cats are sensitive to being left for long periods of time and refuse to eat. Once home again, they usually start to eat and gain back any lost weight.

FEEDING DISHES

Serve food in individual clean bowls or dishes. Wash them between each meal or refill. Bowls or dishes should be sterilized periodically. Never use these containers for any other purpose. Store them separately from the family's. Ceramic, stainless steel or plastic dishes can be used for feeding. Always offer food at the same time and in the same place. Cats appreciate routine because it makes them feel secure.

HOW MUCH TO FEED

Cats have a small stomach in relation to their weight. They need more than one meal per day. Give your cat small, nourishing, concentrated meals. Metabolism varies, so one cat may need more than another. One ounce (30mg) of food for each 2-1/2 pounds (1kg) of body weight keeps a cat healthy. Some breeds, such as Burmese, need more food. The amounts and kinds of food a cat needs depend on its age, condition and activity.

KITTENS

Young kittens need four meals a day; two with milk and two of meat. Meat can be steak or fish. Milk meals may include finely textured cereal, egg yolk, a complete liquid food or one of the formulas developed for hand rearing and weaning young kittens.

QUEENS

Once a queen is pregnant she needs more to eat. She does not need *larger* meals but *more* meals per day. A pregnant female needs at least one and a half times as much as usual. She may go off her food just before giving birth. It may be the first sign that she is going into labor.

When the kittens are born, the mother needs twice as much food as usual. Some say it is impossible to overfeed a lactating female. If there is a large litter, feeding may seem to be an unending task, particularly with some breeds. When kittens begin to eat a

Spoon feeding a complete liquid diet to a kitten. Sick cats can also be fed this way. The extra care and attention may be necessary to save their lives.

little, the mother's appetite usually decreases. Anything put down for the kittens is also eaten by the queen.

While she is feeding the kittens, the queen should be in perfect health. If she is too thin, she may require more food. Kittens should be plump, not thin. If they are thin, the mother may not have enough milk. Supplement her milk with formula fed by bottle. Wean them on solid foods earlier than normal.

WORKING STUD CATS

Stud cats need generous rations. Mating is hard work. Give extra protein and good doses of vitamin E to promote virility and fertility. Besides meat, stud cats need vitamins, minerals and carbohydrates. One stud may want to eat before mating. Another may go off his food as soon as the queen arrives and refuse to eat until he has mated. Queens usually prefer to mate before eating, then they are ravenous!

NEUTERS

Neuters need less food than stud cats. If a neuter puts on too much weight, it is eating too much food. Cut down its rations.

OLD CATS

An older cat needs less food than a young adult cat. Reduce the size of its meals rather than completely cutting out one meal. If it has lost some teeth, it needs puréed food instead of chunks of raw meat.

If it goes off its food, it may have gum or tooth trouble. If this occurs, the cat may need to see a vet.

DIETS FOR DISEASED CATS

Some diseases require special diets. These are best prescribed for each cat individually by a vet. He can assess the situation and advise you accordingly. Be sure to follow your vet's diet as closely as you can. Your cat will respond more quickly to the correct food.

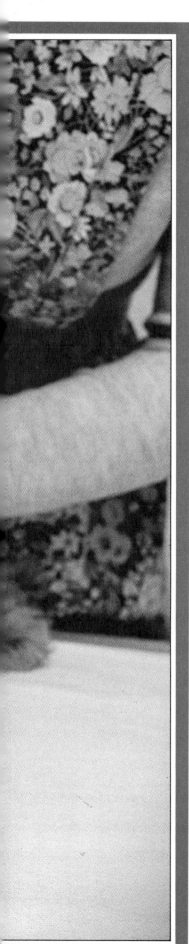

5

GROOMING YOUR CAT

Your cat needs daily grooming for health and beauty. Daily grooming removes dirt, grease, dead hairs and dead skin, and stimulates blood circulation. This improves the condition of the hair and skin.

Many cats groom themselves, but most enjoy grooming by their owners. If there is more than one cat in the house, they often groom each other. A mother cat washes newborn kittens to keep their coats clean, and to stimulate circulation and the production of urine and feces. Washing is an instinctive process. Newborn kittens begin to make ineffective washing movements at about three weeks of age. By the time they are six weeks old, most kittens can do a good job of washing

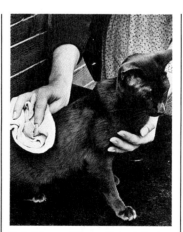

Polishing an Ebony Oriental Shorthair with a chamois cloth. Grooming is a simple daily routine, which keeps the coat healthy and shining.

Combing a Blue Persian removes loose hairs and prevents knots from forming in the coat.

themselves. Often the first sign of a queen coming into heat is the way she washes all over, particularly in the vaginal area.

Oriental Foreign Shorthairs, with their short coats and long noses, are efficient at self-grooming, because their tongues are longer. Longhair cats with long coats and short noses are less able to cope. Some cats need help with grooming.

Develop a daily grooming routine. Your cat needs to get used to combing and brushing. An important part of grooming is removing dead hairs. This prevents fur balls forming in the stomach. In nature, fur balls are regurgitated with birds' feathers and rodents' skins. In domestic cats, fur balls accumulate in a cat's stomach, particularly in longhair

Wiping around the eyes with moist cotton removes tear streaks. It may prevent infection, too.

The outer parts of the ears can be cleaned carefully with a cotton swab if wax builds up. Do not probe into the ear.

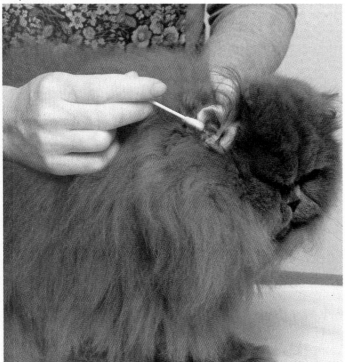

varieties. If not regurgitated, the balls may form intestinal obstructions. They may have to be removed surgically. Prevention by daily combing is better than surgery.

The daily grooming session can establish a bond between owner and cat. This practice should start when the cat is a kitten and continue into adulthood. It is a game to kittens and they try to bite and fight with the brush or comb. Queens appreciate attention to the parts they cannot reach during pregnancy. Stud cats look forward to the daily attention from their owner. An ill cat appreciates a cleanup when unable to do it themselves. Elderly cats find contentment in their owners looking after them. Grooming serves the cat physically and emotionally.

NOSE

Equipment: *Cotton and saline solution.*

Any sign of a runny nose, sneezing or nasal discharge is a warning that something needs attention. Because respiratory infections may be serious, consult your vet immediately. If powder has been used for grooming, make sure the cat is not allergic to it. Isolate any sneezing cat from others.

EYES

Equipment — *Cotton and saline solution.*

The normal eye is clear and alert. If a third eyelid begins to come across the eye from the inner corner, something is wrong. It may be an indication of a temperature or an early sign of infection. A single visible third eyelid may indicate an accident to one eye only. If the condition persists, consult your vet.

If tear ducts are blocked, tears course down the cheeks and may discolor the area from the eye to the nose. This mark can be removed by wiping with cotton dipped in a saline solution. Make this by adding one teaspoonful of salt to a pint of cooled boiled water. A brown discharge from an eye may be a sign of respiratory infection and a vet must be consulted. Check eyes once a week and bathe more often if necessary. Blocked tear ducts may have to be unblocked surgically.

EARS

Equipment: *Cotton swabs, mineral oil and ear-mite solution.*

If there is any trouble inside the ears, the cat may scratch them. This may be an indication of ear wax or ear mites. If it is mites, dark waxy specks appear at the entrance of the ear. These specks result from ear mange mites or *Otodectes synotis*, which are contagious among dogs and cats. Isolate the cat from other animals until cured.

You can remove the wax and dirt with a cotton swab dipped in mineral oil or ear-mite solution. Pour some of the ear-mite solution into the ear daily. Be sure the cat does not shake its head and throw the contents out before it penetrates to the deeper parts of the ear. Massage the warm liquid into the ear before letting the cat's head move. Do not poke down into the cat's ear. Inspect ears once a week and take care of them daily when necessary.

Basic Grooming Equipment

1. Bristle and wire brushes for grooming. Be careful when using the wire side. Hard brushing can strip the coat.
2. Pure-bristle brush, with short, soft bristles. Good for shorthair cats.
3. Rubber brush with short, flexible filaments, and a rigid plastic type for general grooming.
4. Blunt-end scissors for cutting through mats in a longhair coat.

5. Toothbrush for brushing the coat up around the ears and eyes of a longhair cat.
6. Cotton swabs for cleaning the outer parts of ears.
7. Wide, flat-tail comb to separate each hair on the tail of a longhair cat. Also called a *slicker brush.*

8. Specially shaped scissors for trimming claws.
9. Fine-tooth comb for shorthair cats. Smooths the coat and removes fleas and dirt.
10. Wide-tooth comb for removing tangles in fur of longhair cats.
11. Metal dual-purpose comb with wide- and medium-space teeth. Ideal as general-purpose groomer.

12. Non-toxic shampoo, safe for cleaning.
13. Bay rum spirit conditioner. Removes grease from the coat.
14. Alcohol for removing stains from pale coats.
15. Cotton for cleaning eyes, ears and nose.
16. Non-toxic grooming powder gives body to the coat. Sprinkle into the fur and brush out completely.

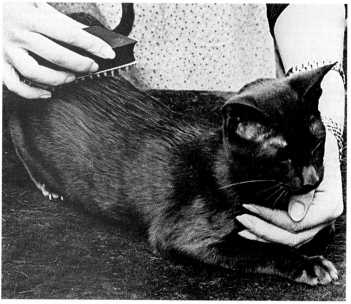

Groom a shorthair cat with a rubber brush to remove dead hairs and stimulate the blood circulation in the skin.

TRIMMING CLAWS

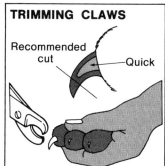

Recommended cut

Quick

Check your cat's claws every month. Trim the tips as shown here. Outdoor cats usually wear their claws down naturally.

CLAWS

Equipment: *Claw scissors or clippers and a scratching post.* Cats normally scratch against trees or a scratching post to sharpen and clean their claws. Give your cat a place it can use to sharpen its nails. An outdoor cat trims its claws by walking on the ground and scratching tree trunks. An indoor cat's claws may grow long and get caught in carpet and upholstery. Claws should be shortened at the tips only. Sit the cat in your lap with its back facing you. Use one hand to hold up a paw. Press on the pad and the top of the foot to make the claws spring forward. Clip the claws with the scissors or clipper held in your other hand. The end of each claw is dead tissue and the cat

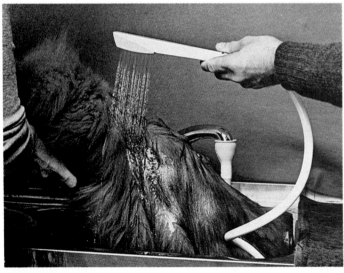

First stage in shampooing a longhair cat. Soak the fur with warm water. Keep the head dry. If necessary, plug the cat's ears with cotton.

Pour on shampoo and massage gently into fur to make a lather. Two people make the task easier.

To add shine, polish the coat with a silk handkerchief or chamois leather. When brushing shorthairs, brush along the lie of the fur. In a longhair cat, the coat can be gently combed up so each hair stands away from the body and the ruff makes a wide frill or halo round the head. The tail should be brushed up and gently shaken, holding the tip. When every hair is separate and stands away from the body, the cat is in perfect show condition. It is not possible to attain this condition in one session. It is the result of twice-daily grooming every day.

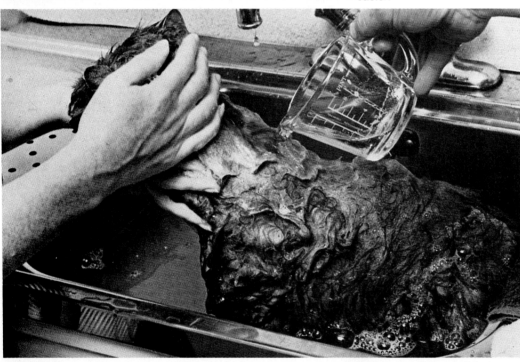

After shampooing, rinse the coat under a gentle stream of warm water. Be sure all shampoo is rinsed out of the fur before drying.

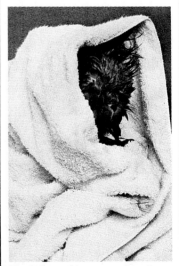

Wrap the cat in a warm towel. With the cat on your knees, rub briskly but gently to remove excess moisture. The cat's face can be cleaned separately.

feels nothing. The pink part, or quick, should not be touched. This contains the nerves and blood vessels bringing blood to the claw. The scissors or clipper must be sharp enough so it does not split the claw. Check nails monthly. Do not declaw a cat.

TEETH

Equipment: *A wooden tongue depressor, for opening and examining the mouth.* Discoloration of teeth or gums, pale gums or bad breath require veterinary attention. There may be tartar on the teeth, which the vet can remove. Loss of appetite may be due to sore gums. Dribbling may be a sign of poisoning or an ulcerated mouth. The best way to open the mouth is to tilt the head back with one hand and open the mouth with the forefinger of the other hand. Inspect mouth and teeth weekly.

COAT

Equipment: *Brushes, combs, grooming powders, cotton, silk cloth or chamois leather cloth.* Regular combing helps keep the coat free from dirt and parasites. Start at the head and gradually move toward the tail. Pay attention to the ears, chin, hind legs and underparts, especially in a longhair cat. If mats have formed, they must be cut out with blunt scissors. This spoils the cat's appearance for the show bench.

When the head, back and tail have been combed, turn the cat over on its back. Work on the underparts and legs. If this is done regularly from kittenhood, the cat enjoys it and does not struggle. The first combing should be done with a wide-tooth comb to remove tangles. Follow this with a medium- or fine-tooth comb to separate each hair. Then finish the cat with a brush.

Gentle stroking along the lie of the fur may be the best grooming for shorthairs. It removes dirt and stimulates blood circulation.

A show cat may need to be shampooed a week before a show if it is dirty or greasy. Marks show in pale-color cats. Choose a shampoo that is non-toxic to cats, with no bleach or carbolic acid. A soft soap, such as a baby shampoo, is best. Choose preparations for grooming cats carefully. Lists of dangerous substances are frequently published in cat publications. When in doubt, consult your veterinarian.

SHAMPOOING YOUR CAT

Shampooing is a task for two people. First, get cat, people and equipment in the bathroom or kitchen. Close the doors and windows. The kitchen sink is the best place to work because bathing can be done at a comfortable height. A rubber mat in the bottom of the sink prevents the cat's paws from slipping. Fill the sink to a depth of 2 to 3 inches (5 to 7cm) with water at about 101F (38C).

Plug the cat's ears with cotton in case it struggles. Lower the cat into the water and hold it by the scruff of the neck. Soothing words help keep the cat calm at this stage. Wet the fur all over with a sponge, except for the head. Rub the shampoo all over the body to produce a lather. If your cat hates standing in the sink, put its forelegs on the side of the sink.

After shampooing the cat, rinse thoroughly with warm water. A spray attachment on a short hose helps if the pressure is gentle. It may be necessary to give a second shampoo, but make sure the final rinse removes all the shampoo from the coat.

Remove the cat from the sink and wrap it in a large, warm towel. The face can be washed by the second person using warm, wet cotton. Any stubborn marks on the face can be removed with alcohol but keep it away from the eyes.

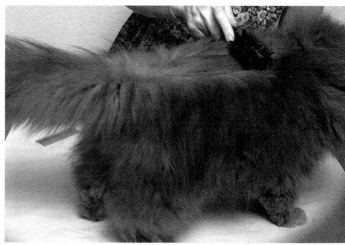

When the fur is almost dry, use a brush and fluff up the coat so hairs stand away from the body.

To finish grooming, brush the coat up and add finishing touches.

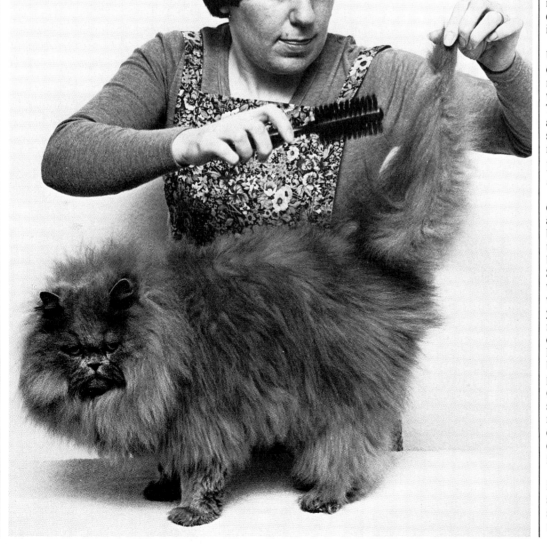

Some cats enjoy being dried with a hair dryer. Many are frightened by the noise. One person can hold the cat, with four feet on the table, while the other dries the hair. Be careful not to get too close or to singe the fur. Put the cat into a drying cage or a carrier in a warm place. Do not let the cat out or leave it in a draft until the coat is thoroughly dry. When the coat is almost dry, gently comb it to separate the hairs.

A bath leaves the coat soft. Until show day, give the coat a daily powdering with a non-toxic powder. Rub it in well, then brush it out again. This puts body back into the fur and helps keep every hair separate. No trace of powder must be found on show day.

DRY CLEANING A SHORTHAIR CAT

Dry cleaning cats with short dark coats is a suitable alternative to bathing. A bran bath is the usual method. Put 1 to 2 pounds (0.45 to 0.9kg) of bran into the oven and warm it. Stand the cat on a table covered with newspaper. Massage the warm bran into the fur with your hands. Most cats love the motion and warmth, and purr contentedly. When all the fur has been covered with the bran, move the cat to a clean piece of newspaper and comb out the bran. The coat should shine. A bran bath is not recommended for longhair cats. Particles of bran left in the coat could cause painful knots in the fur.

Another convenient method is to use a dry shampoo. These shampoos are available at pet stores. Follow directions for use.

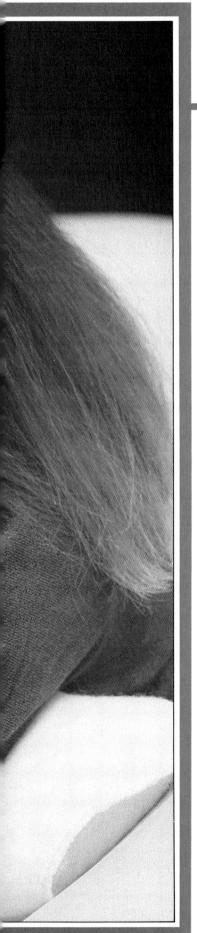

6

BASIC HEALTH CARE

Keeping a cat healthy means many things. Basically, you must feed and groom the cat correctly and have the cat inoculated at required intervals.

CORRECT FEEDING

This involves feeding your cat the correct food, in correct proportions, at the proper time. Tidbits between meals are not recommended. A cat knows by repetition when and where to expect meals. The cat is usually in the right place at the right time to eat.

GROOMING

Regular daily grooming is necessary for the health of your cat. Twice a day is ideal. A well-groomed cat has a glossy coat with no tangles. Weekly attention must be given to eyes, ears, teeth and claws.

A veterinarian injects a vaccine as part of a series of inoculations recommended for all cats.

A sick cat responds to human affection. Keep the cat warm and clean to help it return to full health.

HOUSING

All cats need a place of their own. A pet cat needs a bed in a warm, dark, draft-free part of a room. A breeding queen needs her own quarters. If your pet is a Siamese or Burmese, it may need warm bedding or even a heated bed. These breeds feel the cold more than others.

INOCULATIONS

The most serious diseases may be prevented by the right injection at the right time. Kittens receive some immunity from their mother's milk the first 8 weeks of life. After this, they need their first vaccinations for *feline enteritis,* a potentially fatal disease, and inoculations against respiratory diseases. Your vet will provide a certificate of inoculation after they are given to your cat.

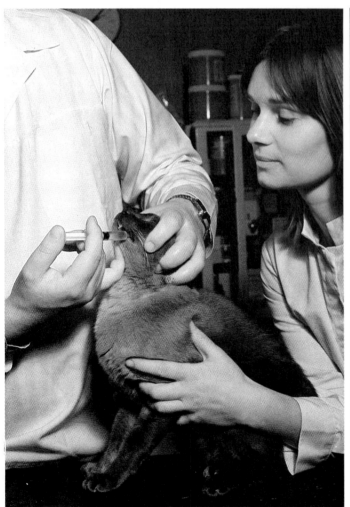

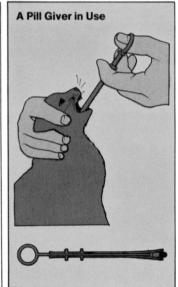

Commercial pill givers consist of a plastic tube split at the end to hold the pill. A plunger pushes the pill out at the back of the throat.

A vet uses a syringe without a needle to give liquid medicine. He holds the cat's head up and puts the syringe into the side of the mouth.

Taking a cat's temperature rectally. Two people should do this together. One restrains the cat, the other introduces the thermometer.

LOVING

No cat is completely happy without attention from its owner. It needs to be stroked, petted and talked to each day. Most cats respond to any attention they receive.

NURSING A SICK CAT

A healthy cat is alert and friendly, with clear shining eyes and clean fur. It purrs often. Any deviation means something is wrong. In a sick cat, the trouble may be an injury. Nursing is an important part of recovery. It can be even more important in illness due to disease. A sick cat can give up its will to live unless a human friend nurses it back to health.

Water is more important than food to a sick cat. The cat must not become dehydrated. Even when unable to eat or drink, the sick cat can take water from an eye dropper or bottle. If the animal can drink or eat normally, serve it food for invalid cats, such as a beaten egg, soup or something else nutritious and easy to eat. Hold its head up if you must, to give food and drink. Put the bottle or dropper in the side of the mouth, toward the back. Sponge the mouth clean afterward. In critical situations,

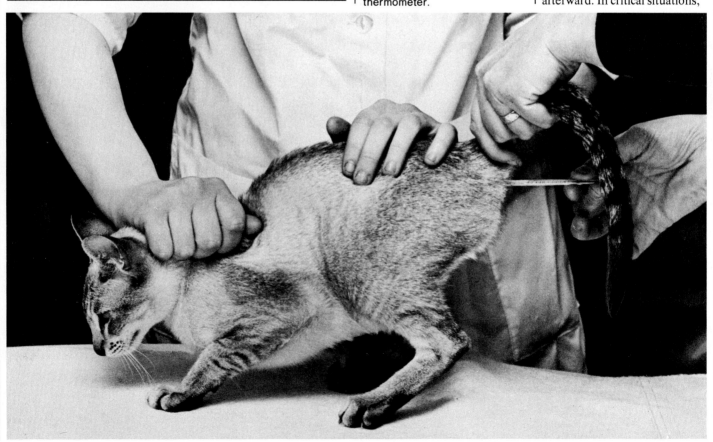

Eyedrops can be given at home. Hold the cat firmly or wrap it in a towel to keep it from struggling while you administer the drops.

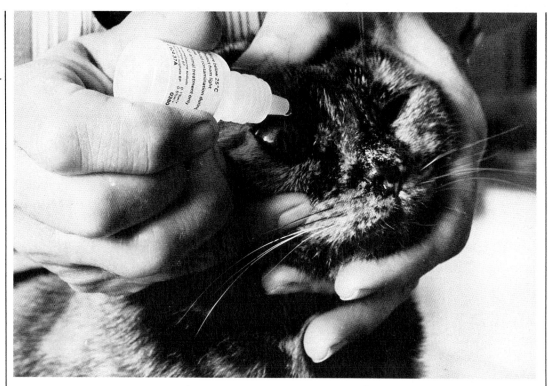

your vet can inject sterile hydrolyzed protein directly into the bloodstream.

You may have to give pills or capsules, put drops into the eyes or ears, apply bandages or take your cat's temperature, depending on your vet's instructions. Administer liquid medicines in a bottle, syringe or dropper. Crush a pill or empty a capsule and mix the powder with some butter, a piece of sardine or some other food. Drop the food to the back of the cat's tongue. You can buy a pill-giver designed to help put pills in the back of the cat's mouth without getting your fingers bitten. Open its mouth with one hand, insert the pill-giver with the other, then push the plunger forward.

Taking a cat's temperature may require two people. First lubricate the thermometer with petroleum jelly. One person must hold the cat's head and front feet. The other puts the thermometer into the rectum. The second person may also have to hold the rear feet.

Eyedrops are put into the eye while the head is lifted and kept still. It may be necessary to hold the front paws or wrap the whole cat in a bath towel to keep it from interfering with you.

If your cat is bedridden, you may have to turn it from time to time to prevent bedsores. If it has diarrhea, you must clean it up. If the cat is off its feet for some time, you may have to trim its claws.

Your vet may recommend a steambath. Put the cat in a plastic basket, cover the top and sides of the basket with a towel and stand it in steam rising from hot water. The cat breathes in the vapor, which helps relieve congestion. Sponge away any mucus around the nose, eyes or mouth with damp cotton. Do not add inhalant to the bath without veterinary instruction.

Sick cats often try to run away and hide. Do not allow your cat to do this. Place a sick cat in a dark, quiet place, with heat, if required. Talk to it reassuringly without fussing. If the disease is contagious, keep the cat isolated.

After an illness has subsided, restrict diet until the cat's stomach can cope with normal food. Most sick cats do not groom themselves but appreciate your doing it for them.

COMMON ACCIDENTS AND CONDITIONS

Abcesses—These often occur in free-roaming cats and may be the result of fighting or bites from rodents. Confined cats seldom have abcesses.

Signs and symptoms. Swelling under the fur, which is hot or hard, and painful to the animal when touched. The swelling is caused by bacterial infection.
What to do. Put hot packs on the swelling to draw the pus to one point. Abscesses should be treated by a vet, but if you cannot visit your vet, treat it yourself. Cut away long fur if this prevents access to the swelling. When the abscess comes to a point, lance it with a sterilized scalpel. As the pus begins to ooze, gently squeeze the abcess to extract all the liquid. When the wound is empty, clean it with hydrogen peroxide. Do not allow the wound to close up until all the pus is out. This may mean daily removal of the scab with repeated squeezing until the wound is clean. It should then heal normally. If the cat has a temperature, take it to the vet immediately.

Swelling of one or both ear flaps may be the result of a blood blister called a *hematoma*. This requires your vet's attention. He will drain and fix the ear flaps flat. He will also check the ear region for any infection or irritation as a cause of the hematoma.

An abscess on the cheek shows as a swelling. Simple abscesses may be treated at home. This one needs expert veterinary attention.

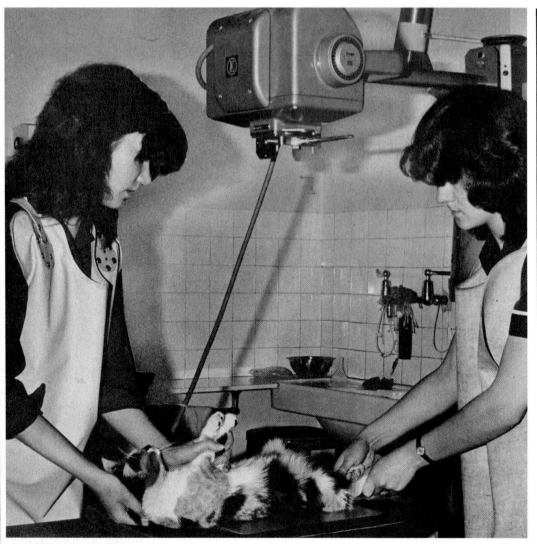

Fractures—Fractures are often sustained in accidents, falls or by heavy objects falling on a cat. They are most common among free-roaming cats and are found in legs, jaw, pelvis and spine.
Signs and symptoms. Bones sticking through fur, bones at wrong angles, an inability to move or eat, a limping gait, irritablity when touched, complete or partial paralysis.
What to do. Take the cat to the vet as soon as possible. Try not to disturb the cat's body if possible. If the wound oozes blood, stem the flow with a bandage. If the mouth is bleeding, hold the head lower than the body, face down, so blood does not run down the throat. If the body is bleeding, keep the head higher than the body.

Burns—These are most often caused by hot liquids, electrical appliances or chemicals.
Signs and symptoms. Hair pulls out or is lost spontaneously, signs of burns visible at contact points, shock, collapse and unconsciousness.
What to do. Call the vet for advice. Remove the cat from the source of further burns. In severe cases, treatment such as artificial respiration and warmth should be applied. If there are chemicals on the skin, bathe the cat in a mild shampoo. Do not allow the cat to lick burns. Treatment may require a stay at a veterinarian hospital.

Poisoning—Cats may eat poisonous plants if they do not have access to grass. Drugs should not be left lying around the house. Cats are sensitive to commonplace drugs such as aspirin. If you think your cat has eaten a drug, contact your vet immediately. When urgent treatment is necessary, a

Preparing a cat for an X-ray. Vets usually take X-rays to judge the type and extent of an injury, particularly for broken limbs.

This commercially produced *Elizabethan collar* is made of flexible plastic. It can be fit around the cat's neck to prevent it from licking medicated or sore areas.

sample of the material or an exact description of the suspected substance can help the vet treat your cat.
Signs and symptoms. Salivation, convulsions, tremors or fits, vomiting, pain, weakness or dullness, excitability. Can result in death.
What to do. Cats can be made to vomit, if within minutes of swallowing the substance. After 30 minutes, the toxin may be absorbed. Good emetics are strong salt-and-water or mustard-and-water solutions.

INTERNAL PARASITES
Small organisms live on or in cats. When large numbers occur, they may impair the animal's health. Most spread from one cat to another through feces or contact. A few may pass to kittens through the mother's milk.
Roundworms—These are threadlike, off-white creatures, 2 to 5 inches (5 to 13cm) long. They live in the gut of the cat and may be coughed up or passed in feces.
Signs and symptoms. Severe coughing, distended stomach, diarrhea, dull coat and eyes, ravenous appetite, third eyelid visible.
What to do. The vet will probably prescribe medication based on the size, age and weight of the cat. Worm kittens and cats every year, giving a second dose two weeks after the first. Never worm a sick cat because it could be fatal. Worm queens before they are mated, not when they are pregnant. Regularly worm studs. Cleanliness is important in the control of worms.

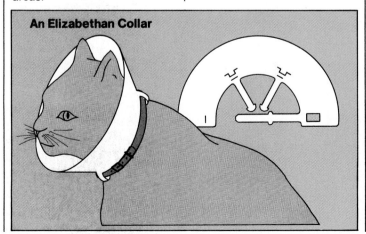

An Elizabethan Collar

Hookworms—These suck the blood from inside the intestines. Anemia can be a symptom of this parasite.

Tapeworms—These are segmented flatworms. A tapeworm lives in the gut with its head attached to the cat's intestine. From the tail end of the tapeworm, eggs drop off and are passed in the cat's feces. *Signs and symptoms.* Small ricelike segments, sometimes still moving, appear on the fur around the anus. They show up better on dark cats than light ones.

What to do. Fleas are the intermediate hosts in the tapeworm cycle. You must get rid of fleas as well as the tapeworm. Worm cats regularly. There are drugs that will get rid of tapeworms easily, with a minimum of side effects. These may have to be repeated because the animal can become reinfested. Seek advice from your veterinarian on the best dosage.

Coccidia—These are microscopic unicellular organisms living in the intestine. A variety of symptoms are attributed to them. They are rarely a major problem. *Signs and symptoms.* Persistent, intermittent diarrhea, loss of weight and condition, blood in feces.

What to do. Hygiene is important. Dispose of soiled litter. Drugs are available from veterinarians to eradicate coccidia.

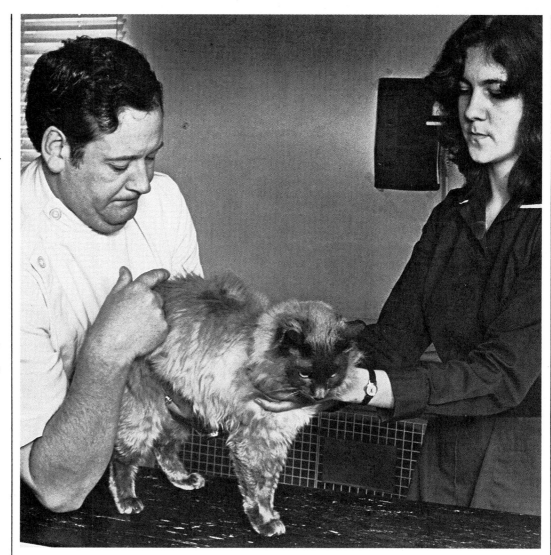

A vet gives this cat a thorough exam. He checks fur and skin, which could host various parasites.

INTERNAL PARASITES

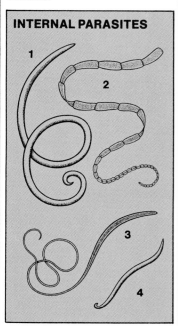

The principal internal parasites that can affect cats. The drawings show the basic shapes of the parasites but are not in scale with each other. The most common species are listed.
1. Roundworm, *Toxocara canis* and *Toxocara leonina.*
2. Tapeworm, *Dipylidium caninum.*
3. Whipworm, *Trichuris sp.*
4. Hookworm, *Ancylostoma caninum.*

EXTERNAL PARASITES

Fleas—These are hard-back, brown, wingless insects, flattened from side to side. Fleas live in the fur and feed off the blood. Cat fleas bite dogs and humans but seldom stay on either. Fleas are found mostly around the back and bib. Heavy flea infestation can lead to anemia, eczema and other troubles. *Signs and symptoms.* Dermatitis or eczema, scratching, restlessness, skin feels gritty, visible evidence of fleas.

What to do. Many insecticides are effective against fleas. They are found in powder or aerosol form and may be supplemented by a flea collar. Cats can be bathed in severe cases.

Fleas breed off the cat. Clean the cat's bedding and furnishings. Ordinary household insecticides are satisfactory for this purpose. Do not use these when the cat is in the room.

Lice—These are pale gray, wingless, insect parasites, flattened from top to bottom. They attach by their mouths to the skin of the cat. They glue their eggs to the cat's hair and spend their entire life on one host. *Signs and symptoms.* Scratching, visible lice nits on the cat's head and their eggs attached to some of its hair.

What to do. Give the same treatment as for fleas. Repeat the treatment weekly because lice are difficult to kill. Comb out all visible nits. You can also pick off lice with eyebrow tweezers and drop them into disinfectant.

Mange Mites—There are three main offenders:
Cheyletiella—Affects all parts of the body and is transmitted to human beings.
Notoedres—Causes scabs, hair loss and intense irritation around the cat's head.

Trombicula—Found on the lower parts of the body.
Signs and symptoms. Hair loss and secondary scabs. You cannot see mites without a microscope, except for *Trombicula,* which are barely visible to the naked eye.
What to do: Treat as for fleas.

Ear Mites—These mites live in the ear canals and can be transmitted from one cat to the other.
Signs and symptoms. Vigorous scratching, head shaking, ears twitching or at odd angles, head held on one side, brown or red blobs of wax on insides of ears.
What to do. You can detect ear mites by wiping the outer ear with a cotton swab and examining the debris under a magnifying glass. Mites show up as tiny, moving white objects, and their excreta appear as a red-brown debris. If a severe condition exists, the vet may wash out the ear, then prescribe daily drops. Massage drops into the lower ear before releasing the cat's head.

Treatment must continue for several weeks. Ears need regular inspection to guard against recurrence. In an emergency, put warm mineral oil in each ear. This softens ear wax and helps remove it from the ear. If a cat has ear mites, it is likely other cats in the household will have to be treated.

A vet uses an auroscope to look into the deeper recesses of the ear. Inspection may reveal ear mites, a bacterial infection or blockage.

Ticks—A tick fastens onto a cat's skin with its mouth and sucks blood. Cats are seldom aware of ticks.
Signs and symptoms. If there are ticks in your area and your cat goes outside, daily grooming is necessary. You can see ticks hanging from the body of the cat. They may be white and flat when first attached or gray, fat and pea size when engorged with blood.

In some areas, ticks infect cats with a fever that causes partial paralysis of the hind legs and eventual death if not treated. The disease is transmitted in a toxin secreted by the salivary glands of the ticks.
What to do. Avoid pulling ticks off without preparation. The head remains embedded, producing a septic lesion. Dab the tick with a small amount of petroleum jelly. The tick suffocates or pulls its head out of the animal because of lack of oxygen. Remove the tick carefully with tweezers. Do not burn ticks off because you could also burn the cat's fur.

The principal types of external parasites found on cats are shown on the right. The species and severity of infestation vary. In some geographical areas, parasites carry diseases.

INFECTIONS

Ringworm—This fungus infection is spread by spores. It produces bald patches that are more obvious in shorthairs than in longhairs. It is contagious and can be contracted from and by cats, dogs, rodents or people.
Signs and symptoms. Bald, scaly patches and scurf in the fur.
What to do. The vet can confirm the presence of ringworm by ultraviolet light or microscopic examination of scales. Treatment may involve bathing or applications of lotions and tablets. If liquids must soak into the skin, clip the hair around the area for maximum penetration. Isolate the animal. Handle the cat with gloves and other protective clothing. Wash or replace the cat's bedding and other things it frequently comes in contact with. Treatment can be lengthy. Precautions and sanitation are necessary, but cats and people have differing resistance to this fungus. One case of ringworm does not mean other cats in the house or family members will become infected.

Rabies—This disease is fatal to mammals, including man, and must be reported to health authorities. It is caused by a virus that attacks the nervous system. Rabies is spread by bites or saliva from infected animals. The incubation period varies, but rabies usually manifests itself in the cat within two months of contact. Cats can contract it from each other, dogs or wild animals.
Signs and symptoms. Behavioral change, such as ferocity, salivation, dilated pupils, lack of coordination, convulsions, paralysis. Results in death.
What to do. Take the cat to the vet if it is bitten by a wild animal. Cats allowed to run free where rabies occurs should be vaccinated at 3 to 4 months old, with boosters every year.

Feline Viral Rhino-Tracheitis (FVR)—This is also called *cat flu* and *pneumonitis.* It involves severe congestion of the nasal passages and is highly contagious, especially to kittens. Preventive vaccines are available.
Signs and symptoms. Sudden onset, coughing, sneezing, high temperature, red and sore eyes, discharge from nose and eyes, lack of appetite and lethargy.
What to do. If some of the symptoms are present, do not wait to take your cat to the vet. Waiting a week could be fatal. If only one cat shows the symptoms, isolate it from the others. Even if the cat is cured, it can still infect others. Permanent damage may be done and the cat can suffer nasal congestion for the rest of its life.

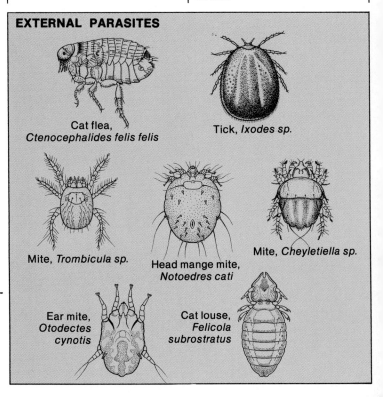

EXTERNAL PARASITES

Cat flea,
Ctenocephalides felis felis

Tick, *Ixodes sp.*

Mite, *Trombicula sp.*

Head mange mite,
Notoedres cati

Mite, *Cheyletiella sp.*

Ear mite,
Otodectes cynotis

Cat louse,
Felicola subrostratus

Feline Infectious Enteritis—
This is the chief killer of cats. Early inoculations are almost totally effective. All cats and kittens should be vaccinated.
Signs and symptoms. Pain, listlessness, subnormal temperature, loss of appetite, diarrhea, vomiting, collapse, severe dehydration. Can result in sudden death.
What to do. Take your cat to the vet immediately. Keep it in a dark, quiet place. Without serum, death can follow within 24 hours. Kittens are naturally immune for the first few weeks through mother's milk. The vet will tell you when to have your cat vaccinated. If your cat dies, wait six months before bringing a new kitten into the house.

Feline Leukemia—Feline leukemia is a fatal condition of the blood, caused by a virus. It occurs in epidemic proportions in some breeds.
Signs and symptoms. Weight loss, lack of appetite, collapse. Results in death.
What to do. There is no cure. The cat should be put to sleep. There is no evidence this virus is a risk to humans.

Kidney Disease—Kidney disease is more likely to occur in old cats.
Signs and symptoms. Excessive water intake, excessive urination, bad breath, listlessness, repeated vomiting, lack of appetite, weight loss.
What to do. This condition is usually irreversible. Once the kidneys have started to degenerate, they need increasing amounts of water to flush out the same amount of body waste. There may be accidents around the house. Do not blame the cat, it can no longer hold its water. Drugs may prolong life, but kidney disease is progressive and fatal. It is kinder to have the cat put to sleep.

This vet is using a Wood's lamp to check for ringworm, a highly contagious fungal infection of the skin. Under the lamp's ultraviolet light, the affected circular patches glow green.

Bladder Troubles—Two common conditions are *cystitis,* an inflamed bladder, and *urolithiasis,* a urinary obstruction. The first is usually due to infection; the second to crystals in urine blocking the urethral canal. Cystitis causes pain and frequent urination. In urolithiasis, blood may appear in urine as the cat strains to pass urine through a blocked canal. Pressure from a distended bladder may damage the kidneys. Neutered male cats are most susceptible to urinary obstruction, but this condition may affect other cats.
Signs and symptoms. Small quantities of cloudy urine, bloody urine, obvious pain, possible inability to urinate, weakness, loss of condition.
What to do. Contact your vet. He will probably give an antibiotic injection for cystitis and surgically or manually remove any obstruction blocking a male cat's urethral passage. If left unattended, an obstruction could be fatal. Encourage the cat to drink plenty of fluids. Offer barley water instead of tap water. To prevent urolithiasis in male cats, avoid a total diet of dried cat food that produces crystals in the urine. Feed dry food only to cats that normally drink a lot of water. Keep the litter tray clean to encourage the cat to use it often. Using the tray often helps prevent the build-up of crystals in the bladder.

TEMPERATURE-INDUCED ILLNESSES
Heatstroke—This affects cats of all ages that are subjected to extreme heat without sufficient ventilation. It can happen at cat shows, in a closed car or if the cat is taken to a warm climate from a cooler one. The cat's temperature may rise to 106F (41C).
Signs and symptoms. Vacant expression, prostrate posture, heavy panting, increased pulse rate, vomiting, unconsciousness.

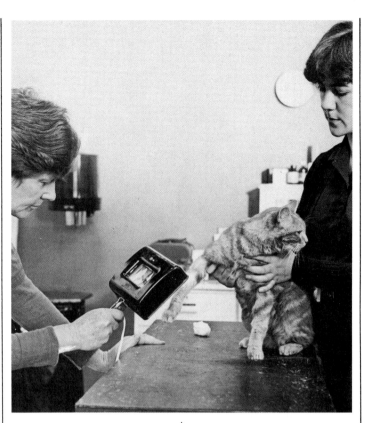

What to do. Immerse the cat in cold water to reduce body temperature. If this is not possible, lots of fresh air, an ice pack or cold water on the face and a body massage will suffice. Take the cat to the vet.

To prevent heatstroke in a car, supply water. Leave windows open so the cat can get fresh air. Never leave a cat unattended in a closed car.

Hypothermia—This is a sometimes-fatal drop in body temperature.
Signs and symptoms. Decreased pulse rate, cat feels cold to the touch.
What to do. If a kitten seems cold to the touch, it could die of hypothermia. Hold the kitten in your hand until it warms up, then place on a warm pad. An infrared lamp may be used. Hot-water bottles cool too quickly but may be used in an emergency. Hypothermia is a problem when the queen dies during birth and her kittens are not warmed by her body. Provide artificial heat for the first few days. Old cats may be subject to hypothermia. As they get older, their metabolism slows, keeping their body temperature low—especially when surroundings are cold. Artificial heat is required to reduce the risk of chilling and death.

PSYCHOLOGICAL DISORDERS
Some cats object to being left alone, to a new cat in the house or a new human addition to the family. These cats may express their feelings by odd behavioral patterns.
Signs and symptoms. Spraying in unusual places, spraying on owner's possessions, defecating in the house, aggressive behavior.
What to do. Find out what the cat is objecting to. A disturbed cat is seeking attention because it thinks it is being neglected or displaced in your affections by something else. Once you renew your attention and show affection, the problem usually clears up. If the cat is objecting to being left all day without human companionship, the best thing to do is to provide it with a dog or another cat as a companion.

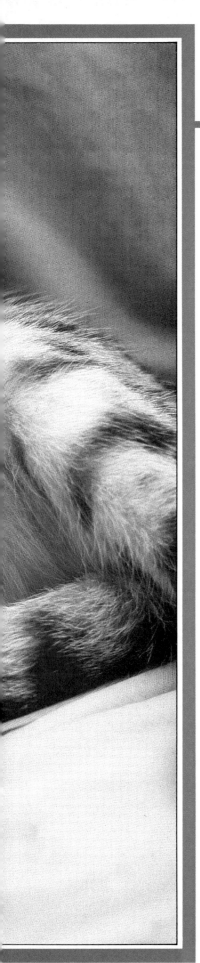

7

Breeding & Rearing

It is not a good idea to let cats breed freely because we would be overrun with them. To preserve the species at its best, only the healthiest, finest-looking, best-natured cats should be bred. Selective breeding for health, appearance and temperament has made today's pedigree cats superior to those in the past. There is a risk inbreeding develops hereditary defects, but responsible breeders guard against this.

Unaltered non-pedigree cats that roam free at night breed. Kittens may be of any color and type according to the colors and types of the sire and dam. There can even be more than one sire to the same litter of kittens. Crossbreeding produces mongrel or alley cats

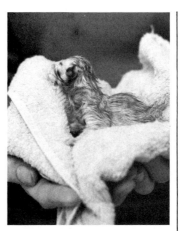

A newborn kitten still wet from the fluid in the amniotic sac in which it was born. The owner dries the kitten with a towel.

A Silver Tabby mother with nursing kittens. Moving to the nipples is an instinctive reaction for a newborn kitten.

that are robust but may not find homes. If you want a specific type and color, restrict breeding to certain pedigree animals to give predictable results when mated, according to genetic makeup.

KEEPING A QUEEN

A queen is an unaltered female. When the queen is ready to be mated, send her to a stud of the same breed. She may be anywhere from six months to two years old. Wait until she is a year old so her body has a chance to mature. Foreign breeds usually *call* much earlier than other cats. *Calling* is the term given to queens who come into heat and are ready to mate. This term is used because most queens are vocal at this time. Their loud cries are accompanied by rolling on the floor, head down

Look for a suitable stud of the same breed while waiting for your young adult queen to call. The breeder who sold her to you may have some suggestions. Check the pedigrees of several studs and compare them with the queen's own pedigree. The stud should be a champion and fairly experienced if he is to mate a maiden queen. A more mature queen can be sent to an experienced stud. Choose a stud to complement the queen. If her only defect is poor eye color, choose a stud with superbly colored eyes. You can sometimes assess him by seeing his kittens on the show bench.

Book the stud in advance and give the stud's owner some idea of when to expect the queen. You can judge a suitable date if you keep records of her calling cycle once it starts. Some cats go off call if moved too quickly. Wait a day or two until the cat is ready. If she goes off call when she is moved, it may be necessary to arrange for her to stay with the stud until she comes on call again. This is not possible unless the owner has a double stud house with room to have a queen in waiting.

Visit the stud in advance to see him and inspect his quarters. Quarters should be clean and roomy, and have a queen's compartment with her own fresh-air run and some heat if she is used to it at home.

and rear end in the air, and rubbing their legs against owners and furniture. Foreign breeds have been known to call as early as four months. Others may be one to two years old before their first call. The average age is the first spring after reaching adulthood, at 8 to 9 months old.

Persians do not usually call between October and March. Many foreign cats call throughout the year. Cats of any breed usually settle into a pattern, which may be every other week for some Orientals to twice a year for others. The cycle is individual.

Calling coincides with a vaginal discharge of clear liquid, which the queen removes with her tongue. A sign of oncoming estrus is frequent washing, particularly in this area.

It is possible for a queen to have as many as five litters in two years if she calls frequently. But it is best for her to be limited to one or two litters per year, depending on the breed and her condition. Some queens go on producing year

after year. Others stop at about eight years old or continue to call and mate but no longer become pregnant. When you want to stop your cat from producing kittens, have her spayed.

PREPARATIONS

When you first see signs the queen is ready, keep her confined or she will choose her own mate. She will be anxious to get out of the house, pacing up and down by the windows and jumping at the door handles. Keep her in a cat-proof wire run attached to sleeping quarters or build a special house and run in the yard where she can be confined. Prepare this before the queen's first call.

These quarters are valuable later for confining the cat and her kittens. Keeping her confined also ensures the queen does not stray before the kittens have been reared. In cold climates, a source of heat should be available, particularly for foreign breeds. When heated, the quarters may be used all year round.

A queen, left, and stud cat are getting to know each other before mating takes place. This familiarization period is essential to the mating ritual. If the queen is not ready, she may hiss at first.

A queen assuming the mating position with the hind legs. This posture is accompanied by head rolling and plaintive cries to attract the attention of male cats. This is a sign of *calling*.

MATING PROCEDURES

The queen must always be taken or sent to stud in a cat-proof container. She is liable to go berserk at the first smell of a stud cat, particularly when she is calling. It is best if she can enter the queen's quarters without going through stud territory before her box is opened. Usually a wire partition separates the queen from the stud so they can see, smell and get to know each other before mating. The queen usually hisses and spits at her suitor on first sight, particularly if she is not ready to mate. This is normal.

As soon as the cats start rubbing together through the wire, it is safe to let the queen out to be mated. A non-slip mat is usually provided in the stud's half of the stud house. The queen runs there. The stud grabs hold of the back of her neck and mounts her from the rear. At her climax she throws him off and rolls violently in circles on the floor. She may even attack him, so he jumps up and out of the way.

The queen may be mated more than once by the stud. If both are allowed to run together there will be many matings in one day. But more matings do not mean more kittens. One mating is sufficient. Litters of 10 have been produced from a single mating.

The stud fee you pay includes the service fee and a portion of the costs of keeping the male at stud throughout the year. In addition, you pay the queen's board and lodging, which may last a few days if she is not ready to be mated on arrival. The stud owner usually insists the queen be inoculated, so produce certificates on arrival. The queen's owner should also inspect the stud's inoculation certificates.

THE PREGNANT QUEEN

When she returns home, the queen may still be calling. Keep her confined until she stops. If she calls again in a few days or weeks, you know the mating failed. She must return to stud.

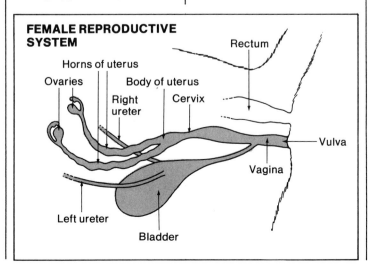

FEMALE REPRODUCTIVE SYSTEM

Rectum
Horns of uterus
Ovaries
Body of uterus
Right ureter
Cervix
Vulva
Vagina
Left ureter
Bladder

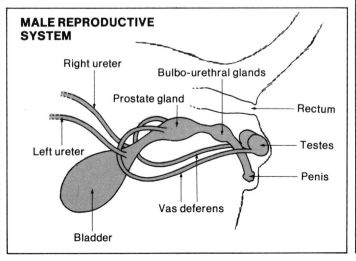

MALE REPRODUCTIVE SYSTEM

Right ureter
Bulbo-urethral glands
Prostate gland
Rectum
Left ureter
Testes
Penis
Vas deferens
Bladder

The stud owner may give a free mating this time, but is not bound to do so. He is entitled to charge a fee to cover boarding.

If the mating is successful, there is usually a period of quiet, though the queen still rushes around. Add extra vitamins and calcium to her diet.

About three weeks after mating, the queen's nipples turn pink and she rolls again but without any vocal accompaniment. Eventually, she begins to look plumper and starts nesting in the house. She needs help grooming during this time, particularly with the parts she cannot reach. Use blunt scissors and carefully cut the fur around the nipples of a longhair queen before kittens come. This keeps the fur from getting wet and drying in hard spikes. It could scratch the kittens' eyes. Fur may also be cut short around the vagina of a longhair before kittening.

Confine the queen to her own quarters during the last week. Make her a kittening box lined with clean newspaper. She will shred it into a comfortable nest for her babies. A cardboard box is good to use. A carton with a top-opening lid is even better. Use a sharp knife to make a round hole at one end to let the queen in and out. The hole should be 4 inches (10cm) above the floor and 6 to 8 inches (15 to 20cm) in diameter. Place the box in a dark, warm, draft-free corner. If it is winter, put the box on an electric pad or other source of heat. Examine the queen's teats and massage them gently with corn or other edible oil.

A pregnant queen is shown here. The nipples show clearly and the cat is plump. During this time, the cat seems contented. Give her extra calcium and vitamins to ensure healthy kittens. Pregnancy lasts 61 to 70 days.

The mother licks one of her kittens immediately after birth. It is an instinctive reaction to clean kittens. Once clean, the kittens are drawn close to the mother's body for warmth. They may start trying to suckle immediately.

GIVING BIRTH

Birth occurs 63 days after mating in some breeds, 65 days for Siamese and other foreign breeds and up to 73 days for Egyptian Maus. Anything from 61 to 70 days can be considered normal if the queen is not distressed. Most queens like to have their owners present when they kitten, particularly the first time. This can mean sitting up all night with your queen or taking her to your bed. If you place the prepared box on the bed beside you, the queen usually stays in it and kittens there. You can return the kittening box to the queen's quarters after the births.

Most cats have their kittens without mishaps. Each kitten comes in a bag called the *amniotic sac*. This has to be broken so the kitten does not suffocate. Usually the queen bursts the sac. If she fails to do so or neglects the kitten, break the sac with clean fingers and wipe the mucus away from the kitten's mouth and nose. It breathes and makes little squeaking noises that immediately causes the queen to take fresh interest in it. She licks it all over and draws it toward her to keep it warm. The kitten may move toward her teats instinctively and try to suckle.

If kittens come in quick succession, you should help. If they are well-spaced, the queen may prefer to do all the work herself. This includes biting off the umbilical cord about 4 inches (10cm) from the body to separate the kitten from the placenta. The placenta attaches the kitten to the womb and comes away during birth. If the mother fails to sever the cord, you must do it. Do not cut it too close or pull it away from the kitten. You can use scissors or pinch it between thumb and forefinger, pulling toward the kitten. After a few weeks the remaining piece of cord withers and falls off. The queen usually eats the placenta, also known as the *afterbirth*. If there are many kittens, the queen may not want to eat all of the placentas. When you see she has no more interest in the placentas, remove them.

BIRTH PROBLEMS

Sometimes a queen fails to give birth after starting labor, a condition when the muscles in the flanks contract at regular intervals. If this happens and she becomes exhausted, call the vet. It may be a breech birth, where the kitten is coming hindquarters first or something else may be wrong. If the queen is not distressed, leave her alone and let things happen naturally. It is unlikely the kittens will be deformed. Have the vet examine them and put malformed kittens to sleep painlessly.

Any kittens born with cleft palates make a shrill, unpleasant noise, easy to distinguish from the soft squeaking of normal kittens. Often the queen lies on such kittens to silence and smother them. The queen can usually determine which kittens to rear and which to discard.

KITTEN CARE

When all the kittens are born, lift the pad of newspaper and the kittens on it out of their box. Prepare a clean bed in the box and return the kittens one at a time. The queen may object to this but soon realizes you are not trying to hurt her kittens. She can safely be left to enjoy her babies. Feed her some warm milk or food mixed with milk. Put the drink in a deep bowl and hold it so she can drink while in the box. Some cats refuse to leave their box for hours, but drink or eat anything offered while they suckle their kittens.

Eventually, the mother leaves her box to visit the litter tray. Keep it nearby. These visits offer you the best time for changing bedding. If possible, shut the queen out of the room for these few minutes. She will try to rush back to the nest at the first vocal sign that her young are being disturbed. Once they settle down, let her back in the room. She will curl up with them in the clean bed. Change the bedding once or twice daily for the first week. The queen will probably still be losing some blood.

Changing bedding is the best time for checking the sex of kittens. They may screech when suddenly picked up. Hold the kitten in one hand with all

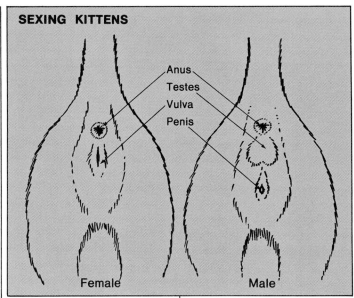
The differences in male and female kittens are easiest to see in the first few days of life. The vulva and anus are close together in the female kitten. The anus, developing testes and penis are farther apart in the male kitten.

These contented kittens are growing strong on their mother's milk. They suckle for 4 or 5 weeks before being weaned on other foods. The mother needs a lot of nourishing foods while she is feeding her kittens.

four feet on the hand. Lift the tail with your other hand. The illustration on this page shows sexual differences.

After a few days, the queen gets hungrier. She should have as much nourishing food, with added vitamins and minerals, as she wants. She needs regular grooming during this time. If kittens have any infection around the eyes, wash her underside with cat-safe shampoo. Clean the kittens' eyes with damp cotton before they are placed back in their box.

If the queen calls again before the kittens are fully weaned, she must be confined with them. If she loses her milk or has no milk, sometimes another queen who has milk can take over the kittens. The second queen will wash the kittens and keep them warm. If you cannot find a foster mother, you must hand-rear them, which is a time-consuming process.

If you must hand-feed the kittens, you need a bottle and substitute milk. Kittens require feeding every two hours, night and day, for the first week. Do not attempt this without the patience to see it through. Feeding is only part of the task. You must also massage the kittens' bellies to stimulate urination, wipe their rear ends clean with damp cotton, change the bedding twice a day and keep the kittens warm. There are heated pads for this purpose. A hot water bottle is not recommended because it has to be replaced every four

hours. A bed heated at one end only is good. Kittens can move to a hotter or colder section as required. When hand rearing, stop some of the night feeds in the second week. Feed only every four hours for the third week.

REARING KITTENS

After giving birth, the queen will not move out of the kittening box for the first week, except to feed herself and use the litter tray. She curls up with the kittens, purring, letting them suckle and washing them.

At about 10 days old, the kittens' eyes begin to open. They start to move around in the box. If there is a litter tray near the breeding box, the mother nudges them into it after feeding them. They instinctively know what to do. They usually start using the litter tray before being weaned, if you provide one for their use. Normal kittens eat some of the litter in the tray or any other dirt. This may help them to add the bacterial organisms vital for digestion.

They will be content with only mother's milk. If she is lacking in milk they will not be as plump as they should in this case. You will need to supplement her milk with a bottle. The smallest kittens, who are not getting enough food, are the first to accept the bottle. Offer the mother a bowl of the milk, too. A week later this can become a milky baby cereal, served to the mother near the nest. Use the same sounds when you serve meals to the kittens as you have used with the mother. They soon associate these sounds with food and mealtime.

The kittens copy their mother and stick their noses in the food. Eventually, they all learn how to lap and look forward to food at regular intervals. In between, they are still nursed by their mother.

At three weeks old, they can be given one meal of raw meat, chicken or fish, finely minced or chopped. Feed this meal four hours after the cereal meal. If kittens seem constipated, mash sardines and bread crumbs together with a little hot water.

After four weeks, give two milk or cereal meals and two meat or fish meals each day.

This young kitten is eating from a curved bottle. By taking the thumb on and off the open end, it is possible to control the flow of fluid.

It is better not to disturb kittens in the first week except to change bedding daily. After the first week, they need to be handled regularly to socialize them.

Add one drop of halibut oil to the food for each kitten. Be sure all kittens get their share. If any kitten is greedy and eats too much, feed it separately. Give food slowly, a little at a time.

Even though kittens are feeding themselves and seem independent of their mother's milk, leave them with her until they are 10 weeks old. During this time, the mother has a chance to finish their education.

KITTEN EDUCATION

When the kittens start crawling out of the nesting box, using the litter tray and eating food other than from their mother, their education begins. The mother teaches them many things before they leave home. A wise breeder handles kittens frequently and affectionately. Those destined for a show career should be handled as a judge will handle them. They will get used to the routine by the time they go to their first show.

One of the first things kittens learn is to wash. They may copy their mother or do it instinctively. They move their paws to their mouths to lick and then pass the paw over the ear.

The next thing they learn is how to play. They sit up and box each other, using paws. If one kitten falls over, another pounces on it. Usually play is between two kittens only. One

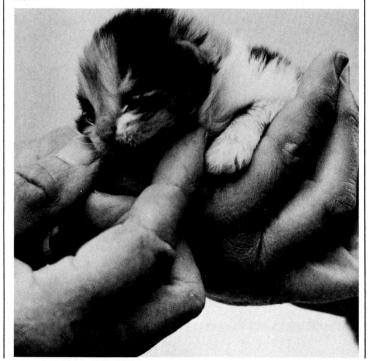

The mother carries young kittens by holding their heads gently in her mouth. As they grow older, they become too heavy to be carried safely this way.

of them will break away and pick on one of the other kittens. They also try to play with mother. She holds them down with one paw and washes them while they try to escape. When she moves her tail, the kittens pounce on it.

The kittens soon graduate to chasing moving objects. There are individual and group toys the whole litter can enjoy. A rattle ball on a string attached to a door handle gives hours of exercise and amusement.

Kittens quickly learn to climb. Even the tiniest kitten is able to climb. They learn to use scratching posts for sharpening their claws, just as their mother does.

In the evening, allow the kittens to socialize with the family. Mother will jump up on a lap and the kittens will try to follow. Gently pick up the kittens. Stroke and talk to them.

The mother teaches the kittens to hunt, pounce and protect their catches. She teaches them which humans to trust and which to avoid.

While the mother is nursing the kittens, the human family can make an attempt to groom the kittens with a brush and comb. It will be considered a game at first. Hold the kitten down with one hand and brush or comb it with the other.

If the queen is allowed out, she will bring home mice and other small creatures. Cats do not regurgitate food from the stomach for their kittens. The mother growls over the prey in front of her kittens, showing them what to do when they catch something. This interests and excites the kittens. Later, she brings in live prey and lets it go in front of them. They soon learn to chase and pounce. Kittens can practice on toy

Kittens play together. This develops the muscles they need for hunting. The home provides many opportunities for games.

mice the owner provides and soon become expert at chasing and catching prey. If allowed out, they may catch something for themselves. Cats that have been taught to hunt and kill prey by their mothers become more efficient mousers.

As the kittens grow, they exercise by chasing each other and playing tag. They cover a lot of ground, so they must have space to exercise and play. They will grow into intelligent, healthy, agile cats.

KEEPING A STUD

Keeping a stud pedigree cat is for professional breeders only. A person should have experience with two or more queens before considering it. Managing a stud cat is not easy. Handling visiting queens requires patience, understanding and knowledge of cats. Stud management is expensive, if done properly. The stud cat needs his own quarters and good food. Another problem is odor. Many people dislike the smell of an unaltered male cat.

It is important to find out if another stud cat is needed. There may be too many, with insufficient work between them. A male cat is unhappy if he is not given enough work to do. If there is no demand for his professional services, have him neutered. Never let a stud cat run loose to mate with local queens. He may catch a disease or get injured in fights. He may not be available when needed to receive a visiting queen.

To keep a stud permanently confined have the largest accommodation you can afford, with room inside for the cats to mate. You must have a waiting room for the owner. A large outdoor run gives the stud cat plenty of fresh air and exercise. Shelves 6 inches (15cm) wide, at different heights around the sides provide the cat with all the exercise he needs. The best-arranged stud houses combine a queen's compartment inside with her own individual run outside. They can both share the same escape run. The queen's coming and going does not have to be carried out through stud territory.

Vinyl flooring is needed inside the stud house. Put vinyl up the walls above spray height. A washable mat or rug in the center of the stud's area provides comfort and a surface feet can grip during mating. In some climates, it may be necessary to heat the area for the stud and queen. A light in the stud house enables feeding and mating to take place at night, if necessary. Concrete runs are best for cleaning, with wire raised about 1/2 inch (1cm) above the concrete.

To be successful, a stud cat must be a champion or potential champion of its breed. Only the best are in demand by owners of pedigree breeding queens. These people want to win prizes with their kittens and build their reputations.

To keep a successful stud in peak condition all year, feed him raw meat, chicken and fish, plus extra vitamins, minerals, egg yolks and milk. It costs a lot to feed him, but each stud fee includes a portion of his keep for the year. He must receive inoculations as required. Visiting queens' owners will want to see necessary certificates.

A stud house with separate queen's quarters and run is shown at the right. The queen can be installed safely behind wire until ready to mate.

The stud house shown below is large and airy, with shelves at different levels for interest and exercise. The cedar frame needs little maintenance. The stud cat awaiting his next queen is a Blue Burmese.

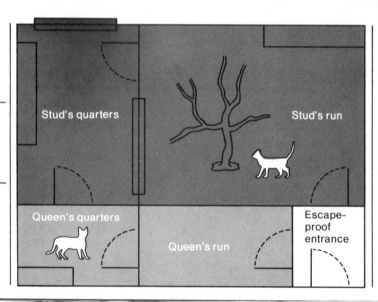

Stud's quarters

Stud's run

Queen's quarters

Queen's run

Escape-proof entrance

USING A STUD

A male cat may become ready to mate a female as early as six months old or not until he is two years old. Readiness is not breed related, but varies with individuals. Some males have mated with their sisters while still together in a litter. A male becomes a proven sire and can be put to stud once he has mated a queen who gives birth. Some breeders limit the number of queens to be served the first year. Others may limit matings at all times. Nature is usually the best judge. As long as the cat appears to be thriving and eating properly, there is no harm in letting him mate as often as he wants.

It is unlikely a stud cat is overworked when well-fed. If he goes into a decline, it is probably for other reasons. The cat who does not get enough work may be a more difficult problem. He could pine away or become bad-tempered. Advertise his services, but if there is no call for him, he should be neutered. This may be done at any age, but it may take six months for him to drop the spraying habit.

A successful working stud can go on for years, even to age 16 or 17. Some studs lose interest or queens no longer become pregnant. When this happens, a stud can spend the rest of his life as a pet.

At the start of his career, mate a young stud only to experienced queens. This builds his confidence. Save maiden queens for later, when he is experienced. If a young, timid stud gets a difficult queen the first time, he may develop problems. Even experienced queens are sometimes troublesome. You may have to steady a queen by hand or leave the couple to run with each other. Some cats mate only if no human is present.

When the queen arrives, it is normal for her to spit at the stud if she is not ready or has gone off call because of the journey. He usually does not mind, because he knows she will change. He waits patiently, wooing her with his voice until she rolls and coos back at him. When the time is right, open the door of the queen's apartment. The queen runs out on to the mat and assumes a mating posture. The stud straddles her, takes her by the scruff with his mouth and penetrates. He may thump her hindquarters until she lifts them to the required level and moves her tail to one side. She may waltz about a bit, moving round in circles or actively try to throw him off. He hangs on, until she climaxes and he has ejaculated. Then he jumps clear.

After mating, the queen rolls around furiously and may even attack him if he fails to get out of the way. A shelf about 18 inches (46cm) high should be provided for this purpose. The stud owner should immediately praise the stud. Make no attempt to handle the queen until she has calmed down. The queen returns to her own quarters voluntarily or with a little persuasion. The couple can be left to clean themselves. They usually enjoy each other's company and eat meals at the same time. If the queen remains for any length of time after she has gone off call, the couple can run together. They may be found curled up together in one bed or enjoying mutual washing.

The stud's owner receives the stud fee when the queen arrives. This fee varies with the breed, popularity or awards held by the stud, the type of stud quarters and the location. It should reflect the stud service and the queen's room and board. It should also include payment toward the stud cat's annual maintenance.

When the queen goes home, the stud's owner gives her owner a mating certificate showing the dates on which matings took place and the date kittens can be expected. The stud's owner also gives the queen's owner a copy of the stud's pedigree. News of the result of the mating is passed on. If the queen does not become pregnant, some stud owners offer a free mating. But they are not obliged to. They may charge a boarding fee for the queen. The stud fee is never returned, but if a stud persistently fails to impregnate his queens, he is withdrawn from stud.

A STUD'S LIFE

The life of the stud cat can be lonely. Most stud cats are not allowed into their owner's house. This is because they routinely spray a foul-smelling liquid designed to attract queens. The stud establishes the boundaries of his territory by spraying. The stud is still an affectionate animal needing attention. His owner must take time to groom him and love him.

Between duties, the stud enjoys the companionship of a female that is not calling or a neutered male placed in the queen's compartment. Two studs together fight, so never try this combination. Two studs in houses 60 feet (18m) apart enjoy watching each other. Only experienced breeders are able to cope with more than one stud cat.

HISTORY & GENETICS

Archeological remains show that cats were domesticated in Egypt as early as 2500 B.C. Hundreds of thousands of cats were mummified. Cats were also present in China as early as 1000 B.C., and later in Japan. The Japanese used cats to protect silkworms, granaries and old manuscripts from damage by rats. Egyptian paintings and Pompeiian relics depict striped or spotted tabby cats. The Egyptians made gods of cats and attributed magical powers to them. By the Middle Ages, the Roman Catholic Church, in an attempt to bring people back to God and to suppress their interest in magic, persecuted cats and their owners. This may account for the bubonic plague that swept through Europe and Asia in the mid-14th century. There were

An Egyptian bronze figure, dated around 30 B.C., is one of many images showing the respect the ancient Egyptians had for cats.

This colorful British Shorthair litter is the result of mating two cats with genes for different colors in their makeup.

few cats left to control the rats that carried the plague. By the end of the 18th century, the value of the cat in rodent control was again realized. The cat was reinstated as a household pet.

At the end of the 19th century, the first cat shows were held. People began to realize the differences between coat colors and patterns. As more was learned about genetics, cat breeders became interested in creating new breeds and colors, and perfecting the ones that existed.

Since 1918, knowledge of genetics has increased. It is now possible to predict the types of cat that will be produced in any color, coat pattern and coat type.

A Seal-point Colorpoint, produced by mating a recessive longhair to a shorthair with the Himalayan coat pattern.

HEALTH AND STAMINA

Do not start a breeding program unless you have healthy stock. Your foundation stock must be the healthiest and best you can afford.

SEX AND COLOR

The cat has 38 chromosomes consisting of 18 identical pairs and one pair that is different. The different pair is for the sexes, male and female. Some breeds seem to produce more male kittens. Some coat colors are sex linked. Tortoiseshells and Calicos are female, in all colors and their dilutions. Occasionally, a male cat is born with tortie or other coloring because he has an extra chromosome. Such a male is usually sterile.

GENES

Genes determine the characteristics of the cat. There are thousands of genes in every chromosome, all with a specific purpose. There are genes for coat color and pattern, temperament, eye shape and eye color, body and hair type, and every other characteristic. During cell division, the gene reproduces itself with great precision. When occasionally a gene does not reproduce itself exactly, or moves to a different location in the chromosome, that gene is a *mutant*, resulting in mutant kittens.

An Exotic Shorthair, the result of mating a longhair cat to shorthair to get a cobby-type body, round face and short hair.

A Scottish Fold. The folded ear is a natural mutation that has been perpetuated by selective breeding.

The front paw of a polydactyl cat, showing six toes instead of the usual five. Some cats may have seven toes.

A Seal-point Siamese. This slender Oriental-type breed was found in the East in Himalayan and other coat colors.

An elegant blue-eye Angora is one of the longhair breeds with a fine-boned, slender-type of body and wedge-shape head.

BODY TYPES

There are two basic body types: the cobby shape with a round skull, typified by the show quality Persian and Exotic Shorthair; and the finer boned, lithe, slender type with a wedge-shape head, as seen in the Angora, Balinese, Siamese, Colorpoint and Oriental.

Some cats are natural breeds from different areas of the world. Others are attempts to create new breeds by mating different types together to combine features from both. Occasionally, a new type occurs as a natural mutation. Some examples of this are the Manx, without a tail or with various degrees of shortness of tail; the Japanese Bobtail, with a curled tail; the folded-ear cat, the Scottish Fold, which was a natural mutation; and the polydactyl cat, with extra toes. With the exception of the Scottish Fold, these mutations occurred long ago. They were perpetuated because they were geographically confined and in-breeding intensified the characteristics. The gene for taillessness in the Manx is a recessive gene. Folded ears are a dominant gene. The polydactyl gene is dominant over the one for normal toes, producing that characteristic.

COAT COLOR AND PATTERN

Various coat colors and patterns are all inherent within the cat species. It is doubtful whether they would all have appeared with random matings of the cat population. Some colors are dominant over others. Recessive colors would be repressed if breeding had not come about from some cats being confined within a geographical location. This may have produced the Korat and Siamese.

These are Bicolor Rex cats. The curly, or rex, coat was a natural mutation that appeared in various locations. There are two genetic types: Cornish and Devon.

This is a Seal-point Showshoe. It is a Himalayan-patterned shorthair with an added gene for white spotting, which was deliberately introduced.

Now that breeders are beginning to understand selective breeding, all possible colors can be produced in all coat patterns, in each body and hair type or mixture of types. What constitutes a breed is becoming uncertain.

Governing bodies of the cat fancies worldwide should meet. They should reassess the situation and finalize a new system of classification acceptable to all, based on sound principles of genetics.

EYES

It is believed hazel eyes developed naturally in cats in temperate regions. That color was a good camouflage for them in the undergrowth. Red and cream color cats with amber eyes may originally have come from desert regions, where such coloring would have added to their chance of survival. On the show bench, dramatic colorings are sometimes desired by the breeder, such as red cats with green eyes. The study of genetics has made this possible.

TEMPERAMENT

Genes for temperament vary with different breeds and can be manipulated along with other features. When one breed is crossed with another, the resulting breed has an intermediate temperament. When some Siamese breeds are crossed with longhairs, the resulting Himalayan-color longhairs are less aggressive, less vocal and less destructive than the original Siamese.

HEAD SHAPE

During the 20th century, the Persian cat has been selectively bred from a long-nose cat with a long tongue, to a short-face cat with a short tongue. The length of its tongue is important for grooming purposes. The short tongue is not as efficient for grooming.

The reverse has happened with the Siamese. At the end of the 19th century, the Siamese was a short, round-face animal. Selective breeding has produced a long head, with a long tongue. Fashion has dictated such changes.

Some think selective breeding is not always in the best interests of the cat. In extreme cases, such as the Peke-Face Persian, the short nose produces breathing problems, blocked tear ducts and difficulty in feeding. Inexperienced breeders should beware of experimental breeding and concentrate on improving the looks and practicality of each cat within various breeds.

FEATURE FIXING

The way to fix a feature is to take a female that has one or more of the features you wish to fix. Mate her to a male with similar features or other features you wish to introduce into your strain.

Out of the resulting kittens, sell those not showing the desired features. Mate the others together or back to their parents. Keep the ones showing desired features and sell the others as pets. When the next generation is old enough, mate them with each other or back to the foundation stock. In this way, a strain is built carrying desired features. By not using undesirable offspring, some of these features become fixed and appear in all future offspring. Do not outcross, which undoes all the work you have built up.

It is better to have more than one program going at the same time. Cross over to the other strain built up by you or another breeder attempting the same program. This is not always as easy as it sounds. You sometimes come across a feature that is different because it is recessive or sex linked.

A completely tailless cat is the result of genes for skeletal deformity. Manx-mated-to-Manx results in a high percentage of prenatal deaths.

Red color in cats is sometimes sex linked. Diluted colors are recessive to dominant colors.

DOMINANCE

In considering a dominant against a recessive feature, if both cats show the dominant feature, all the offspring will show the dominant feature. If both cats display the recessive feature, all offspring will display the recessive feature. If a cat with a recessive feature is mated to a cat with a dominant feature and all the kittens show the dominant feature, the dominant cat is probably not carrying the recessive feature. If half the offspring display the dominant feature and half display the recessive feature, this proves the cat displaying the dominant feature also carries the recessive gene. A pair of recessive genes—one from each parent—is necessary to produce a recessive feature.

This is an important discovery affecting future matings. A table of dominant and recessive features is shown on the right. Using these charts, the breeder can decide how to go about building a strain within a breed or creating a new breed, new color variety or new combination of coat type, coat color and eye color. It may take many generations and much hard work. The creation of the Himalayan took 10 years of specialized breeding.

SUMMARY

Every characteristic of the cat is capable of manipulation today. It is hoped breeders will be responsible in their creative skills to create beautiful cats that are also practical. No one wants to perpetuate deformities.

DOMINANT AND RECESSIVE CHARACTERISTICS

COLORS

BLACK
dominant over
Blue

BLACK
dominant over
Chocolate

CHOCOLATE
dominant over
Lilac

CHOCOLATE
dominant over
Cinnamon

RED
dominant over
Cream

WHITE
dominant over
All other colors

TORTOISESHELL
dominant over
Siamese

CALICO
dominant over
Dilute Calico
Blue-cream and white

SOLID COLOR
dominant over
Siamese

SOLID COLOR
dominant over
Burmese

SIAMESE
dominant over
Blue-eye albino

BLUE-EYE ALBINO
dominant over
Pink-eye albino

PIEBALD
Mostly white
dominant over
Solid color

TICKED TABBY
Agouti
dominant over
All other tabbies

TICKED TABBY
dominant over
Black

MACKEREL TABBY
dominant over
Classic or blotched tabby

WHITE SPOTTING
dominant over
Solid Color
There is also a recessive white spotting.

WHITE UNDERCOAT
dominant over
Solid color

COAT TYPES

SHORTHAIR
dominant over
Longhair

SHORTHAIR
dominant over
Hairless

WIREHAIR
dominant over
Normal hair

NORMAL HAIR
dominant over
Rex coat

OTHER FEATURES

FOLDED EAR
dominant over
Normal ear

MANX TAIL
dominant over
Normal tail

POLYDACTYL
Extra toes
dominant over
Normal toes

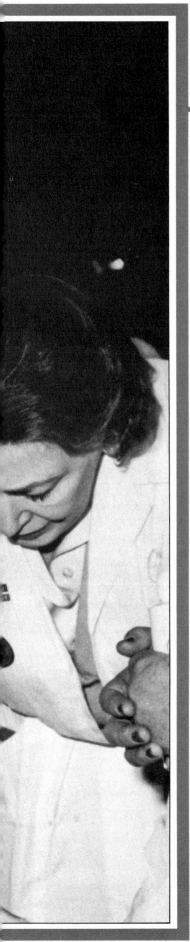

SHOWING YOUR CAT

Showing cats is a hobby that brings people with similar interests together. It can be exciting. It helps give breeders scientific insight into the characteristics cats inherit from their parents.

Visit a local cat show and study exhibits. This can be an enjoyable day for the family. If it is an all-breed show, there will be many different cats.

You may find kittens for sale at the show. If not, exhibitors often have kittens at home or know where to find them. They may help you purchase a kitten, show it and breed it. You may have to wait for a show quality kitten of a rare breed, but it is worthwhile. There is no point showing or breeding an inferior specimen.

A proud young owner holds her prize-winning Siamese kitten.

A steward holds a Silver Tabby British Shorthair kitten while the judge writes her report on the cat.

If you intend to show but not breed, have the animal spayed or neutered. Altered cats may be exhibited in special classes. This gives you a choice of male or female. Or purchase a female because only an experienced breeder with several queens should attempt to keep a stud.

If you wish to become a serious cat breeder, you must have your own prefix, or name, which will apply to all the kittens bred by you. This name is registered with the governing council or cat association before the kittens are born. Act as soon as you make your decision. Once you understand genetics, it is possible for you to produce champions.

HISTORY OF SHOWING

Cat shows have been held only during the last hundred years. The first official show in the United States took place at Bunnels Museum in New York in March 1881. It was followed by one at Madison Square Garden in New York in 1895.

Shows are now also held on a regular basis in Australia, New Zealand, throughout Europe, South Africa and Japan. Mexico conducted its first cat show in 1978, and Hong Kong its first in 1979. The largest shows are in the United Kingdom, with over 2,000 entries at the National Cat Show.

Persians form the largest classes at American shows, followed by Himalayans, Siamese, Burmese and Abyssinians. Chinchillas are the largest single group of longhair exhibits at Australian shows, where Orientals are popular. In the United Kingdom, Persians are most numerous, followed by Siamese and Burmese.

Most shows have classes for household pets, which are non-pedigree, sexually altered cats. A pretty kitten found on a doorstep or a gift from a friend might become a winner in these classes. Some larger shows offer prizes for household pets in categories such as Any Color Longhair, Best Black Shorthair, Most Attractively Marked Ginger Cat or Cat With The Sweetest Disposition. To qualify as a household pet for showing, the cat must be of unknown or unregistered parentage.

Shows last from one to three days. Cats are kept in pens decorated with curtains, cushions and ribbons from previous shows. The judging takes place elsewhere. Stewards call the cats for each class to come to the judging ring, which is often in another room.

SHOW LIFE OF A CAT

A good cat is shown regularly for one or two seasons, gradually picking up points. The luxury of time is not available to Siamese and some Himalayan cats because when their coats change color, they are not shown. All cats are shown as kittens until they are eight months old. Although the experience is good for them, they do not acquire any permanent points. Siamese and Himalayans are shown a great deal between 8 and 12 months of age to get their Grand Championships before their coats start to darken. There has been an effort to breed cats with light coats and more Blue-points for a longer show career.

Other breeds, such as Manx, are shown as kittens and then disappear from the show scene while they go through their rangy stage. When they start to look cobby again at two or three years, they compete for adult honors.

FILLING IN THE ENTRY FORM

The classes you enter may not be clear for your first show. Consult the breeder who sold you the kitten, an experienced cat show friend or cat club member.

There may be one entry form for all breeds. At larger shows, there are often separate forms for the Longhair, Shorthair and Siamese sections. Household Pets always have a separate entry form. Study the form carefully.

Use your cat's registration or transfer certificate for the correct information. The cat's name, sire, dam, sex, date of birth, breed number, registration number and breeder's name must be filled in on the form as they appear on the certificate. If you do not do this, your cat may be disqualified. Experimental breeds may only be shown in assessment classes.

Select the classes and check your cat's eligibility for each. There may be a separate space for the open class number. Be sure you write it in. Look up the entry fees for each class in the schedule. Enter the correct

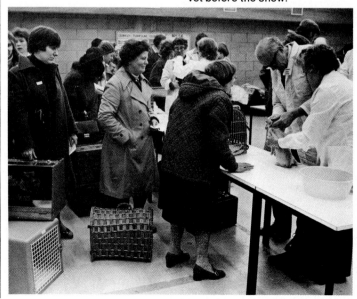

After vetting in, cats are put into pens by owners.

amounts. Many shows offer double pens, which cost more than the ordinary benching. These are in short supply so they are usually allowed only for adult males and neuters. If you are booking a double pen, and enter more than one cat in the show, indicate which cat the double pen is for.

There may be spaces for other information on the form. Fill these in if you wish. Fill in your name, address and telephone number. Include the names of clubs of which you are a member. Sign and date the form. Send the form off in time to be registered. The earlier you send your form in, the more chance you have of being entered in the show. Send a check with the completed form.

If you have entered your cat and then cannot go to the show, inform the show manager. If the cat cannot go because of illness, send a veterinary certificate stating this. If you send these to the show manager before the show, all or part of your entry fees may be refunded.

Never enter a cat that is sick or pregnant. Be sure your cat is inoculated before a show.

Once your application is accepted, groom the cat daily with show equipment until show day. Preparing a cat for a show career involves handling it regularly from kittenhood. If several people handle it, the animal should grow used to strangers and remain calm when scrutinized by judges.

Groom the cat daily and feed it correctly so your exhibit is in good condition for each show.

SHOW EQUIPMENT

Take the items your cat needs for the day to the show: a blanket, litter tray, feeding dish, water bowl and ribbon or elastic to tie the cat's number around its neck.

Choose curtains and a cushion to match or contrast with your cat's coat or eyes. Some pens carry other ornaments, such as flowers. All these enhance the show scene for the visitor. Exhibition pens, containing cats not entered for competition, may be decorated. These pens contain cats for sale, cats as advertisements for breeder's stock or new varieties.

LAST-MINUTE PREPARATIONS

Get everything ready the night before the show. Gather together the show equipment, cat food and litter. Keep the cat indoors so it is not missing when you are ready to leave.

Choose comfortable, attractive clothes for show day. There is a great deal of standing and walking around. Do not put the show blanket in the carrier for the journey. Keep the blanket for the pen itself and use an old blanket for traveling.

If the show is far from home, you may have to stay in a hotel or motel. Make sure the place accepts cats. Put the cat litter tray in the bathroom. If you leave the room, put a notice on the door stating there is a cat in the room. Or take along a wire cage with a roof and put the cat in it with a litter tray while you are out of the room. This is for the cat's protection.

Take along enough food for your cat for the trip. Canned or semimoist food is ideal.

A prize-winning Chinchilla adult poses with its trophies at a longhair-only show. Its coat is in perfect show condition.

HELPFUL HINTS FOR SHOW DAY

On the morning of show day, get up early. *Vetting in* usually starts about 8 a.m. This is a medical check to make sure every cat is healthy. If your cat does not pass the vetting in, it cannot participate in the show. Once past the vet, your cat can be penned. You can feed and water it and make the pen ready for the judging. Remove all food around 9:30 a.m. and clean the pen. Change the litter if necessary. Place your cat's cage under the show bench.

Catalogs for the show may be sold at the show. Buy one to check the details of your cat and the classes you have entered. If there is any mistake, see the show manager. If your cat has been left out of a class or is in the wrong one, it may be possible to change it before judging has finished in the class.

The first time a cat is mentioned, all the details of sire, dam and date of birth are given and there is a list of other classes it is entered in.

If there are many entries, classes may be split. Two or more classes may be put together if there are few entries, except Open Championship classes.

There may be a change of judges. These must be displayed on a board just inside the exhibition room.

An Abyssinian in a pen decorated for the Christmas season. Care goes into decorations. At some shows, prizes are awarded for the most attractive pens.

new breeds and colors can be registered and shown before achieving CFA acceptance. Some of the minority associations are strong in certain regions of the country. These shows give the public and exhibitors the chance to participate in more shows than if there were just one association. It is not unusual for a cat to be registered with several associations and to hold titles in each. It is possible, particularly on the East or West Coast, to show your cats almost every weekend if you want to and can afford it.

Most American shows have the same format. Cats are brought to the show area, which may be an auditorium or a large room in a hotel. They are checked in by a clerk and assigned a cage for the show. All cats shown by the same person(s) are benched together regardless of breed. Exhibitors may request to be benched next to other exhibitors. Cats of a particular breed may be in one part of the room.

AFTER THE SHOW

You will be tired after the show. Go home and rest. If you have other cats at home, isolate the show cat for two weeks, in case it has caught an infection. Disinfect all the show equipment and wash your clothes.

If you have won a cup or other prize, you may have to wait to receive it. But you can often bring home cards or ribbons on show day.

You may want to help with show organization. There are many jobs you might do, such as stewarding for a judge, helping enter results, fixing cards on pens and placing result slips on awards boards. Check with sponsors.

A STEWARD'S JOB

A steward makes certain everything is ready for the judge to begin judging. All necessary items are supplied, but it is the steward's job to make sure the judge has everything required. It is also the steward's job to get the cat out of the pen and to replace it in the pen after the judging. It is helpful to be an expert cat handler because cats are sometimes nervous at shows

and take it out on the steward. A steward must clean his hands before handling each cat; the scent of one cat could upset the next.

Once all the cats in one class have been judged, it is the steward's job to take the award slips to the awards table. When all the classes have been judged, the steward takes the equipment back to the show manager.

At the Best in Show judging, the steward takes the cats the judge has nominated for Best in Show to the table. It is the steward's job to be sure the cat is placed in the Best In Show pen in front of the stage or taken back to its pen.

Stewards are unpaid. But the rewards for cat lovers or young people wanting to be a judge are many. Stewards are not expected to offer their opinions on judging cats unless asked to do so by their judge. If you are a steward and are known to be an expert on a certain breed, you may be asked for your opinion.

After many years of breeding and showing, you may consider becoming a judge or show manager. Many judges are asked to judge at shows in other countries.

SHOWING IN THE UNITED STATES

The United States has seven registering associations, each with its own standards and rules. The largest and most powerful is the Cat Fancier's Association (CFA). Most of the smaller associations accept a CFA registration without question, but the courtesy does not always go both ways. It is beneficial for the cat fancier to join other associations where

Owners and other interested people check the results of the judging.

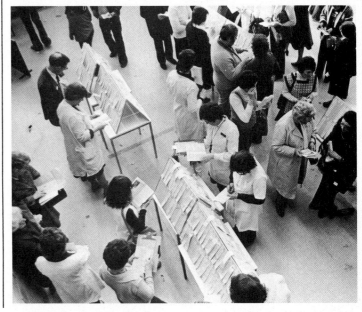

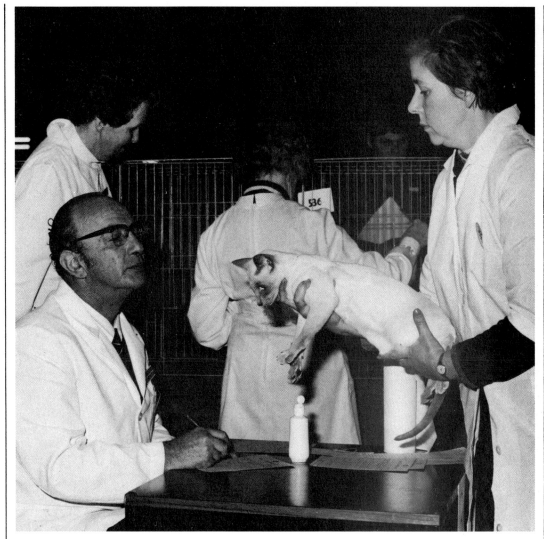

Steward and judge work as a team. The judge takes detailed notes about each cat.

Each cat has a number that corresponds to its listing in the show catalog. The listing includes the name of the cat, the names of its parents, owner, exhibitor and breeder, and the cat's date of birth. It also shows the cat's show status in that particular association—Novice, Open, Champion, Grand Champion, Premier, Grand Premier. It is not unusual for an Open to be a Champion in one association and a Grand Champion in another. These other association titles are not indicated in the catalog.

Judging—Judging tables are set up in a section of the room or around the edges. Behind each table is a row of 10 cages. In front of the tables are rows of chairs for the spectators and exhibitors.

Show committees schedule the classes so each cat is evaluated by each judge. Most shows have four judges, but larger, more-prestigious shows may have as many as six or eight. In the past, two-day shows were common. Due to inflation and the cost of transportation, many shows are trying to finish in one day.

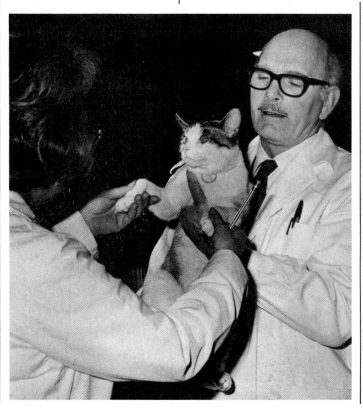

This cat is being judged at a show. The cat's show entry number disk is tied around its neck.

Judging usually begins at about 10 a.m. and may last until 6 or 7 p.m. Cats are called by breed and color, 10 at a time. A large class, such as the Burmese, may take a long time to judge. The judge examines the cat from all angles and assesses its merits. He then makes notes about the cat and sprays a sterilant on the table and his hands before handling the next cat. This first handling tells the owner and the audience little. When the cat is called back to be compared to other outstanding cats, it becomes apparent that the cat is being considered for an award.

The process of elimination is followed by each judge. The judges work independently. Although they all follow the same standard, it is not surprising when a cat does well with one judge and not another. It takes an extraordinary cat to meet the standard and personal preferences of four experts.

The day culminates in the judging of the Best of the Best. The 10 cats that gain the most points during the course of the show are called for a final judging.

Points are collected for each Champion. If a cat has no disqualifying faults, it is not difficult to become a Champion at one show. When that status is achieved, the competition becomes more intense. In some of the smaller associations, as few as 15 points may be required to become a Grand Champion. In CFA, most breeds must have 250 points to become Grand Champions.

Most shows in the United States have between 200 and 500 entries. In a 300-cat show, 40 might be Household Pets (no points), 60 might be Kittens and the Premier

A Birman has been chosen third prize winner. This competitor seems at home amidst the bustling show scene.

The class may be divided into longhairs or shorthairs, males or females for judging purposes. The Household Pets may or may not be judged by the same people who judge purebreds.

Some associations have a separate class for pets that look like purebreds but are pet quality or do not have pedigrees. This category removes purebred look-alikes from the Household Pet competition. It eliminates possible prejudice for or against them from the judges.

New Breeds—There is also a Provisional class for breeds being considered for championship status. Cats are handled and evaluated by the judges, but are not really in competition. Some breeds spend as long as five years as a Provisional breed before becoming eligible for championship competition.

Cats that may be shown but are not handled by the judges are classed as For Exhibition Only or For Sale. Breeds which are experimental and have not achieved Provisional status may be displayed to acquaint the public with them and to get unofficial reaction of judges and other exhibitors.

Kittens over four months old and cats brought to shows to sell on the spot are often found at shows. More often, breeders put up signs and hand out cards to prospective buyers to protect their kittens from the stress and exposure of the show environment. This gives the breeder a better opportunity to screen would-be owners to make sure the cat gets a good home.

(Alter/Neuter) class might be as large as 30 to 40. The adult purebreds do not compete with any of the above classes, so it is almost impossible for a cat to become a Grand Champion at a single CFA show. It can be done at some of the large shows, but such winnings are rare.

Some cats are retired when they achieve their Grand Championship and may be used for breeding. But many continue to be shown. These cats compete for Regional and National wins. Points continue to be gained as they were before the cat became a Grand Champion. These points determine the top 10 or 20 cats in each section of the country. With many fine cats vying for these honors, campaigns are planned so the cat is entered in one or two shows almost every weekend of the season. The cat may be shipped coast to coast and shown by other exhibitors, called agents. It is estimated that entry fees, shipping and travel expenses may cost as much as $18,000 to $25,000 to get the title of Best Cat of the Year. If the cat is a male and well-adjusted, he may offset some of his expenses by accepting stud dates in various cities. Usually a cat on the show circuit is not a dependable sire and the risk of exposing the cat to different females every weekend is great. A scratch or disease might end his show career.

Cats are shown for prestige and for increased value of future kittens, but not for immediate money. There are no substantial money prizes at cat shows. Ribbons and trophies are given. There has been a trend in recent years toward non-trophies.

Conventional trophies are handsome, but become dust collectors at home. Show committees now favor plaques, trays, silver and crystal as prizes. These useful, less space-consuming awards are appreciated by exhibitors.

Household Pets—The most enjoyable prizes are often given in the Household Pet competition. Wine, cheese and chocolates for the owners, and pillows, toys and catnip for the cats are common.

The Household Pet class at most shows is quite large. This is the entry level, where most people start showing. After winning, some buy a purebred kitten and begin serious competition.

The criteria for Household Pets are condition and grooming. Cats may be of any age, size or description. In most associations, they must be neutered after eight months of age and must not be declawed.

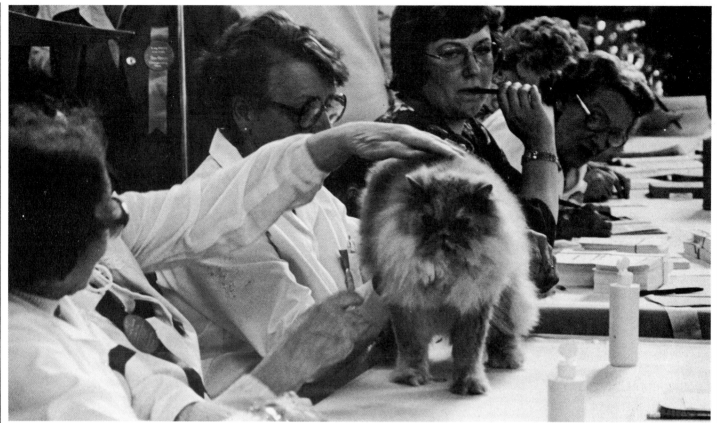

This cat is being examined in the Best in Show judging. Cats nominated from the winners of the breed classes are taken to a separate table and seen by a panel of judges.

Cost Of Cat Shows—Cat shows are designed to give people the opportunity to show their cats and to be revenue producing. The average entry fee is about $15 per cat for purebreds and Household Pets alike. Sometimes there is a small discount for people who enter several cats. Admission for spectators may be $1.50 to $2.00. Areas around the show hall are rented to vendors who put up booths to sell cat supplies, T-shirts, books, magazines and anything else that is cat related. Usually there is a food booth for people who do not want to go out for lunch. Many shows hold a raffle to raise money. A show with 500 entries, 5,000 spectators and 20 vendors can make a lot of money. After all the costs have been paid, the sponsoring club may donate all or most of the profits to charities such as shelters or feline research projects.

Cat shows are the heart of the cat fancy in America. The millions of cats owned and the billions of dollars spent on them are widely publicized. Cats are the most popular pet in America. Only a small percentage of cats are purebreds. Fewer still are used for breeding. Breeders hope to cover the costs of keeping and showing their cats. Purebred cats are expensive. No one makes money with cat shows. The money raised is used to support shelters, neuter and spay clinics, advertising campaigns and research programs to improve the health and population-control of cats.

Many spectators go to the Household Pet judging because cats are like the ones they have at home. They talk to exhibitors and learn how to give their cats better care.

Without purebreds, there would be no cat shows. The result of exhibition of these cats is a benefit to all cats.

SHOWING IN OTHER COUNTRIES

Show procedures vary from one country to another. Point standards for different breeds also vary. Vetting-in regulations in each country depend on diseases there.

The United Kingdom—Open classes are open to all exhibitors, not only members of the club holding the show. Any registered cat whose parents and grandparents are also registered, is eligible to enter the Open class for its own breed, sex and age. If eligible, it must be entered in this class.

At a Championship or Sanction Show, there are Open classes with separate adult Open classes for males and females in all breeds with Championship status. Adults are cats nine months of age or more. Neuters, which are castrated males or spayed females, always have separate Open classes.

Kittens under nine months have separate Open classes for all breeds. Kitten classes for popular breeds may be split into males and females or be divided by age.

Open classes are the most important ones. Cats compete against all others in the same category of breed, sex and age.

Miscellaneous classes are open to all exhibitors. They are split into categories for cats which have won a certain number of points, have been bred by the exhibitor or come from specific areas. They are divided into sections and sections are divided into cats, kittens and neuters.

Debutante classes are for cats that have never been exhibited before. Maiden classes are for cats that have never won a first, second or third prize. Novice classes are for cats that have never won a first prize. The Special Limit class is for cats that have not won more than two first prizes. Limit classes are for cats that have not won more than four first prizes.

Adolescents are cats between 9 and 15 months of age. Juniors are cats under two years old. Seniors are cats two years or older. Veterans are cats seven years and older.

Radius classes are for cats residing within a certain distance of the show. Visitor classes are for cats residing outside that area.

A Novice exhibitor is an owner who has never won a money prize. An Aristocrat is a cat with one or more Challenge Certificates, but is not a full Champion.

Charity Classes are classes in which all cats and owners are eligible but entry fees are

Each judge nominates a best cat, kitten and neuter. A panel of judges, usually the five most senior judges, sees all the nominations that have won their breed class. The judges vote secretly for the Best Cat, Best Kitten and Best Neuter. They may choose the Best Exhibit in show from the Best Cat and Best Kitten. Neuters do not compete against full cats. A Best Neuter is chosen from other neuters nominated.

Europe—In Europe, there are many cat fancies. Some are linked together under the Federation Internationale Feline d'Europe (FIFE), which has member organizations in 12 European countries. FIFE does not recognize registrations with other bodies in Europe. A cat may not be concurrently registered with FIFE members and others. FIFE members may not buy kittens from non-members or use their studs.

FIFE shows are all Championship shows and may last one to three days. Cats are judged on a point scale.

Excellent	88 to 100 points
Very Good	76 to 87 points
Good	61 to 75 points
Fair	46 to 60 points

Major classes are: International Champion for Longhair and Shorthair Full International Champions; International Premier for Longhair and Shorthair Full International Premiers; and Champion for Full Champions with classes for both sexes of each breed. A Certificat d'Aptitude au Championnat Internationale de Beaute (CACIB) is awarded to the winner of each class if it gains at least 95 points.

Premiers classes are for full Premiers, with classes for each breed. A Certificat d'Aptitude de Premier Internationale de Beaute (CAPIB) is awarded in the same way. Open classes are for cats 10 months and over, not including Champions or International Champions with separate classes. A Certificat

donated to a cat charity. Club classes are put on by the club holding the show and other cat clubs. They are entered only by members of the club sponsoring the class.

The Household Pet Classes are for unregistered cats of unknown pedigree and are split into Open, Miscellaneous and Club classes. At a small show, Open classes may only be split into Longhair cats and kittens and Shorthair cats and kittens. At a large show they may be divided into several color categories. Household Pets are expected to be neutered when they are old enough. There are no separate classes for neuters.

Stewards find the cats to be judged in a class and let the judge examine each one. The cat is judged against a standard of points laid down for each breed. Body shape, coat texture, coat color and eye color have points allotted to them, adding up to 100. Most judges do not actually award points but put remarks in their judging books that enable them to assess the cat's standard. If they think it is not high enough, the Challenge Certificate may be withheld.

The results appear on an awards board showing each class with the cats entered marked 1st, 2nd and 3rd. The letters CC mean Challenge Certificate, an award granted to the best cat in an Open class. Winning three Challenge Certificates at three shows under three different judges makes a cat eligible to apply for recognition as a Full Champion. Premier Certificates are awarded to the winners of Open neuter classes for championship status breeds only if the judge deems the cat to be of sufficient merit. Three certificates must be won under three judges for a cat to be awarded Premier status.

The best Lilac-point Siamese cat is proudly held by the Show Manager.

d'Aptitude au Championnat (CAC) is awarded to each class winner if it gains at least 93 points.

Neuter classes are for neuters 10 months and older of each breed. A Certificat d'Aptitude de Premier (CAP) is awarded to winners gaining at least 93 points. Kitten classes are held for kittens 3 to 6 month old, and 6 to 10 months old of each sex and breed. Litter classes are held for kittens 8 weeks to 3 months old, with at least three in each litter.

Four places are given in each class: 1st, 2nd, 3rd and mentioned. The judges' reports on each cat are given to the exhibitors at the show.

To become a Champion, a cat must win three CACs under three different judges. To gain International Championship, the cat must be awarded three CACIBs under three judges, at least one of these being won in a different European country.

In addition to the major classes, there are classes for imported cats, progeny classes and novice classes in which unregistered cats may be entered. If the latter gain sufficient points, they are registered.

Cats are confined in decorated pens with cats belonging to one owner grouped together. Stewards carry cats to a separate room for judging. The cats are penned anonymously in plain pens. The International classes are judged first, followed by Champions, Premiers, Opens and the others. Afterward, judges form a panel to select the Best Longhair cat, kitten and neuter; and Best Shorthair cat, kitten and neuter; and finally the Best in Show.

In addition to the shows run by members of FIFE, there are also independent shows in most European countries.

New Zealand—In New Zealand, there is only one cat fancy consisting of many clubs, each running shows. Individuals must have bred cats for at least five years to be eligible to be judges. Foreign judges are often invited to judge at larger shows. Only Championship shows are held, but there are usually classes for Household Pets.

The shows last one day and cats are penned anonymously, grouped according to breed. In addition to the Open classes, there are Side classes, including type classes in which the cats are judged on type alone. Coat color and pattern are disregarded.

Sweepstake classes are also held in which the winners each get a percentage of the entry money. Challenge Certificates are awarded to Open class winners of sufficient merit. Three Certificates under three different judges give the cat its Championship.

Australia—There are seven states in Australia, each with at least one cat fancy. They all cooperate with each other. They use judges from other fancies, recognize each other's registrations and exhibit at shows run by clubs belonging to other fancies.

Judges have to train hard and are not accepted on breeding and stewarding experience. Only their expenses are paid.

All judging, including Best in Show, is done by the judge going to the cats in their pens. Cats are judged only against others of their own breed, unless they are nominated for Best in Show. Then they compete against other breeds.

South Africa—At South African cat shows, judges go from pen to pen. Two stewards take the cats out for the judge, who dictates his remarks to a notetaker or scribe. There is a sheet of paper for each cat, giving details of breed, sex and age on which the judge makes a written report. These reports are later circulated to exhibitors.

All the classes a cat may be entered at any one show are judged by the same person. Best of Breed or Best in Show is determined by a panel of judges. The panel sits in a separate area and stewards bring cats to it.

Training to become a judge is rigorous. Clubs nominate candidates, who then go through a course of lectures and demonstrations and take an exam. Judges are unpaid, receiving only their expenses.

TRAVEL & BOARDING

Sometimes you may want to take your cat on a journey to the vet, a boarding cattery or a show. The most docile cat can become lively, even uncontrollable, when frightened by unusual smells, noises or surroundings. Never carry a cat any distance in your arms. It may leap out of your arms and never be seen again. This can also happen if you leave a cat in a car with the door or window open more than a crack for air circulation.

A cat-proof container is necessary for travel. The ideal container is lightweight and easy to clean, with plenty of ventilation, but escape-proof.

If you are preparing for a long trip, confine the cat in advance. You will be sure it is not missing when you want to leave. Put the cat in its litter

Cats should be taken on outings in a cat-proof carrier. This plastic one is hygenic and well-ventilated.

This cat enjoys its stay at a boarding cattery. Its pen has an individual run and high-level shelves for viewing and interest.

tray before you leave. The cat usually uses it before leaving. Make calming noises to the cat during transit to reassure it.

SEDATIVES
Tranquilizers are sometimes prescribed for cats before a long trip. But they can have the opposite effect on cats. Cats may be less controllable or more ferocious after taking sedatives. Most travel happily without them. Unless you find they make your cat easier to manage, do not use them.

SHORT TRIPS
For short trips, such as a visit to the vet, put the cat's blanket in the carrier, so it is not cut off from everything familiar. Prepare the carrier in advance. Show it to the cat only inside a room with closed doors and windows. Some cats, knowing

something strange is about to happen, disappear at the sight of a container. Use the same procedure for moving to a new home or travel to a boarding cattery if these trips are also short. On such occasions, place a toy or some favorite object in the carrier.

LONG TRIPS

Long trips may include going to a show, away to stud or on vacation with you. If a show is held a long way from home, you may have to start early or spend a night in a hotel. Do not use the show blanket for the journey because it may get dirty. Keep it for the show pen. Traveling long distances with a cat means taking food and water, and making provision for it to use the litter tray. If traveling by car, stop occasionally. Close all doors and windows before letting the cat out of its carrier to use the litter tray. Put it back after it has stretched its legs and has been offered water. This routine is not possible when you are traveling by bus, plane or train. For these occasions,

This cat is going on a visit to the vet in a see-through carrier. Some cats prefer to be invisible when traveling.

use a container large enough to fix a small litter tray, and food and water dishes. Dry food is best for a long trip because it does not attract flies and does not spoil.

If traveling to another country, find out whether there are any quarantine restrictions at the point of entry.

VACATIONS

If you have two homes, you may find your cat adjusts quickly to spending time at each place. If you are visiting a place unfamiliar to the cat, keep it inside its wire pen and take it for walks on a harness and leash. Do not tether a cat. Most cats are great escapers.

Cats from one household do not mix readily with those from another. Cats have a strong sense of territorial rights and each feels threatened if a strange cat enters its territory.

CAT CONTAINERS AND CAGES

1. This plastic-coated wire carrier is well-ventilated and easy to clean.
2. This small breeding unit has two compartments, one private.
3. A solid cardboard carrier with air holes in the sides folds flat when not in use. It is inexpensive and useful.
4. This vinyl carrier has a see-through clear plastic viewing window. It is easy to carry.
5. Designed specifically for cats, this carrier can be used at home as two beds or for whelping. The two halves fit together and you can lock it. A small litter pan and cups can be used for long journeys.
6. This is a smaller but heavier plastic carrier.
7. See-through containers are popular. This one is sold in a box for self-assembly.
8. Fiberglass carriers have metal doors with locks. They are good-quality, but expensive.
9. These fiberglass cages are ideal for one night at a boarding cattery, for use as an isolation unit or for recovery after an operation.
10. The large plastic-coated wire playpen with fiberglass base is an ideal place to put kittens while you are out or busy.

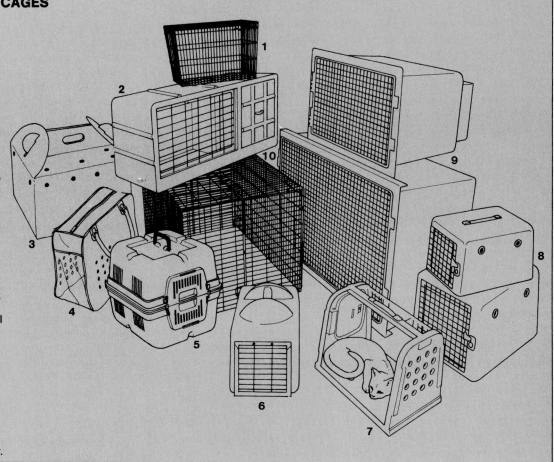

This boarding cattery has a house for each cat and a separate outdoor run. Only cats from the same household can be put together. These two Siamese watch other cats with interest.

There are exceptions, but it is better for a cat to stay in its own home or to go to a boarding cattery than to accompany its owner to an unknown place where another cat may be present.

A cat can be left at home by itself for one night if you leave water and set a timed feeder to provide food when necessary. There are several types of feeders available. If you are away for more than one night, have someone live in as a cat sitter or visit and feed the cat on a regular basis and change the litter tray. The animal stays in its own familiar surroundings and enjoys human company each day.

BOARDING CATTERY

If no responsible friend or neighbor can care for your cat while you are away, the cat must go to a boarding cattery. This is like a kennel dogs board at when owners are away.

Two young owners bring their cat in for boarding and get it settled in. Its own blanket and basket help the cat feel at home. The owners can now enjoy their own vacation.

Reserve one as soon as you know the dates of travel. You might need to inspect several catteries. Pick one with an individual house and fresh-air run for each cat, where it can view other cats, but not come into direct contact. Keep your cat confined indoors before taking it to the cattery.

Buy a package of instant grass. Plant some in a portable container a week before leaving so your cat will have a supply of grass while you are gone. Buy some catnip, too. A favorite toy and blanket makes your cat feel at home. Tell the boarding cattery about any medications that need to be given. Some catteries groom longhair cats for an extra charge. A good cattery gives individual time to each cat while feeding, watering, changing the litter tray or bed making.

TRAVEL AND QUARANTINE

Cats in quarantine are put in a boarding cattery. The stay can be six weeks in some countries to six months in others. These cats need care. Six months without seeing their owners is a trial for most cats. Frequent visits maintain the bond between the cat and its owner.

STUD VISITS

A queen who is calling may be taken or sent to a male cat for stud service. A fight may start when the stud meets the queen. It is important for a container to be cat-proof. Do not open the container on arrival until the queen is inside her quarters.

Two household pets relax together after receiving their rabies inoculations. Inoculation regulations are in effect to protect cats and people.

11

THE LAW & YOUR CAT

Cats are considered untrainable. By law, owners are not usually held responsible for their cat's actions, particularly if these actions are instinctive. Owning a cat gives the owner a moral responsibility for it.

QUARANTINE LAWS
Strict quarantine measures have kept Hawaii, the United Kingdom, Australia and New Zealand free of rabies.

Hawaii—When a person takes a cat to Hawaii, the cat must be quarantined for a period of 120 days. This is done to isolate any cases of rabies and keep the islands rabies-free.

The United Kingdom—Animals that could transmit rabies must be quarantined for six months when entering the United Kingdom. This includes all cats. Some countries have a quarantine law, but most accept animals from the United Kingdom as rabies safe if they have a health certificate. Anyone bringing undeclared animals into the United Kingdom is liable to a fine and imprisonment. Only by strict enforcement of quarantine laws is the United Kingdom free of rabies.

Australia—Dogs and cats may be imported only from the United Kingdom, Ireland, Hawaii, Fiji, New Guinea, Norfolk Island and New Zealand. The animals must have been in the country of export for six months previously, not in an import quarantine kennel. They must arrive in Australia with the correct documents, including a health certificate.

Importing cats from New Zealand does not require special permission. The animal must have a health certificate showing it has been treated for tapeworm within a specified period before entering. Quarantine is not required.

New Zealand—All cats being imported must be quarantined for one month. Animals from Australia do not have to be quarantined. Persons smuggling cats into New Zealand may be fined and imprisoned. By strictly enforcing quarantine laws, New Zealand has been rabies-free.

STRAY CATS
Indiscriminate breeding results in more cats around than people want. Cat owners should neuter pets. In some areas, abandoned wild cats form packs that live around garbage dumps. This causes health hazards. Unwanted animals are often taken to the pound. Most are destroyed.

Over 18 million cats are put to sleep in the United States each year. Most of these are healthy but unwanted.

CAT CHARITIES
These began as organizations to fight cruelty to cats caused by neglect or ignorant owners. Some cat charities have been around for a long time. There are many cat charities, some with membership fees to pay expenses. Some produce magazines or newsletters.

These charities accept donations. Some cat charities have been left large sums. Individual cats have also received money to assure their comfort after the death of their owners. The record amount was $415,000, left to a cat in San Diego in 1960.

CATS AND PROPERTY
A cat owner is usually not responsible for acts which are ordinarily committed by a cat. These include fighting, unless there is a known history of fighting with vicious intent, or watching and catching birds. The owner is usually not responsible when a cat trespasses and does damage if it is merely following its own instincts. A few cities have experimented with cat licensing and leash laws. Usually cats are perceived as wild animals in the eyes of the law. Cat owners are not held responsible for damage their cats may do. They also have little recourse if damage is done to their cat.

> ## PRINCIPAL ANIMAL CHARITIES
> **ASPCA (American Society for the Prevention of Cruelty to Animals)**
> **AHA (American Humane Association)**
> **API (Animal Protection Institute)**
> **American Anti-Vivisection Society**
> **Bide-a-Wee Home Association**
> **California Humane Council**
> **FOA (Friends of Animals)**
> **Fund for Animals**
> **HSUS (Humane Society of the United States)**
> **Mercy Crusade Inc.**
> **Morris Animal Foundation**
> **National Anti-Vivisection Society**
> **Pet Assistance Foundation Inc.**
> **Pet Pride**
> **Society for Animal Rights**
> **United Action for Animals**

CATS' RIGHTS
Cats are protected by the Federal Laboratory Animal Welfare Act of 1966. This deals more with the housing and transportation of laboratory animals than with actual experiments performed on them.

Cats are protected against cruelty, injury, abandonment, theft and ill treatment. The Animal Welfare Act is overseen by the United States Department of Agriculture (USDA) and requires care and treatment of animals in research laboratories be humane. All research institutions must register with the USDA and report to it annually.

Hundreds of thousands of cats are used annually in scientific experiments worldwide. Scientists use few stray cats, preferring cats with a known history, especially those bred specifically for research and known to be pathogen-free. Such animals are costly to replace. This may help to ensure they are reasonably treated.

RESPONSIBLE OWNERSHIP
Feeding a cat on your premises may constitute ownership. You can be held legally responsible for the animal if you move or go on vacation without providing for it. Ownership continues to apply to you until another owner takes over.

A Silver Tabby American Shorthair.

GLOSSARY & INDEX

GLOSSARY

A

Agouti—A tabby coat pattern speckled with another color.
Aural hematoma—A blood blister in the ear flap of a cat.

B

Bicolor—Coat of 2 colors. Coat may be black and white, blue and white, or red and white. It should be mostly white on underparts and symmetrical elsewhere, with an inverted *V* covering the nose.
Bran bath—Cleaning a cat using a dry method. Bran is heated, rubbed into the coat and brushed out. This removes dirt and grease. Use this method only on shorthair cats.

C

Calico—A female-only pattern. The three colors in the coat are white, black and red, with white mainly on the underparts. Also called tortoiseshell and white.
Calling—Term describing female cats that have come into heat and are ready to mate. Most queens are vocal at this time.
Cattery—A place for the breeding, raising or care of cats. Often used for boarding a cat when owners go on vacation.
Chinchilla—A coat pattern in which guard hairs are tipped with a darker color for about 1/32 of their length.
Cobby—A cat with a short, compact, round body.
Combination coat—A coat that is a combination of different coat patterns.

D

Dilution—A lighter-color coat achieved by mating a dark-color cat with a light-color cat. Sometimes a diluted color appears to be a different color than the original. Lilac is the dilute form of chocolate.

G

Ground color—Base color of the coat. It is the most predominant color.
Guard hairs—Long, coarse hairs forming a protective coat over the undercoat of a cat.

H

Harlequin--A piebald-color cat.
Himalayan coat—A coat pattern in which color is concentrated in the points—the mask, ears, legs and tail.
Himalayan combination coat—A Himalayan coat pattern with four symmetrical white feet.
Household pet—An unregistered cat of unknown pedigree.
Hybrid breed—A cross between two pedigreed cats.

K

Kittening—A queen giving birth to kittens.

L

Longy—A Manx with a medium-length tail.

M

Mackerel tabby—A coat pattern with vertical stripes down the flanks.
Manx—A cat with no tail. This is a genetic mutation.
Mutation—A variation in an inherited characteristic.

N

Natural breed—A breed which has evolved naturally. Breeders have not outcrossed cats to produce the breed.
Neuters—Castrated males or spayed females.
Nose break—The depression between and in front of the eyes, roughly corresponding to the bridge of the nose on humans.

O

Outcross—Breeding a cat of one breed to a cat of a different breed.

P

Patched tabby—A tabby with tortoiseshell patches. May be brown, blue or silver tabby with bold patches of red, cream, or red and cream.
Piebald—An almost-white cat with color restricted to odd patches on head and tail.

Points—The mask, ears, legs and tail of the cat. On a Siamese Seal-point, points are seal color.

Q

Queen—An unaltered female.

R

Riser—A Manx with a small number of vertebrae in the tail. The tail is usually immobile.
Rumpy—Another name for a Manx with a complete absence of a tail.

S

Self-color—A solid-color cat.
Shaded—A coat pattern in which guard hairs in the coat are tipped for 1/3 of their length with a darker color.

Shell cameo—A coat pattern in which guard hairs in the coat are tipped for 1/32 of their length with a darker color.
Sire—Father of a kitten.
Smoke—A coat pattern in which guard hairs in the coat are tipped for 3/4 of their length with a darker color.
Spotted tabby—In this coat pattern, stripes have been broken into spots, giving a pattern like a leopard's.
Stubby—A Manx with a short tail.
Stud—A male cat used for breeding.
Stumpy-tailed—A cat with a short tail.

T

Tabby—The ground color of the coat is a good contrast with the overlying pattern color.
Third eyelid—Also called a *haw*. An additional eyelid coming across the eye from the inner corner. It is an indication of a temperature or an early sign of infection.
Ticked tabby—A tabby coat pattern speckled with another color.
Torbie—A patched tabby.
Tortie—Another name for tortoiseshell.
Tortoiseshell—A female-only pattern. The black and red or cream coats are intermingled rather than patched.

INDEX OF BREEDS

INDEX

ACKNOWLEDGEMENTS

COLOR AND LINE ARTWORK

John Francis, Alan Hollingbery, Keeller-Cross, Gordon Riley, Clive Spong.

PHOTOGRAPHS

Catac, Creszentia, Anne Cumbers, Folkestone Herald, Fox Photos Ltd., Marc Henrie, Jane Howard, Roger Hyde, Kathleen Koopman, Panther Photographic International, Robert Pearcy, Hugh Smith, Alice Su, Kentfield Taylor.

7.6348624241161